Elder Statesman, adviser to F
banker, humanitarian—Bernard b
earned a unique position in the affections
of the American people. Here, for the first
time, is a highly readable summary and
commentary upon the most significant recommendations he has made to our last six
Presidents, both Democratic and Republican.

What is Bernard Baruch's position on such

Morris Vict timely topics as national security, inflation, focusing
public atte taxes, mobilization, foreign aid, etc.?   rity, was
prompted   Herein lie the answers. Here, too, is the NGTH:
Bernard Ba author's opinion, based upon careful study mulative
effect of his combined with a personal knowledge of
             Bernard Baruch's views, of what Mr. Baruch
Mr. Rosenb might be expected to recommend to Presi- rve with
the War Pro dent Eisenhower and his Administration as unteered
for active   a nine-point blueprint for security.   manding
Officer of a submarine chaser in the South Pacific.

Since Korea, he has held key positions in the defense program,
including that of Executive Director of the Defense Materials
Committees of the Defense Production Administration. In 1951,
he organized and directed the Institute on the Economics of Defense Mobilization, sponsored by The American University, in
Washington, with the cooperation of the Office of Defense
Mobilization.

Morris V. Rosenbloom's previous works on industrial and economic subjects have been highly regarded. His current book,
PEACE THROUGH STRENGTH, is a review of Bernard
Baruch's recommendations on preparedness over the years . . .
and Mr. Rosenbloom's urgent plea that America will pay heed
to the lessons of the past in planning for the future.

PEACE THROUGH STRENGTH

Bernard Baruch and a Blueprint for Security

Courtesy of the artist, Douglas Chandor

PEACE *through* STRENGTH

Bernard Baruch and a Blueprint for Security

by

MORRIS V. ROSENBLOOM

Foreword by
ELEANOR ROOSEVELT

Afterword by
CHARLES E. WILSON

PUBLISHED BY
AMERICAN SURVEYS
WASHINGTON, D. C.

IN ASSOCIATION WITH
FARRAR, STRAUS AND YOUNG
NEW YORK

1953

DEDICATED

to those patriotic men and women — in active military service, in supporting civilian roles, and in our government agencies — who serve loyally and unselfishly in helping mobilize America's strength to keep the peace, to defend freedom and liberty, and to preserve the security of the Free World

Thanksgiving Day
November 27, 1952

Contents

Each Chapter Title is a Quotation by or about Mr. Baruch

PEACE THROUGH STRENGTH

Bernard Baruch and a Blueprint for Security

"There is only one way to protect yourself from a possible aggressor," Bernard Baruch has warned again and again. "Be strong. Be so strong he cannot dare attack you without fear of self destruction. In that way you achieve peace, and only in that way. There are certain people who only understand strength. They sneer at weakness, no matter how noble the aim of the seeker after peace."

ACKNOWLEDGMENTS

For much of the biographical data in this book I am indebted to the books by Carter Field, W. L. White and Harry Irving Shumway, as well as to the three-part profile by John Hersey in *The New Yorker*.

The Bibliography lists sources which have been useful either for information about Mr. Baruch or for background material. My thanks, naturally, go to all these authors. I believe it appropriate, however, to mention that the following works have been especially helpful:

Speaking Frankly, by James F. Byrnes; *Roosevelt and Hopkins*, by Robert E. Sherwood; *Bernard Baruch, Portrait of a Citizen*, by W. L. White; *Bernard Baruch, Park Bench Statesman*, by Carter Field; *Industrial America in the World War*, by Grosvenor B. Clarkson; *The Blue Eagle from Egg to Earth*, by Hugh S. Johnson; *This Is My Story* and *This I Remember*, by Eleanor Roosevelt; *Arsenal of Democracy*, by Donald M. Nelson; *How to Get Rich in Washington*, by Blair Bolles; *The Struggle for Survival*, by Eliot Janeway. Also, articles in *The Saturday Evening Post* by Ralph E. Lapp, Alan Moorehead and Ernest O. Hauser; in *Look* Magazine of September 26, 1950 and July 17, 1951.

It can hardly be overemphasized that without the availability of Mr. Baruch's own published writings—not to mention the transcripts and reports of his Congressional testimony over the years— *Peace Through Strength* could not have been written. In this connection, I am in the debt of *The New York Times* for its thorough reporting of history in the making.

Preface
by
The Author

TODAY, AS THESE WORDS are written, Americans are commemorating Armistice Day of 1952. Ironically, a large part of the world is again under arms—thirty-four years after Bernard M. Baruch played such a major role in mobilizing our country's resources during World War I.

Since that time, Mr. Baruch has continued to serve the cause of preparedness. He has pointed out "to all who would listen," as General Eisenhower has said, "the lesson of that First War and what we had to do to remain safe."

Bernard Baruch was among the first to recognize the danger of totalitarian aggression to the United States and the other democracies and to warn that it could lead to another world conflict. Today, less than four weeks before another tragic anniversary of our unpreparedness at the time of Pearl Harbor, it is fitting that *Peace Through Strength*—largely concerned with the preparedness efforts of Mr. Baruch—should be completed.

It seems to me that a review and analysis of his efforts over the years to strengthen the country militarily and economically has a special timeliness in the light of current world developments. Once again our country is faced with the task of becoming so powerful that not only will it be impregnable within itself, but strong enough and sound enough to assist other free peoples in protecting themselves against the Communist threat.

It is likely that in the crucial days ahead the new President

15

will call upon Mr. Baruch for advice, as have the last six Presidents, both Republican and Democratic. When Eisenhower, in August of 1952, was awarded the first Bernard Baruch Peace Medal by the Veterans of Foreign Wars, he referred to his friend, as quoted above, adding: "I was one of those who for the past quarter century has had the privilege of sitting at his feet and listening to his words of wisdom, words that are still mighty."

Just two weeks after Eisenhower voiced this tribute, Mr. Baruch was honored once again. A bench, hand-hewn out of California redwood, was publicly dedicated to him at Dyerville, California, its bronze plaque carrying this inscription:

> *"Dedicated to Bernard M. Baruch, philosopher, philanthropist, stalwart American on his 82nd birthday. His stature is that of the redwoods."*

This book is intended as a study of Bernard Baruch as "stalwart American"—the man who perhaps more than any other citizen of our time has been devoted to, and has *worked at,* keeping the United States strong and free. I have also attempted to outline in Chapter VIII a blueprint for security which Mr. Baruch might suggest to the new Administration. This blueprint is a nine-point forecast based upon a study and analysis of his counsel and published writings which have been presented to the Congress and the people—with each point supported by quotations cited from Mr. Baruch's past statements.

When I first told Mr. Baruch of my desire to write a book on his contributions to national security, he said he doubted that many people would be interested in such a book and that he definitely did not want to encourage me. In his characteristic way, after I mentioned my intention to be as impartial as possible, he said, "Son, if you want your book to be well accepted, be sure to keep it that way. And if you find I have made any mistakes, give me both barrels."

16

My initial meeting with Mr. Baruch occurred in the spacious industrial conference room of the War Production Board not long after Pearl Harbor. As the senior economist for one of the WPB industry branches then being established to aid war production, I had prepared a preliminary requirements program to be discussed by industrial leaders at an advisory committee meeting. Since this was to be one of hundreds of such committee meetings, the reception accorded our plan for converting a large proportion of the facilities of their industry to war work was of the utmost importance.

Although the room was large, it was filled to overflowing. Around the long T-shaped conference table sat high-ranking executives of many of the country's largest corporations. Seated along the walls were representatives of the Government agencies concerned: Army, Navy, Maritime Commission, Lend-Lease, Board of Economic Warfare, and the War Production Board itself. Scarcely had the meeting started when strong objections to our program were raised by several industry representatives. They were firm in stressing the essentiality of this industry's normal production.

In the midst of high-pitched controversy, Bernard Baruch entered the room. As one of Donald Nelson's aides ushered the tall, white-haired figure to the head of the table, a surprised hush fell over the entire group.

It was explained that Mr. Nelson had asked Mr. Baruch to stop by and say a few words to the advisory group. Mr. Baruch, in his direct way, made clear his concern as to the outcome of the work of that early committee. He spoke with vigor of the country's need for industrial conversion, and for the aid which only the wholehearted cooperation of this industry could provide toward meeting that objective. He touched briefly upon the reasons for haste in rearming and the need for speedy and continuous production of war equipment. He told the industry's executives that he knew they could be counted upon to do their part.

Mr. Baruch made a decisive, convincing talk that lasted less than seven minutes. As he spoke I looked about me, studying particularly the faces of the men who had been most outspoken in their opposition to the proposed program. An amazing change had taken place. Each man was listening with almost rapt attention to the words of the distinguished speaker. Mr. Baruch concluded his remarks by voicing his appreciation for the opportunity given him to address the group. Then, quietly, he left the conference room.

As the applause died down and the door closed behind Bernard Baruch, the man who had been the acknowledged leader and spokesman of the industry sprang to his feet. "Mr. Chairman," he said, "I want to register a change in my position. The complete facilities of my company are at the disposal of the Government. I only hope that we of this industry will measure up to the trust that has been placed in us."

As he sat down others arose, in turn. Each pledged the full cooperation of his firm. The tide of opposition had been turned in a matter of minutes. A great industry, with an enormous capacity for vital war production, had been swung solidly behind the conversion program by the words of a single man. In the days and months ahead, that particular industry proved —through miraculous production feats—how completely its leaders had been won over to the convictions of a man they knew and respected.

The subsequent curtailment of civilian production for this industry was important news for the nation in those early days of the war. Undoubtedly, the cooperation of this industry played a significant role in the later acceptance by others of deep cuts and, in some cases, complete blackouts of their normal products. Those few words of Mr. Baruch's—never before recounted, to my knowledge, except in a sketch I wrote about Mr. Baruch in

1945–left a mark of immeasurable import on the tremendous industrial strides through which this country mobilized for all-out war. Yet I very much doubt if Mr. Baruch ever realized how important a contribution he made that morning, accustomed as he has been to the effects of his persuasive powers.

This episode impressed upon me the validity of one of Bernard Baruch's favorite concepts–the importance of "human equations and natural economic laws" in dealing with people. Several months later, partly as a result of my friendship with the late Justice Brandeis, I came to know Mr. Baruch personally.

My own work then and later–both as Commanding Officer of a Submarine Chaser in the Pacific during the war and in industry experience before and since–has stimulated a special interest in the concepts and significance of the pronouncements on preparedness which Mr. Baruch has advanced over the years.

In brief, I have had many opportunities to evaluate Mr. Baruch's oft-repeated defense recommendations in the light of day-to-day Government and industry practice. After World War II, I re-entered industry as an executive of a concern manufacturing industrial equipment. A few years later, in June of 1950, I returned to Washington to handle program coordination as an assistant in the office of W. Stuart Symington, then Chairman of the National Security Resources Board. In December of that year, General William H. Harrison, Defense Production Administrator, asked me to transfer as Special Assistant to his Deputy Administrator. Since that time I have been active in helping set the rate of stockpile acquisition for strategic and critical materials, and for some months have been Executive Director of the Defense Materials Committees of DPA. In the spring of 1952, I was especially fortunate to gain first-hand knowledge as a participant, at the invitation of the Secretary of Defense, in the Joint Civilian Orientation Conference. This

Conference provided an opportunity for the members to inspect military installations and be advised of plans and programs of the Armed Services.

Thus, I believe, this experience has qualified me somewhat to prepare this study of Mr. Baruch's recommendations. There are other reasons for my writing at this time. First, I am convinced that greater public attention should be focused on the status and urgencies of our national security. Second, because I believe that totalitarian aggression is a menace to our freedom today, I wanted to present as soon as possible a review of Mr. Baruch's efforts to strengthen our country.

Actually, this book has been prepared only through the co-operation of a few friends and associates. To all who have contributed so unstintingly of their time and of their enthusiastic support, I am deeply indebted. Of course, the responsibility for the opinions expressed, where not otherwise credited, is mine.

As noted in the Bibliography, a vast amount of material has been drawn upon in the research and writing of this volume. Sources of particular aid are listed in the Acknowledgments.

Mrs. Eleanor Roosevelt has graciously written the Foreword, from the vantage point of a humanist and active participant in world affairs. She has had the unique privilege of being a close observer of Mr. Baruch's devoted service to her husband and to the nation.

Mr. Charles E. Wilson, former President of General Electric and first Director of the Office of Defense Mobilization, has contributed the Afterword as an appraisal of Mr. Baruch seen through the eyes of a leading industrialist. Perhaps no other American today is in a better position—by virtue of having faced such responsibilities himself during World War II and since Korea in mobilizing American industry for war—to evaluate Mr. Baruch's service in the cause of preparedness.

Just a year ago, when Mr. Wilson was Defense Mobilizer, he kindly served as Honorary Chairman of the Institute on the

Economics of Defense Mobilization, which I directed. The Institute was sponsored by The American University in Washington, D. C., with the cooperation of the ODM.

It is especially pertinent and timely—in consideration of the theme of this book—to quote from Mr. Wilson's special message to the opening session of the sixteen-week Institute:

> "It looks as if we'll be in this defense business for a long, long time. Each one of us—businessman, factory and office worker, farmer, professional person, student, and government employee—has a vital stake in our Government's defense mobilization program.
>
> "We alone can make it work—but only if we clearly understand where we're going, and then put our heads together to produce a bold, imaginative program that says to any potential enemy, 'We're ready . . . we're more than ready.'"

In conclusion, if this book appears to be a tribute to Baruch the patriot, as well as to Baruch the adviser and planner, credit should go not to the author but to that distinguished Elder Statesman whose deeds—and whose words as well—have for so long richly merited the world's respect.

Morris V. Rosenbloom

Washington, D. C.
November 11, 1952

Foreword

by

Mrs. Eleanor Roosevelt

THROUGH MANY YEARS of association, I have found Bernard Baruch to be a man who has placed his country above all personal considerations.

I like to think of Mr. Baruch as the practical visionary. All too often in our political and economic life, there is the tendency to scoff at someone who is labelled a visionary. But then someone comes along like Mr. Baruch who is the embodiment of the fact that the visionary also can possess realism and practicality.

If you do not know, from your own experience, the answer to any given problem, then you try to find the right people to work out the answer. This, I think, is a quality which my husband possessed in a great degree—and it is one which Mr. Baruch possesses in equal measure. It is the quality of leadership that comes from one's own confidence in his or her ability to deal with problems and with the people who are capable of solving these problems.

To this end, you can never be afraid of the potentialities of any set of facts. You evaluate the facts and place the conclusions against the problems so as to best meet any eventuality. This has been, and is, the genius of Mr. Baruch.

In his public life—and how, I ask you, could a man of his wisdom and vision have escaped prominence in public life? —Mr. Baruch always has been conscious of the welfare of the people as a whole. Always, he has worked to keep the various segments of our economic life in balance.

For example, it is so easy for many of us to forget that, in the early Twenties, Mr. Baruch took careful note of the sad economic plight of agriculture; and that he recruited two able men—George Peek and Hugh Johnson—to work out a program of "Equality for Agriculture." This purely public-spirited interest in agriculture, I have always felt, shows the tremendous depth of a man whose adult life, prior to his initiation in government service in World War I, had been spent in an entirely different field.

It is a unique position, indeed, that Mr. Baruch has filled in this country.

His many appearances before Congressional Committees have served a much broader purpose than merely their effect upon the thinking of Senators and Representatives. They have been splendid courses in adult education.

We have come to associate the necessity of preparedness for national security with his name. He has stressed this policy with great foresightedness. And his recommendations on atomic energy control, made to the United Nations, still stand, even after some years have elapsed, as the wisest counsel in the membership of the United States Commission on Atomic Energy that formulated our policy.

Significantly, his vision does not diminish with age. Rather, it becomes enlarged. He foresees the great possibilities of the cooperative use of atomic power for peaceful purposes and the building up, with the cooperative spirit of free nations, of the under-developed areas of the world. His mind is constantly at work on ways to establish the fuller life for all peoples. And no one could hope more passionately that this troubled world will soon have both peace and freedom.

Mr. Baruch was a trusted adviser to my husband, both in

Albany and in Washington. Around any President there will always be at times personal jealousies which lead to stresses and misunderstandings, but Mr. Baruch, in his relationship with my husband, always rose above such conditions. And to me, personally, he has been a much appreciated adviser and warm friend. I have sought his help frequently on projects I have been interested in—and he has never failed in lending his support and guidance.

Mr. Baruch is a very independent gentleman. He differed at times with my husband on both policy and procedure. And there were times when some of those immediately associated with my husband—in the so-called "official family"—were jealous of outside advisers such as Mr. Baruch. Under normal circumstances, these jealousies would have made it difficult for cordial relations to exist. But the President was impervious to stories or rumors about anyone when he felt they could give wise counsel and be of useful service; and, since Mr. Baruch is one of those all-too-uncommon people who can ignore past difficulties, he was always ready to be of service, when called upon. Thus, I am happy to say, the personal relationship remained unbroken through all of my husband's years in the White House.

It is this desire—yes, this very yearning—to be of service that dominates Mr. Baruch. He has served his country well in the past, and I feel sure that his advice, if followed, will be of great benefit in the years to come.

This book fills an important need for a better understanding of the great contributions Bernard Baruch has made over the years. The book has been prepared with care to highlight significant portions of his recommendations, portrayed against the events and background of the times. They have the mark of Mr. Baruch's long and deep thought—and so, to a large extent, it is Mr. Baruch, again, giving us the benefit of his mature judgment. Mr. Rosenbloom has captured the very essence of this man's great wisdom and vision.

Peace Through Strength: Bernard Baruch and a Blueprint for Security is a valuable book. It is one to be considered with attention, as it so directly concerns itself with our national welfare.

Eleanor Roosevelt

"I was one of those who for the past quarter century has had the privilege of sitting at his [Baruch's] feet and listening to his words of wisdom, words that are still mighty. Beyond this, he is one of those who has shown to us that if a man forgets all else except service to country, then indeed the country will remember him with respect and affection."

— From Dwight D. Eisenhower's speech to the Veterans of Foreign Wars on August 5, 1952.

CHAPTER 1

"The Country
Will Remember Him"

THE FIVE-STAR GENERAL, who had just
been selected the Republican candi-
date for President of the United States, was receiving the first
Peace Medal to be presented by the Veterans of Foreign Wars
in the name of Bernard Baruch. The date was August 5, 1952;
the place Los Angeles. Said General Eisenhower, in accepting
the award:

> "As long ago as World War I he [Baruch] was the
> director of our mobilization effort and one of the great
> figures that brought victory in that war. Between the
> wars, he never ceased to point out to all who would listen
> the lessons of that First War and what we had to do to
> remain safe, particularly in the field of economic
> strength, that no one would dare again repeat the mad
> venture of World War I. But his words were not heeded.
> "I was one of those who for the past quarter century
> has had the privilege of sitting at his feet and listening
> to his words of wisdom, words that are still mighty.
> Beyond this, he is one of those who has shown to us
> that if a man forgets all else except service to country,
> then indeed the country will remember him with re-
> spect and affection. . . ."

This sort of tribute was nothing new to Bernard Mannes Baruch—even though it came from a man soon to be the next President of the United States—for our Elder Statesman has been a guiding influence on Presidents for nearly one-half of his eighty-two eventful years.

Baruch's place in American life has no precedent and may never have a parallel. To the public he is the park bench philosopher, always ready to advise a Senate Committee or a school boy. To the Bulls and Bears of Wall Street he is one of the shrewdest speculators ever to scan a ticker tape. To Government administrators and Members of Congress he is the mobilization expert par excellence, the man whom President Wilson finally put in charge of the all-powerful War Industries Board in 1918. To liberals and humanists the world over he is the spokesman for the plea that the atomic bomb is too awesome a weapon to be entrusted to all nations, unless restrictions can be enforced to prevent the use of the bomb to destroy mankind.

Specifically, however, what recommendations on preparedness has Bernard Baruch *actually made* over the years? Many people —well aware of the respect and esteem in which he is held—ask that question. This, then, is what this book is about.

Before sketching these recommendations against the historical events of the times in which they were made—as well as the results or lack of results of his urgings—it is well to note, in summary and highlight form, the background and experience upon which he has drawn and from which his convictions have been shaped, In short, what sort of man is this Bernard Baruch who, in the words of one of his oldest friends, Governor James F. Byrnes, "has behind him a career of that universal quality rarely achieved since the days of the great figures of the American Revolutionary era"?

Bernard Baruch was born in Camden, South Carolina, on August 19, 1870. His father, Dr. Simon Baruch, was a German immigrant who had dashed off to serve as a surgeon in the Confederate Army as soon as he received his medical diploma. Captured, released and recaptured by the enemy, Dr. Baruch settled in Camden after the Civil War and married Belle Wolfe, the daughter of a planter whose family had lived in the South for seven generations.

Bernard was the second of four sons. When he was eleven his father moved the family to New York City in search of more opportunity than Camden offered. There Dr. Baruch became a professor at the College of Physicians of Columbia University, where he still is credited with diagnosing and helping to perform the first successful appendectomy on record. Many years later his famous son would give more than a million dollars to establish university research foundations for the promotion of physical medicine in honor of his father.

Young Bernard entered the College of the City of New York at the age of fourteen and graduated in 1889, with a major in classical languages. A fair student, he was a better athlete, being especially good in lacrosse, boxing and baseball. Well over six feet tall, muscular and quick on his feet, Bernard early developed the strong constitution which was to stand him in such good stead in the years to come that at eighty-two he still has the health and vigor of a much younger man.

Baruch's first job after leaving college was as errand boy and office clerk in a firm that sold glassware to druggists. His salary was $3.00 a week. His second employer was a small banking concern which paid him the same wage, plus a chance to learn something about finance.

Next came a trip to Europe with his father, followed by a job in a gold mine in Colorado. Back in New York once more, he was employed by A. A. Housman & Company, brokers—at $5.00 a week. At this point he had about decided to make finance

31

a career—thus putting into effect a prophecy made earlier by a phrenologist.

To equip himself better in this field, Bernard Baruch studied bookkeeping and law at night school. Blessed with a good memory, he made excellent progress in his courses. Moreover, his study of railroad data, in particular, soon prompted people from other offices, in addition to Housman's, to consult him as though he had the industrial map of America in his head.

This was a compliment which Baruch appreciated. Unfortunately, however, he didn't always live up to his reputation for research and analysis. The ticker tape was irresistible. Couldn't he read it as well as the next man? He began to make small purchases of ten shares, through another brokerage house, and if he won a little one day he often would lose it soon after. What was the key to gambling in the market? He began to try to discover the answer and questioned the people he worked with, as well as other brokers and speculators.

He soon reached the conclusion that the answer lay in *facts*—facts about the companies in which he was buying stock, facts about the people who were running them, and facts about their past performances and future prospects. There arose in him that insatiable zest for information which later led President Wilson to dub an older and wiser Bernard Baruch "Dr. Facts."

The time came when the young man asked the Housman Company for a raise. He had received several salary increases, and in 1896 was drawing $25.00 a week, but he thought he was worth more. His employers agreed. Instead of a raise which the company could not afford, however, he was offered a one-eighth interest in the business itself. He accepted and in that year made $6,000 in commissions as a customers' man, in addition to his salary.

In 1898 Baruch earned a large commission for his firm by obtaining a major interest in the Liggett & Myers Tobacco Company for Thomas Fortune Ryan, who already controlled the Union Tobacco Company. By this time Baruch had a one-third interest in the firm, and his total earnings for the year came to more than $160,000. Wall Streeters were beginning to talk about him as a smart young trader, and he himself felt that he had "arrived" as a speculator. He was not so certain, when a bad investment in the stock of a distilling firm, bought without his usual thorough investigation, resulted in a substantial loss.

Within a year, however, young Baruch had recovered from that setback. In 1901 he decided to sell Amalgamated Copper short, against the advice of some of the wisest heads on Wall Street, and was reported to have made $700,000. Not long afterward, he cleared a considerable sum which could have been considered consolation money, as the Morgan group had prevented him from gaining control of the Louisville & Nashville Railroad.

By 1902 he possessed—in his own phrase—$100,000 for every one of his thirty-two years. He was happily married and had two girls and a boy, but he was far from satisfied with his life. Somehow he felt that he should be doing something more important than piling up money. As a speculator, he was unable to point to a single industrial company in which he had a tangible interest as director or member of the Board. Had he made a mistake in not following in the professional footsteps of Dr. Baruch? Should he take up the study of law?

After a trip to Europe with his wife and his father, Baruch withdrew from A. A. Housman & Company. He opened an office at 111 Broadway, but took on no clients. He had determined that, whatever he would do in the market in the future, he would do alone. He would be a lone operator.

One day a magazine editor said to him, "You know, B. M., you are not really a Wall Street man at heart. You should go into public life, and some day you will." That proved to be an excellent prophecy, but Baruch was not yet ready to act on it.

Instead, he began to collaborate with the Guggenheims, and in one deal purchased control of two smelting companies for them.

When asked by the Guggenheim lawyer what fee he expected for his services, Baruch replied, "One million dollars." Told of this seemingly exorbitant demand, Daniel Guggenheim replied, "If Bernie says he ought to get a million dollars, that is what he will get." Actually, Baruch paid out $600,000 to the men who had assisted him and had legal expenses totalling $100,000. Later, when he thought the Guggenheims were in trouble, Baruch offered to deposit half a million dollars to their account. He was hardly the cold-hearted gambler, as some people on the Street kept jeering.

The year 1912 was a turning point in Baruch's life. The direction in which he turned was toward national politics. Coming from a Southern state, he always had been a strong Democrat and a regular contributor to his party's campaign funds. Knowing this, William F. McCombs—then promoting the candidacy of Governor Woodrow Wilson for the Presidency —brought the Governor to see Baruch one day.

The two liked each other from the start, but it is probable that Baruch backed Wilson at first merely as a matter of party loyalty. From business training and personal inclination, Baruch himself leaned more toward the economic and social views of Theodore Roosevelt. Nevertheless, he actively worked for Wilson's election. When Wilson entered the White House, however, Baruch distinguished himself by asking nothing in return. He valued Wilson's friendship, but at that time neither man could have guessed that within a few years Baruch would be one of the President's most trusted advisers.

Late in 1916, Wilson appointed Baruch to the Advisory Commission of the Council of National Defense, thus launching him upon a career of distinguished service to his country. A resolution of the Council, dated July 28, 1917, by which the War Industries Board was created, defined its duties in general terms.

Later, with the reorganization of the War Industries Board in March of 1918, Baruch was oppointed its Chairman by President Wilson. It was then that Baruch began to establish the international reputation which he has since maintained as an authority on industrial mobilization.

In view of that reputation, it surprises most people to learn that Baruch has since held only two other key Government jobs. He was a delegate to the Versailles Peace Conference after World War I, and he served as our country's first representative on the United Nations Atomic Energy Commission after World War II. His other activities on behalf of the Government have been advisory. For more than thirty years Baruch has acted as a special consultant to Presidents and the Congress, rather than as an appointive official. Even in his official Government positions, he never accepted any payment for his services.

To quote James F. Byrnes on his friend Baruch, "It is not in the official titles and public reports that one finds his great contributions. It is through his informal advice and assistance ... that his influence for the national good has been most strongly felt."

It is true that Baruch has never been "a prophet without honor in his own country." Indeed, he could hardly have been more honored and respected if he had held a dozen high elective offices. His advice has never been consistently accepted nor profitably used, yet today he remains that paradox—a beloved but sometimes controversial Elder Statesman who has made a popular career of an unpopular task, that of goading the conscience of his countrymen.

The fact that a man's advice is seldom taken at the time it is offered does not mean, of course, that his views are generally wrong. On the contrary, his counsel may be unwelcome, or uncomfortable, or unpolitic—and yet be honored. In fact, it is more than likely that part of the respect shown Baruch in his later years is the belated thanks of a nation accustomed to receiving and appreciating his advice—if not to following it promptly.

After nearly forty years in the forefront of public life, Bernard Baruch has emerged as one of the most highly regarded Elder Statesmen of our day. To a greater degree than any other American over a similar period of time, Baruch has won and kept the esteem of all types of our citizens—rich and poor, young and old, industrialists and laborers, Republicans and Democrats, farmers and city people.

What is more, Baruch's reputation rests upon his lifelong habit of very often being right. In the final analysis, he has consistently been right about important issues—right about the dangers that have confronted us from totalitarian aggression since World War I; right about the steps we should have taken to combat those dangers; right about the price we would have to pay for our failure to take those steps; and right about the things we have been doing wrong.

The faculty of being right so often does not lead to popularity necessarily. Yet Americans have recognized that Mr. Baruch has made an enormous personal investment in time, money and effort to obtain the information upon which he bases his advice to us. We have long known, as well, that his integrity is beyond question. His advice has always been given for our own good.

His passion for the realistic view has led him to face the truth openly and clearly. And he can be stubborn on such a subject. Baruch will add 2 plus 2 and always come up with 4. As Carter Glass once put it, "Yeah, they say Bernie's dogmatic. He's dogmatic, all right. He's dogmatic as hell about that."

Over and above these basic considerations, his readiness to serve has played a very special part in the public affairs of his country. Regardless of the party in power, regardless of the political favor in which his views may be held at the moment, regardless even of the concerted opposition of other men, inevitably there has come a time in the course of each Administration when Baruch is sent for to help solve a tough problem.

Thus he served as Wilson's strong right arm in mobilizing industry for World War I, and was a top economic adviser at the Peace Conference. Baruch was active in the Agricultural Conference of 1922 under Warren G. Harding. Calvin Coolidge asked for his advice; so did Herbert Hoover. With the return of a Democratic Administration under Franklin Delano Roosevelt, the demands Washington made upon Baruch increased. When Harry Truman needed a distinguished American to represent this country on the United Nations Atomic Energy Commission, the appointment almost naturally went to Baruch.

With or without the blessing of 1600 Pennsylvania Avenue, Baruch constantly has occupied himself with jobs that needed doing for the public good, and has coached many others in the nation's service.

What qualities of mind and heart did he bring to his many governmental responsibilities? Exacting knowledge, for one. As mentioned earlier, President Wilson called him "Dr. Facts," and, in World War I, weighed him down with assignments that depended upon precise information, properly interpreted, for their successful completion.

Personal character? As Chairman of the War Industries Board, Baruch had almost complete authority to mobilize our industrial resources—an authority which he was unwilling to assume until he had sold his seat on the New York Stock Exchange, disposed of all shares in corporations that could possibly be affected by Government action, and otherwise freed himself from such private interests as might have influenced his public decisions.

Selfless devotion to duty? It is well-known that Baruch, as a close friend, urged President Wilson to accept Senate ratification of the Versailles peace terms with compromise rather than risk having the Treaty rejected. It is perhaps less well-known that he refused a reward for his services—appointment as Secretary of the Treasury.

Perseverance? Mr. Baruch, a lifelong and ardent Democrat, continued to be on call as an adviser to the Republican Presidents who followed Woodrow Wilson into the White House. During the G.O.P. regimes he was, as always, a constant and outspoken advocate of industrial preparedness for any emergency that might arise, and a persistent opponent of plans on paper in the place of actual and tangible readiness to meet attack.

Consistency? From World War I to the present day he has continued to advance his oft-repeated plans for taking the profit out of war.

Foresight? From the middle 1930's to the outbreak of World War II, "Bernie," as President Roosevelt called him, urged the Administration to stockpile tin, rubber and other strategic materials. Late in World War II, he was instrumental in establishing the procedures to be followed in terminating Government contracts with industry and in converting our economy back to a peacetime basis.

Sometimes Baruch's warnings were popular; sometimes not. In his insistence upon the all-important aspects of national strength—military strength, industrial strength, actual strength in being, planned strength in reserve—Baruch sometimes proved to be more demanding than the framework or traditions of democracy allowed, except in time of peril.

In the period between the World Wars—the "normalcy" era of the three Republican Presidents and the emergency period of FDR—what Baruch had to tell the American people about foreign relations often seemed to them out of date, almost alarmist. In the days when they were persuading themselves that the U. S. had made the world "safe for Democracy," Baruch was explaining before the Army Industrial College or the

Congress and in his published writings that, during peace, we must plan for what is to be done in the event of war. In brief, he preached that peace through strength—armed strength and economic preparedness—is the only safe foundation for our security, and perhaps for the security of the free world as well.

Always aware of the need for a well-informed public, Baruch periodically put his views in print. A select list of his published works between 1920 and 1951 indicates the trend of his thinking: *The Making of the Reparation and Economic Sections of the Treaty* (1920); *Taking the Profit Out of War* (1926, reprinted in 1936); *Priorities—the Synchronizing Force* (1941); *American Industry in the War* (1941); *Preventing Inflation* (1942); *War and Postwar Adjustment Policies* (1944); *The International Control of Atomic Energy* (1946); *What of Our Future?* (1949); *Spiritual Armageddon Is Here—Now* (1951).

By 1920 he had settled down to what he considered his job—"to keep the country prepared industrially for any emergency that might come," as Carter Field has written. Having personally taken part in the Versailles Peace negotiations, he was none too sure about the world remaining at peace for very long. Shortly after Harding's inauguration, therefore, he embarked on a mission he considered even more important than his work on the War Industries Board. He began a one-man crusade to have the U. S. always ready for war. First, we had to have an adequate armed force, trained and equipped. In addition, as Field has written, "He wanted a skeleton directing body always working on industrial preparedness, backed by powers lodged in the President that could instantly, in emergency, be brought into play. He wanted to assure not only military strength, but also government control of prices. Thus he would prevent inflation, hold down the cost of war, avoid civilian hardship, and avert the hitherto inevitable postwar depression following demobilization of fighters and war workers."

For thirty years Baruch has been making regular trips to Europe, to observe conditions there at first hand. On his return, he would pour out his observations and inside information to all those who would listen. As the Thirties grew more critical and the clouds of war became visible to certain eyes, he tried again and again to warn the American people about their danger. Few would take him seriously.

Baruch has been able to be bold and firm in his ideas because of his unbounded confidence in the United States. Testifying in May, 1952, at a Senate Subcommittee hearing, he put it this way: Americans are people "of huge pride." Set them doing something and then let somebody tell them they cannot do it, and they will outdo themselves. "We did it in the last world war, and we can do it again. But you must let the people know what our peril is and what steps and why you are taking them, and you need not worry about deficits, because they will supply the goods at whatever cost. . . ."

"Of course we can fix the world," Baruch has said on many occasions. He doesn't even like to hear people joke about this matter. Once a friend said, "If we can't fix the world, at least we can talk about horses." Baruch commented to his nurse: "Did you hear what that young man said? He said, 'If we can't fix the world.' I don't like to hear the young men of this country talking that way. We *can* fix the world. We've got to believe we can, and then we will."

But sometimes Baruch has lost faith in those who are in charge of fixing the world. In a letter to the author, dated September 2, 1950, Mr. Baruch advised:

"I fear that the people in Washington do not realize the full extent of the difficulties that lie before us. They are going at it piecemeal, with all the tragic costs that will come from that kind of approach."

40

In the chapters that follow, the concepts which Bernard Baruch has recommended and supported are explained and analyzed. The next chapter describes some of the nation's efforts toward peace through strength since World War II. It focuses on Baruch's recommendations since 1945 for action to achieve military and economic security.

The testimony of Bernard M. Baruch on May 28, 1952 before the Preparedness Subcommittee of the Senate Committee on Armed Services was printed under the title, "Only Strength Will Win the Peace." Baruch's testimony included an admonition he has frequently emphasized: "We must strengthen ourselves militarily if we are to succeed in our objective of preventing a third world war and building and keeping a lasting peace."

CHAPTER 2

"Building ...
A Lasting Peace"

Bernard Baruch stands in the forefront of that small group of Americans who, after the Yalta Conference of 1945, became increasingly suspicious of Soviet Russia's post-war ambitions. Like many others, he was at first more disheartened than alarmed by the growls of the Russian bear in the halls of the United Nations. But when the bear began to gobble up country after country in Eastern Europe, there was no doubt in Baruch's mind of the new peril facing the world, and he prepared once again—as so many times in the past—to rouse the American public to its danger. It was not an easy task, or especially rewarding.

Weary from the long war against the Axis powers, the average American was in no mood to believe that Hitler's prophecy was coming true—that the war-time alliance between Soviet Russia and the West could not survive the difficult days of peace. Not until the hammer and sickle were firmly riveted on Czechoslovakia in 1948 did millions of Americans begin to open their eyes to what Moscow was plotting—and achieving.

Other millions became aware of the national peril only when the Communists struck in Korea on June 25, 1950. This invasion revealed the urgency of a rapid strengthening of the whole free world in the face of Communist aggression. As always, however, many of our national figures were not so easily alerted.

Senator Taft immediately questioned the legal right of the President to send American troops to fight abroad, without authorization of the Congress. Two years later, the Republican platform charged that the Administration "plunged us into war in Korea without the consent of our citizens through their authorized representatives in Congress. . . ."

Even among those who saw the danger to the United States, many clung to a false sense of security, or wrapped themselves in the thought that this country is the strongest on earth. Many remained complacent despite the testimony of General Omar Bradley, Chairman of the Joint Chiefs of Staff, when—at the signing of the North Atlantic Defense Treaty—he pointed out that it would require from three to five years to build a minimum defense force in Western Europe, at the rate of rearming then being planned.

Even such distinguished patriots as Herbert Hoover and the late Senator Brien McMahon, Chairman of the Joint Congressional Committee on Atomic Energy, argued that adequate national defense no longer required the so-called "conventional" armament and land forces, but rather the fullest development of atomic weapons and of air power. There were others, as Hanson Baldwin pointed out in the *New York Times* Magazine in the summer of 1952, who claimed that "Fortress America" no longer required balanced military forces or friends and allies overseas. We can, said these neo-isolationists, virtually go it alone, relying on our aircraft carriers, our bombers and our A-weapons "in the deadly reprisal strategy of a rattlesnake."

Baruch considered those views not only false but dangerous. When he testified on May 28, 1952 before the Preparedness Subcommittee of the Senate Armed Services Committee, he declared that world peace and national security demand total diplomacy and greater speed in building up a full complement of armament and armed forces, as well as greater economic and industrial strength. "We simply cannot make peace," he emphasized, "unless we are militarily stronger." Total diplomacy "necessitates an overall global strategy in which military, diplomatic, political, economic and spiritual factors are parts of one whole, embracing all the many factors in the struggle for peace." Solemnly he warned that disaster inevitably would result from "piecemeal patchwork, waiting for the next crisis to hit us."

While grieved by the tragic fact that "we have been forced into an arms race with our very survival at stake," Baruch emphasized "the present disparity in military strength between Soviet Russia and ourselves and our allies." He added, "No decisive victory in the cold war is possible as long as the Soviets hold as terrifying an edge in military readiness over the West as they do today." He called upon the Subcommittee to give the public the facts "so that the American people will know whether the tempo of re-arming is really being changed on the basis of a fully thought-through master plan of defense."

Always insistent upon the necessity for such an overall blueprint for defense, Baruch has been equally insistent that "no aggressor was ever stopped by blueprints"—a view he repeated to the Subcommittee.

He asked that "the whole defense program" be reviewed "to determine whether too heavy an emphasis has not been placed on building new facilities and too little on turning out weapons."

Baruch discounted the "much talked-of matter of 'obsolescence.'" Admitting that "we must strive constantly to improve our weapons," he said that what is "obsolete" must also "be judged by what the enemy has and by the value of even older weapons in dire emergency." Such obsolete weapons, as our over-age destroyers and stocks of Lee-Enfield rifles left from World War I helped save Britain from Hitler, he pointed out. Moreover, he asked, "What would we be doing today without our mothball fleet, air reserves, and ammunition stocks left over from the last war?"

He called for the stockpiling of actual weapons "considerably in excess of our own troop requirement." Such weapons, he said, "could be deployed around the globe so as to pin down and immobilize a sizeable portion of Russia's own armed strength, if she decided to go to war. . . . We could take instant advantage of any opportunity that might arise for arming some ally. We would be prepared if events forced an abrupt increase in our Armed Forces, since men can be recruited more rapidly than munitions."

Many Americans, convinced by this reasoning, deeply regretted that Baruch took it one step further. "To forestall persistent Soviet aggression," he said, "we must be capable of opening other fronts where we can choose the conditions of struggle—where we can take the initiative." Firm resistance to aggression was necessary, these cautious Americans agreed, but talk of taking the initiative and opening other fronts was talk of hastening, not deterring, global war. Had Baruch forgotten that the American people strike back at aggression but do not take the war-making initiative, and do not open up new fronts until war has been forced upon them?

In support of his own suggestion, Baruch might have called attention to a Congressional appropriation passed in the spring of 1952, which aroused little comment at the time. As part of the Mutual Security Act of 1952, the Congress had appropriated $100 million as a special fund for militant help to anti-Communist persons and groups in the Soviet-dominated areas of Europe. The fund was intended primarily to aid the escape of people behind the Iron Curtain who wished to join combat units for the ultimate liberation of their homelands.

The Soviets, who follow official Congressional action far more closely than do most Americans, protested to our Government, and Foreign Minister Vishinsky screamed in the United Nations General Assembly that the U. S. appropriation was a violation of the 1933 exchange of letters between President Roosevelt and Maxim Litvinoff, in which both nations promised not to interfere in each other's internal affairs. American delegates in the Assembly asked Andrei Vishinsky to specify dates and occasions when the Soviets and their agents had *not* interfered in American affairs. Furthermore, they asked, since when had Hungary, Czechoslovakia and the other countries officially become parts of the Soviet Union?

Baruch, in brief, was simply bringing into the open, as he always has, what others discuss behind closed doors. Thus, he may have been surprised at the furor caused in the press by President-elect Eisenhower's remarks in a speech before the American Legion during the election campaign. Eisenhower declared that the United States should encourage the subjugated peoples behind the Iron Curtain to rise up and overthrow their oppressors.

There resulted such a flood of criticism of his statement, and not only from the Democrats, that Eisenhower did not repeat the subject again in his campaign speeches. The country as a whole was not yet prepared for open sponsorship of an underground movement in Europe, just as Baruch's advocacy of another front before the Senate Subcommittee was criticized in newspaper editorials and columns. Yet molders of public opinion approved several other recommendations which Baruch made at the same time. They liked such blunt statements as "I do not think that the huge sums which have been appropriated for defense are being expended as economically and effectively as they should be. . . . Other nations get more fighting power for the same resources than we do. Why?"

Some, however, withheld approval of his equally blunt reiteration, "I am opposed to the ceiling on defense expenditures, even as I opposed the earlier reduction by the Executive." Anticipating this reaction, Baruch added that he appreciated "the justifiable concern of those who are worried over how long we can continue to spend such huge sums on defense without wrecking our economy."

He urged Congress "to regain control of the military budget," employing a greatly expanded staff, as the Hoover Commission had recommended, to work with the Defense Department through every step of the budgetary process. "Go beyond these mere requests for money to how the appropriations are actually being spent," Baruch suggested, "and even into such basic problems of military organization as to why so large an overhead is required in relation to the forces actually fighting."

The armed services, he insisted, "need a driving production authority of their own—of the caliber of the late William Knudsen—to see that orders are properly placed and followed up, vigorously, constantly. The services also need a clear-cut point of decision to determine when designs are to be frozen and weapons put into production. Changes in design are costly both in time and dollars."

Other Baruch recommendations to the Subcommittee on May 28, 1952 were: "That you lay bare the basis of our so-called calculated risk so the public can judge whether we are being needlessly exposed to unwarranted danger," and, "that Congress adopt a defense budget which fits the risks we face." He also wanted the Congress to insist that the arms program be reduced to specific production targets, and that mobilization controls be adjusted accordingly.

Baruch emphasized that the President should be given all the power he needed to carry through this program, "including price and priority controls." Finally, he urged that the Senate Subcommittee "obtain from the military a single, unified strategy, covering the whole defense establishment, and which is part of an over-all, global strategy which integrates our own defense efforts with what our allies can do."

With this "single unified strategy," Baruch insisted, there must be "a sense of disciplined urgency" without which the "whole mobilization may fall to pieces," and added, "Of course we cannot rearm to the extent that our security requires if we persist in profits as usual, social reforms as usual, and politics as usual. . . . Our economy can do all that our security requires —and more—provided there is the will to do so and the courage of administration to channel our resources from less essential to more essential activities and to share the costs of the struggle equitably. . . .

"Our highest military authorities have stated, unequivocally, that from now through 1954 will be the period of maximum peril for this nation. Yet we deliberately are doing less than we can do to achieve readiness by that date." He called on the Subcommittee to give the American people full information "so they can demand a defense program which will mobilize our strength in time to prevent further aggression."

There was and has been, naturally, considerable doubt as to when this nation will face its greatest danger. On November 11, 1952, Defense Secretary Lovett released a letter written by him to Chairman Johnson of the Senate Preparedness Subcommittee.

The Evening Star of Washington, D.C., quoted Lovett as writing, "The Joint Chiefs of Staff do not state that 'the years of 1953 and 1954 will constitute the period of our greatest peril.' They mention the general period of 1954 as a date by which Russian capabilities will become 'very dangerous.' They do not estimate that Russian intention is to make war in 1954 or imply that after that year danger will be less. Obviously, if we knew Russian intentions, we could gear our mobilization accordingly."

Since Baruch made his recommendations in May, 1952, we are once again close to becoming the "arsenal of democracy." The Munitions Board of the Defense Department told Congress in its semi-annual report, on August 15, 1952, that $480,000,000 worth of strategic and critical materials had been added to the nation's war-emergency stockpile during the first half of 1952. This was accomplished despite the diversion of millions of dollars worth of scarce metals to the current rearmament program, and despite other withdrawals from the stockpile in the same period to speed the military buildup.

A new type of stockpiling was publicly announced in late November by Defense Mobilizer Henry H. Fowler. He reported that President Truman would recommend in the 1953-1954 military budget the creation of a billion-dollar reserve of heavy machine tools and other production facilities. Fowler explained that this would cost less than a huge stockpile of arms and would smooth the transition to all-out war mobilization if that should become necessary.

In August the Defense Department revealed that in the fiscal year ending June 30, 1952, it had spent or obligated $61,900,-000,000 in expanding our military forces, making a total expenditure for the two-year period following the outbreak of war in Korea of $111,500,000,000.

War and the security measures taken to prevent it are clearly becoming more and more expensive. Is a "ceiling" really possible in defense spending? Listening to Republican campaign speeches in the 1952 election, one might have thought that nothing in the world was easier than to bring economy to Government and to reduce the huge tax load now bearing down on all Americans. With Republican control of the White House and the Congress, it remains to be seen whether the campaign promises will be able to be realized.

In Hoover's time there still was talk of trying to collect from European nations the debts incurred during World War I and its immediate aftermath. Twenty years later we were not concerned with billing foreign nations for the Second World War, but rather with preventing economic collapses in Europe that could help bring on still a third world conflagration. We also were concerned lest the neighbors of Soviet Russia remain so weak as to invite Soviet penetration or absorption.

That explains why, in the fiscal year ending June 30, 1952, the United States spent an additional $1,900,000,000 for military aid around the globe—an increase of 72 percent over the previous year. During the first six months of 1952, U. S. arms shipments to our European allies jumped more than 100% over the previous year. Government officials predicted on September 20, 1952 that, at the current rate, American defense spending in Europe might reach a total of $8,000,000,000 in the next twelve months.

On the previous day, a report had been published in the press regarding the defense time-table laid down at Lisbon for the Council of the North Atlantic Treaty Organization. Its retiring Chairman, Lester B. Pearson, announced that the schedule was not being met in all respects but added, "Progress has been substantial and encouraging . . . the next year of NATO may well decide whether . . . we will reach our goal of security from which we can keep moving toward other and greater goals of increased human welfare and constructive peace."

September of 1952 also saw the announcement of less encouraging news. The United Nations Economic Commission for Europe reported that industrial expansion in all Western Europe "has been slowing down, while industrial capacity in the traditionally low-producing Eastern European countries had expanded rapidly"—with an average 20 percent increase over the same period of the previous year in each of the Soviet satellites. No estimate was included for Russia itself, for obvious reasons.

How would the industrial slowdown of Western Europe affect her defense buildup? Ernest O. Hauser, in a *Saturday Evening Post* article on General Matthew B. Ridgway in the issue of October 25, 1952, reported that the covering force of 25 combat-ready divisions, originally scheduled to be ready in the fall of 1952, would not be complete until sometime in 1953. As for the reserve divisions, he thought Ridgway would be lucky to have half of them by the spring of 1953. Hauser summarized the NATO picture in these words: "And the total NATO force of ninety-seven divisions—exclusive of Greek and Turkish units —envisaged for the end of 1954, will almost surely remain the 'phantom army' former President Herbert Hoover recently chose to call it. With a far-from-phantom Soviet juggernaut of 175 divisions, including more than sixty armored ones, in readiness behind the Iron Curtain, Western Europe still has little reason for complacency."

Our Department of State, as late as September, 1952, did not take quite so somber a view of the military situation. John M. Allison, an Assistant Secretary of State, in commenting on the global situation at that time, declared that the military strength already built up by the NATO countries would make it difficult for Soviet forces to undertake European aggression without "an all-out war." He felt that, though conditions in Asia were better than a year before, Communist imperialism was still "a greater immediate threat" in that area than in Europe—either through subversion or infiltration.

He singled out Communist China, Indo-China and Korea as the most serious trouble spots. Events since September confirmed Mr. Allison's fears. Heavy fighting again broke out in Indo-China and almost all of France's military power was concentrated there in the hope of crushing the Viet Minh rebels. According to French sources, French casualties since 1948 exceeded American casualties in Korea, and France was finding it difficult to replace her lost fighting men.

As for the truce negotiations in Korea, they were in indefinite recess as of late November. Simultaneously, the tempo of the war was being stepped up and the fighting was the heaviest since 1951. The United Nations' forces battled the Chinese and

Korean Communists in a futile recapture of one small hill after another, with success going first to one side and then to the other. The only certain result of this type of warfare was the increase in casualties for both sides. The Defense Department announced that, as of November 26, 1952, American battle casualties totalled 126,997. In thirty months of fighting in Korea we had suffered 22,258 dead, 91,933 wounded, 9,444 missing and the remainder captured.

Baruch had been reasonably successful, back in April, 1949, in foreseeing the general nature of our foreign developments. In a *Saturday Evening Post* article titled "What of Our Future?" he summarized the obvious threats to world peace at that time. He made no attempt to pinpoint the exact zones of peril and there was no reference to Korea. In fact, he predicted that the "show-down" with Russia would come when the effort was made to rejoin partitioned Germany—a show-down that still hovers just over the threshold three and one-half years later.

Baruch's main thesis in this article was: "The stakes are too immense to trust to improvisation or luck." He proposed a central "think-body" or General Staff, "continuously deliberating over the whole of our peace-waging, adjusting the balance to changing conditions and our evolving peace strategy."

Baruch stated in his *Post* article that before the end of World War II he had suggested to President Roosevelt the creation of two deliberative bodies: a Supreme Reconstruction Council in Europe, and an Advisory Peace Council at home. The latter was to consist of the Secretaries of State, War, Navy, Treasury, James F. Byrnes, then Director of the Office of War Mobilization and Reconversion, and Harry Hopkins, plus a small fact-finding staff, and a counselor who enjoyed Roosevelt's confidence. Roosevelt approved the second part of this dual suggestion, and spoke of naming Byrnes as Chairman of the Peace Council and Judge Samuel Rosenman as its counselor. Rosenman at that time was in London. Baruch, sent there on a special

mission by the President, told him of the suggestion and won his
interest. Two days later the President died, and the Peace Council idea was forgotten officially.

But Baruch, who gets maximum mileage out of his ideas,
has continued to revise and recommend this one, too. It was
recapped and renamed later by John Foster Dulles, when he
was the Republican strategist and former foreign policy adviser
to the Department of State, but Dulles perhaps conceived it
independently. As the Secretary of State, he may have the opportunity of establishing such a Peace Council.

When the idea became the core of Baruch's *Saturday Evening
Post* article, he noted that American business and industry had
"a bad case of jitters." Indeed, he thought that phrase too weak.
"All business," he declared, "is now on a fear-to-fear basis."
Why? The nation was "neither at peace nor war"—a condition
that "clashes violently with every American tradition." (He did
not add that this condition had prevailed also between 1914
and 1917, and between 1938 and 1941.) New technological
developments, Baruch continued, and new armaments including atomic weapons, have destroyed the "buffer of time which
formerly cushioned" our isolation, and "war and peace have
become an interconnecting stream."

A new kind of peace-waging therefore was required, Baruch
said. For this, he considered the National Security Council
neither broad enough nor well enough organized to reach
effective decisions. That Council, he insisted, should be replaced
by a new board, which might enable us "to develop a new sense
of the inter-relationship between war and peace, between home
and abroad, between each of us and 'those bureaucrats in Washington.'"

Such a Peace Council, Baruch declared, should review all
American foreign-aid commitments. "If a greater outlay of
resources will break the stalemate on any front, let's pour it
on," he said, "if no decision is possible, let us cut expenditures

and insist that these nations do more for themselves." Having made this his main contention when testifying on January 19, 1948 on the Marshall Plan, Baruch added, "As to the argument that some countries may turn Communist, we do not have enough to buy the political convictions of other nations. Let us not be blackjacked by threats 'to join Russia.' . . . We can help those with will to save themselves."

The Peace Council proposed by Baruch should, he said, decide whether "serious danger may be forced upon us in a few years." If so, "then the program for rebuilding the defenses of Western Europe is recklessly slow" and "a peace-time equivalent of the War Production Board should already be functioning." Moreover, "with the continuous threat of war, we cannot trust blindly to a self-regulating economy."

This time, he insisted, "we must take our stand before the bullets have begun to fly," and at the same time accept "disciplines such as rationing and price control." This time, he reemphasized, the nation must "mobilize economic, military and spiritual power . . . in advance of war." Just how the people would be persuaded to accept those war disciplines before war came, he did not specify.

In concluding his *Post* article of April, 1949, Baruch made a charge that has been reiterated many times: "The inflation that has racked the country since the war's end had its start in the price control law of 1942. . . . That law legalized inflation."

Several months before the Economic Stabilization Act of 1942 became law, Baruch had advised that, in all fairness, wages should be allowed to move with living costs and farm prices should be tied to parity. His specific recommendations at that time are quoted in Chapter Six, which also sets forth their bearing on subsequent economic changes.

When the time came to overhaul the price and wage control machinery early in 1946, Baruch again testified before the House Banking and Currency Committee. His statement of March 26 ran to seventeen closely printed pages, but began, as he said, with certain of his ideas in capsule form. They are as follows:

"Increase production. This is the Law and Prophets—without it the rest of my suggestions are meaningless. . . .

"Stop increasing money supply. Stop decreasing taxes until the budget is balanced.

"Stop bunking the public by saying wage increases can be granted without increase in price levels.

"Do not fear to increase prices or wages where necessary to get and stimulate production.

"Continue price controls, subject to indicated modifications, for a year. Allow profit but no profiteering.

"Avoid favoritism to any particular group. Take care of those between the millstones—clerks, government employees, pensioners, et al.

"Make surpluses of goods in military hands available to compensate for shortages. Stimulate founding and financing small business.

"Take stock before blindly lending—make inventories of our goods, our cash, our credit before we increase the pressure on these.

"Cut government costs, including Federal, state, county and city. In time of deflation we should spend; in time of inflation we should save.

"Eliminate all strikes or lockouts for a year, but arrange that hardships are guarded against.

"Set up a high court of commerce—a sort of supreme economic counsel which can decide questions involved in the above points and related subjects.

58

"Remember that a sore or rotten spot anywhere in our system spreads and causes an illness everywhere.

"Avoid an economic dictatorship. We are still a free society based on the enterprise system. Let us abolish neither without the consent of the people.

"And, above all, we should keep in mind that the humanities come before the dollars. . . . Our first duty runs to man before business, but we must not forget that sometimes the two are interchangeable."

When Baruch made these recommendations, the steel industry had just won another battle for increased prices following the steel crisis in the spring of 1946. Baruch, as Chairman of the War Industries Board in the First World War, had had to face similar demands. At that time, however, the steel industry was dominated by Judge Elbert H. Gary, who himself seemed to have been molded of steel, while organized labor was comparatively weak, and Hugh A. Frayne, who represented labor on Baruch's Board, was even weaker.

The steel crisis in the spring of 1946 was magnified over that of the First World War by as much as the steel crisis in the spring of 1952 was magnified over that of 1946.

Baruch's friend, James F. Byrnes, was then President Truman's Secretary of State, and already was working closely with Baruch in February, 1946 on the problem of devising a plan for effective international control of atomic energy. Both were called in by the President for advice on the steel strike, which was slowing production in general. The President also called in Fred M. Vinson, who had resigned in April, 1945 as Director of the Office of Economic Stabilization.

The steel industry demanded at least $6 more per ton. Initially offered $4, Chester Bowles, then Price Administrator, insisted $2.50 was all that was justified. President Truman originally said that the steel industry needed no price increase at all, but from its high profits after taxes could well absorb an

18½ cents an hour wage increase for steel workers. He recommended that wage increase to cover their increased living costs.

To reach a compromise, Truman finally agreed to allow what was then called a moderate bulge in the "hold-the-line" order on prices as decreed by President Roosevelt early in 1943. He also promoted Chester Bowles to direct the Office of Economic Stabilization and named Paul A. Porter to Bowles' old job. One of Baruch's biographers, Harry Irving Shumway, was much impressed by Baruch's role in this steel struggle and quoted a commentator who reported, "Baruch was instrumental in breaking one of the stalemates in the steel strike. In this, he devised a secret formula for a speedy solution."

But Baruch, quickly washing his hands of that statement, declared less than a month later to the House Banking and Currency Committee that "indirect control over wages" had been removed "by getting rid of the Little Steel Formula (which was but a weak substitute for wage control), and by granting the 18½ cent increase for steel. This will be followed by increases all along the line, no matter what anybody thinks to the contrary. Call it a bulge, but it is really a break—and a grave one. This was inflationary.

"I do not blame labor," he continued, "for wanting to retain their standard of living. For the decrease of $6,000,000,000 in taxes and the throwing over of the Little Steel Formula naturally made them feel they should take care of themselves. I would want my take-home pay to remain the same. The corporations and smaller income groups benefited mostly from the $6,000,000,000 tax reduction."

Other groups, Baruch prophesied, would demand price and wage increases, and already, he pointed out, the "race between prices and the cost of living is going on here and all over the world. Ask the housewife. She knows better than the economists and statisticians." She certainly did.

Baruch predicted, "With full production, we can escape inflation and have our people resume their leadership." It made Baruch heartsick that "the whole world is watching us, amazed at the exhibition of a giant who cannot put himself together even to take care of his own needs." Whatever he could do to help that giant through exhortation, he would do.

Throughout the remaining months of 1946, all of Baruch's interest in the cause of national security and all his efforts were devoted to his duties as United States representative to the United Nations Atomic Energy Commission. This demanding service is discussed in Chapter Seven.

Soon after he resigned from that post he announced, on January 11, 1947, that he was retiring from public life. Interested onlookers were not overly alarmed. The betting odds were that Baruch would be back at the White House and on Capitol Hill before the month was out. And so he was!

On February 4, 1947, for example, Baruch testified before a Congressional Committee considering appointments to the United States Atomic Energy Commission. On March 4 he attended ceremonies marking the induction of his brother, Dr. Herman Baruch, as Ambassador to the Netherlands.

Meanwhile, Baruch's friend Byrnes had resigned from the Cabinet late in 1946, after frost had gathered on his relationship with Truman. By that time, Truman had grown wary of a number of officials who, it seemed to him, wanted to exercise the power that the people had elected him to use.

Mutual trust seemed to prevail between Baruch and Truman through late January, 1948, when on the 24th they conferred at the White House. Six months later, however, when Truman was rated a poor chance for re-election, Baruch in London publicly denied he was there on a Presidential mission. The press buzzed with speculation about their discord, and the guessing game continued even after William Hillman's book, *Mr. President,* was published early in 1952. By special permission, Hillman quoted a White House letter of August 19, 1948, in which Truman congratulated Baruch on his birthday and asked if he would agree to serve on the Finance Committee of the National Democratic campaign.

The full text of Baruch's reply has never been made public. It was, however, a polite but firm no, and Truman wrote Baruch again on August 31. As quoted by Hillman, the President expressed disappointment, mentioned the many honors that had gone to Baruch and his family, and acidly commented that, in rough going, the street seemed to be one-way. In a postcript, the President mentioned that he had appointed Mrs. William G. McAdoo and Mrs. Thomas J. Watson, along with the Ambassador to the Netherlands, as special representatives at the coronation of Princess Juliana. Nearly a year later, on August 20, 1949, Dr. Baruch resigned as Ambassador, and Truman's announcement stated the cause "was the Netherlands' severe winter."

By this time, it was sub-zero weather between Truman and Bernard Baruch. Only two months earlier the two men had publicly rowed over the National Security Resources Board as explained in detail in Chapter Three. Yet Baruch managed to muster some kind words for the Administration later when he appeared before the Senate Banking and Currency Committee on July 7, 1950, after war broke out in Korea. *The New York Times,* reporting his testimony of that date, carried the following summary:

"Baruch called for immediate all-out national mobilization that would include blanket price, wage and rent control as well as rationing.

"The Administration's proposals for production incentives including priorities and allocations and consumer credit restrictions, he said, were excellent. But the program, he declared, does not go far enough.

"Unless it were expanded as he recommended, the program would become 'an invitation to inflation.' "

According to the *Times,* in testifying on the Administration bill, the Elder Statesman said:

" 'This bill proposes a system over priorities, over production, yet nowhere is there provision made for controlling prices and other costs. Should this bill be enacted—without price control —the government may get what it wants, but with needless delay and ever increasing prices.'

"In other companion proposals, Baruch recommended:

" '1. That taxes be set high enough to cover all defense costs and reduce profiteering.

" '2. That an over-all mobilization agency be created immediately to synchronize the implementation of planning by the National Security Resources Board.

" '3. That a Capital Issues Committee be established under the Secretary of the Treasury to review all capital issues, public and private, deferring less essential projects to make sure housing, schools, hospitals and other more essential needs are met first.

" '4. That the role of the U. N. be strengthened by coordinating our efforts with it in common defense of peace.

" '5. That assistance in rearming nations ready to resist aggression be speeded along with expansion of our own defenses.' He said he would be loath to increase government controls if the exigencies of the world situation did not demand it.

" 'This legislation before you proposes that we deliberately refuse to lock the stable door until the horse is stolen,' Baruch said. 'A stand-by price control law, if it had been on our books before the Korean situation started might have stopped higher prices—but that hope is now dashed,' he added."

Constantly mounting living costs in the next two years would have justified Baruch in saying "I told you so." Testifying on May 28, 1952, before the Senate Preparedness Subcommittee, he declared:

"Congress actually passed the necessary legislation for such an across-the-economy program. But these powers were not used for months during which living costs soared, all savings were cheapened, and the real purchasing power of every defense dollar was slashed by one-fifth.

"This needless inflation already has cost us $12 billions in higher costs of defense and is likely to exact another $10 billions in needless tribute over the next fiscal year. . . ."

When the Defense Production Act became effective in September, 1950, why did President Truman, calling on labor and management to forego special advantages, hold up action on Titles IV and V of that Act—the sections authorizing control of prices, wages, salaries and rents? One clue, obviously, is to be found in a phrase of which Baruch is very fond. "The human equation," he has repeatedly said, "is the greatest of all—the demand to function—the desire to profit."

Another clue was pointed out by The Brookings Institution in a booklet reviewing Eliot Janeway's *The Struggle for Survival,* an account of economic mobilization in World War II. Totalitarian regimes, this summary pointed out, can order mobilization overnight, with full economic controls and rationing, just as Baruch recommended from the start of Korean hostilities. The same summary referred to the belief of Montagu Norman, the perceptive head of the Bank of England, that dictatorships could mobilize speedily and effectively, but only God Almighty could eventually mobilize a democracy. President Wilson and President Roosevelt required many experts and many months in their attempts to coordinate politics, diplomacy and war into an interrelated war economy, while preserving the fundamentals of a democratic system. Never achieving fully coordinated mobilization, each was, nonetheless, able to lead the nation to victory in a war of production. The Brookings summary concluded:

"Now that we are again mobilizing our resources for defense ... we are fortunate to be able to call on some of the experienced people who played key roles in the development and operation of the mobilization agencies, to play similar roles in the present circumstances.

"But experienced people are not enough. Wide public understanding of the interplay of politics and administration in mobilization is also required."

W. Stuart Symington, then NSRB Chairman, put it this way when interviewed by *U. S. News and World Report* magazine on October 20, 1950. Asked whether the people should be given a choice between butter and guns, he replied: "If we are really going to face up to the great and growing menace of international Communism, we must face up to it all the way." Convinced of the willingness of the country to sacrifice under such conditions, he added: "The American people should be agreeable to a curtailment of their standard of living."

Congressional committees themselves make sporadic attempts to develop public understanding of the problems democracy faces—as did one such committee in accumulating nine and one-half million words of testimony and findings while investigating the surprise Japanese attack on Pearl Harbor. Baruch has assisted many such investigating committees. But whatever the Senate Preparedness Subcommittee learned from him and others about the failure to "freeze" prices and wages before January 25, 1951, a new inflationary process was surely under way by then. Here is how Ellis G. Arnall, Price Administrator, described it in his farewell statement late in August, 1952 before turning over the reins to Tighe Woods:

"In the eight months after Korea, in that immense speculative boom that was largely psychological, since few real shortages existed . . . cost of living prices walked right up the side of the blackboard on the price chart. Eight percent in eight months. For a family that was spending $3,600 for living expenses then, the increase was $300.

"OPS froze prices in January of 1951. The record since then is one that plainly makes out the case for the effectiveness of direct price controls, even when those controls are something less than perfect. Since the price freeze your cost of living has advanced at the rate of only two-tenths of one percent a month....

"As you know, the price provisions of the Act passed in June by the Congress have put new severe limitations on the authority of OPS to do much about your cost of living. Fruits and vegetables, both fresh and processed, were taken right out of the possibility of any price control. Appropriations were reduced fifty percent. Our personnel has been cut from 12,000 to approximately 5,000."

It was the Dixiecrat-Republican coalition in June which made the new slits in the umbrella. As a result, the cost of living rose again between mid-July and mid-August to set another record, the Bureau of Labor Statistics reported on September 19. The index as of August 15, 1952 was 191.1 percent of the average from 1935 to 1939. It was 170.2 at the beginning of the Korean war, with foods leading the rise in price. By late 1952, food prices were up 16 percent compared with a rise of 12.3 percent in all living costs.

Meanwhile, Henry H. Fowler was sworn in on September 8, 1952, as Director of Defense Mobilization, retaining his position as Defense Production Administrator. He followed John R. Steelman, who was Acting Director after the resignation of Charles E. Wilson during the summer steel crisis. Though Fowler immediately promised to keep the defense build-up rolling, the *New York Herald Tribune*—struck by the fact that he was a lawyer, not a production expert—commented that his appointment would indicate preparation "for a smooth transition to a system of much less elaborate controls on the economy in the next administration."

Baruch has his critics as well as his admirers, and some of these guffawed at his recommendation in May, 1952 that Congress regain control of the military budget and eliminate waste. When Baruch gave this advice, the Senate had already passed the McClellan Bill to create a Joint Budget Committee. Its members were to be drawn from both the House and Senate Appropriations Committees. Designed to re-seize the purse strings of the nation, this Joint Budget Committee—as the Hoover Commission had advised, with Baruch's later approval —was to be aided by a joint staff of fiscal analysts. Its aim was to eliminate waste and fraud not only in military purchases but in all government spending.

The Washington Post called the McClellan Bill "the most carefully devised fiscal control measure of the past decade." This proposal, too, was defeated by a coalition of Republicans and Democrats. That is, the companion measure introduced in the House by Representative Colmer of Mississippi was killed. The House refused, on July 3, even to debate it.

Regardless of disagreement with his suggestions at times, on one aspect of Baruch's advice to the nation over the years there is no record of any disagreement whatsoever. All authorities concede that his recommendations to promote scientific research and to develop new resources for growth and security have been of inestimable worth to the American people. This counsel, like so many of his other contributions, was shaped during the First World War.

President Woodrow Wilson, in naming Bernard M. Baruch Chairman of the War Industries Board in 1918, stated that Baruch would "act as the general eye" of industrial mobilization. In informal discussion later, Wilson commented, "I like to watch men who are called to Washington for high responsibility. Some of them merely swell — some grow. Bernie grew."

CHAPTER 3

"Some Men Swell— Some Grow. Bernie Grew"

THOUGH NOT TRAINED as an engineer or social scientist, Baruch long ago realized that national security and the continued economic and social well-being of the American people are dependent on both the conservation and the development of the nation's resources through science and technology.

His *War and Postwar Adjustment Policies Report* of 1944 emphasized one phase, stating: "A closer connection between scientific research and its practical application is needed, particularly in view of the great number of products which we must import from abroad. Especially do we have in mind greater research regarding agricultural by-products and the finding of new sources of minerals through better processes that will permit the using of lower grades of ore. The distillation of coal and the extraction of oil from shales are only two instances worthy of pursuit."

Many of Baruch's recommendations over the years have been concerned with the wider implications of this problem, but never with more telling effect than in November, 1945, when he addressed the Senate Committee on Military Affairs.

Baruch felt it was important first to clear up public misconceptions about scientific advances such as radar and nuclear fission, which were being hailed as guaranteeing "push-button"

71

warfare and national safety. The military authorities, he pointed out, warn that such spectacular innovations as atomic weapons and guided missiles are no substitute for trained armed forces, industrial mobilization, and allied unity.

His main concern, however, was to add his influence to that of the nation's most distinguished scientists and educators in advocating the development of an integrated national scientific policy. His recommendations on that November day are an important part of his blueprint for security.

"What should the Government aim for through a peacetime, scientific program such as this Committee contemplates?" Baruch asked. "I would list eight major goals:

'1. Greatly increase our scientific brainpower, using scholarships and other aids to develop new scientific talent in American youth. 2. Continued, vigilant military research in developing new weapons for national defense. 3. Intensify science's war against disease. 4. Offset the depletion of our natural resources. 5. Stimulate basic scientific research to assure a continued flow of new, fundamental, scientific knowledge. 6. The widest, most efficient spread of scientific information, both of as yet undisclosed war discoveries and future findings. 7. Create a new, permanent, government agency to co-ordinate these many activities into an integrated, national, scientific policy. 8. This agency to provide the expert counsel for the freest, worldwide exchange of scientific knowledge and for effective policing of the war-geared science of Germany and Japan.' "

Congress, adopting seven of these recommended goals, soon enacted the necessary enabling legislation. Part of the eighth goal had to be rejected because of Soviet Russia's threats to world peace and the revelations of atomic spying for Russia by Klaus Fuchs and other traitors. The McMahon Act of 1946 halted further exchange of nuclear information with Great Britain and Canada, which had cooperated in the research leading to successful atomic fission and the development of the atomic bomb. The same Act barred exchange of similar information with all other foreign powers. Russia, nevertheless, has become the second major atomic power, though Great Britain and the Scandinavian Atomic Union have made great strides in atomic research and development.

Six years later, in September, 1952, General Omar Bradley was to propose that the United States share some of its atomic weapons secrets with its NATO allies. The necessary legislation was expected to be introduced in Congress at the session beginning January, 1953. General Bradley believed that if plans for the joint defense of Western Europe were to be put on a completely realistic basis, top NATO commanders should be informed as to the tactical capabilities and limitations of atomic weapons, and as to the quantity of such weapons the United States can supply in the event of war.

Congress also has adopted one other recommendation on science and national resources which Baruch made in November, 1945. It authorized a comprehensive inventory of our natural resources—the keystone, as Baruch saw it, for the whole arch of continued scientific development. Indeed, he insisted that such an inventory was essential not only to guide further scientific research but to develop and pursue intelligent financial and economic policies, both domestic and foreign.

His third recommendation at that time—to "intensify science's war against disease"—influenced the enactment of new legislation and appropriations, which continue to help build and safeguard the nation's most important resources—its human resources. An account of these great benefits is included in a later chapter.

Two Federal agencies were established to carry out the scientific work which Baruch and other counselors suggested as vital to national growth and security. They are the National Science Foundation, established in April, 1950, and the National

Security Resources Board, authorized in the National Security Act of 1947.

Dr. Alan T. Waterman, formerly of Yale's Department of Physics, heads the National Science Foundation whose chief purpose Baruch outlined in points 1 and 5 of his 1945 recommendations. Mostly through grants to universities, it stimulates "basic scientific research to assure a continued flow of new, fundamental scientific knowledge." It strives, through university fellowships, to "greatly increase our scientific brainpower," as Baruch put it.

The National Security Resources Board began the post-war comprehensive inventory of resources recommended by Baruch, but before very long he grew impatient at the lack of tangible results. In fact, Baruch quickly lost patience with the whole "lack of decision" in high places over what he considered the number one problem of the cold war—an over-all mobilization plan. Shortly before leaving for Europe and some important conferences with Winston Churchill in July of 1949, he took the bull by the horns in order to get action.

This took the form of a denunciation of the NSRB on June 29 before the officer graduates of the Industrial College of the Armed Forces where, coincidentally, General Eisenhower shared the platform with him. The NSRB was the object of his plain-spoken attack, but by inference it was also an attack on President Truman for allowing the Board to dwindle in prestige and power since its creation two years earlier.

To prevent war, Baruch argued, the United States must be ready to see the Atlantic Pact through, and to defend Free Europe against attack. "Yet with the cold war dragging into its fourth year," he said, "we still lack any effective plan for the swiftest possible mobilization of our resources to insure reaching our Allies in time. . . . Further delay is a needless invitation to disaster."

74

Getting down to particulars, he declared that the NSRB had, under its first Chairman, Arthur M. Hill, presented such an over-all mobilization plan "but when this agency attempted to act ... it was prevented from doing so" and "has still to be heard from." The implication was clear: the Administration had by default or direction failed to act to carry out its mission.

The Congress and the people, as Baruch saw it, were entitled to a full report on the status of the mobilization plans, and the responsibility for this failure had to be established before it was too late. He believed, he said, in civilian control of our national life, but "this responsibility has its price ... a readiness to make the decisions which the military must have to carry on their assigned duties."

The Baruch blast came during the Alger Hiss trial in New York City, and while the Federal Grand Jury in Washington was deliberating Judith Coplon's fate. In this atmosphere Baruch's charges seemed especially pregnant with meaning, and his talk made front-page news, side by side with the sensational coverage of intrigue and espionage activities in our Government.

Baruch's closing remarks to the Army graduates were especially pointed. "Lack of self-discipline, weird economics, strange ethics and perverted logic," he said, "if persisted in, will surely destroy us." There could be little doubt in the minds of his listeners just where the Elder Statesman was laying the blame.

A quick and indignant denial of the charges came from the White House—first from the press secretary, Charles Ross, and later from the angry President himself. Harry Truman was hardly in a mood to accept such a blast lying down—and especially from the man who had refused to serve on the National Democratic Finance Committee in the 1948 election.

Mr. Baruch, it was announced, was "badly informed." The President had not rejected a mobilization plan; in fact, none had been submitted to him. The plan which Baruch undoubtedly referred to, it was explained, had been prepared only by staff members, and had not been approved by the full agency. Hence it had never gotten to the President's desk.

Baruch held his fire until after Truman himself entered the dispute at a press conference the next day. Later, in answer to a reporter's query about the Ross statement, Baruch answered: "My statement goes. I'm not misinformed. . . . They've got to get rid of this vested interest in error." Privately, however, Baruch revealed that the NSRB report in question had been turned down by President Truman, despite approval by seven Cabinet officers.

At the same press conference the President personally denied that such a plan had come before him. When told of the President's denial, Baruch suggested acidly that Mr. Truman might do well to examine his office files. Perhaps the report would turn up. . . .

Former NSRB Chairman Arthur M. Hill, according to Baruch's off-the-record statement, had submitted the report in May or June, 1948, with all the Board members concurring except William C. Foster, then Undersecretary of Commerce. Later, Hill was told by Presidential aide John R. Steelman that Truman disapproved of the plan "as of that time."

Meanwhile, Hill himself stoically refused to shed any light on the controversy. From his home in Washington the former Chairman appeared to strengthen Baruch's case, whether he intended to or not, for his only comment to the press was this: "I'm in a position where I can't say anything."

The issue of the NSRB's role in mobilization planning continued to attract attention in the press. Why had the Board steadily dwindled in prestige and efficiency? For one thing, the President had found it one of the most difficult agencies to staff. Hill served from August, 1947 to December, 1948, when he resigned. When the Senate Armed Services Committee failed to confirm the appointment of Mon C. Wallgren, Truman's friend, the President made no other nomination. Busy John R. Steelman, who was soon named Acting Chairman, could not give the Board much of his time. Other Board Members met only to approve or disapprove recommendations made by the full-time staff, and the staff was seldom at full strength.

During Hill's sixteen months on the job, he had submitted some progress reports to the President, though it could not be easily determined whether any of these constituted a full-dress mobilization plan, according to the *New York Times* of June 30, 1949.

Even before Hill resigned, however, the President was charged by many with "emasculating" the Board. In May, 1948 he had written Hill that the NSRB was no longer to have responsibility for any national security programs which required "directive authority over any Department or Agency or which imply a final power of decision vesting with the Board." The Board was merely to advise the President. Yet it was just this advisory function which the Eberstadt Committee report later attacked so vigorously. Failure to use the NSRB to coordinate and regulate mobilization planning, Eberstadt concluded, "inevitably must mean the domination of the military over the industrial and great areas of civilian life of the United States."

For several months before Baruch spoke out, the military had been criticizing the Board's slowness in reaching decisions on which the Joint Chiefs of Staff could base their own war plans. The Eberstadt report had flatly stated that the Board expected to have a "Preliminary Program for Economic Mobilization" ready by December, 1948. It had not been forthcoming.

Hanson Baldwin, writing in the *New York Times* a few days after the Baruch speech, conceded that the Elder Statesman may have been incorrect in some details of his accusations, but concluded that Baruch's major contention was certainly correct—the Board *was* a weak link in our national security. Echoing the Eberstadt Committee's report, Baldwin too believed that unless the Board was used as a "viable instrument of day-to-day government as well as a planning agency," it was almost certain to drift off into a "useless vacuum" and to "decline into a mere blueprint agency with a certain by-product output of statistical material."

Whatever the final appraisal of the NSRB during this period may be, it still must be credited with providing much of the technical staff of the President's Materials Policy Commission—popularly known as the Paley Commission, from the name of its Chairman—for its five-volume report of June, 1952 titled *Resources for Freedom.* A volume, *The Promise of Technology,* answered Baruch's demand for proposals "to offset the depletion of our natural resources." Volume I, *Foundations for Growth and Security,* contained the summary and recommendations growing out of the sixteen months spent by the Commission in researching anticipated raw materials supply and demand from 1952 to 1975.

William S. Paley, the Chairman, had headed the Columbia Broadcasting System as President or Board Chairman since 1928, but during the war was on leave to serve as deputy chief of psychological warfare at General Eisenhower's European headquarters. Paley was not perturbed when some anti-Administration newspapers overlooked the non-partisan character of the Commission of private citizens, and attacked the massive report as reviving the old "have-not bogey." The facts so carefully assembled and cited in the report—as Paley insisted in various interviews—make it clear that for America the days of "self-sufficiency" are over. In one interview Paley stated: "Our technical people figured that even if we had what we started with—all the materials that were in this country to begin with— it still wouldn't be enough for another 25 years of growing at the rate we've maintained for the last half century."

Our use of metals and fuels, especially, greatly exceeds our production of them, he pointed out, and added: "As a nation we have crossed the great industrial divide. We used to produce more raw materials than we used, but now we are using more than we produce. And this is not a temporary situation. In 1950, we had to import about 10 percent of the raw materials we used. . . . We estimate that by 1975 we may have to import about three times as much in quantity, but only twice as much in percentage—20 percent—because our total consumption will have increased a lot by then. We estimate that, in terms of prewar dollars, we'll be importing about 3 billion out of every 16 billion dollars spent for materials."

Summarizing the inferences from these facts, Paley said:

"First, we will have to become even more worldminded in the future than we have been in the past. . . . We feel that by cooperating more fully with our friends throughout the rest of the free world we can develop additional sources of raw materials for us as well as for other industrial nations, and, at the same time, help resource nations to develop their economies better and faster.

"The second broad inference is that we have to do a better job at home. We have to strengthen and conserve our domestic resources, and more particularly we have to use technology to get more work out of each pound of material and each unit of energy. I say that unless we face up to these new facts in our political and economic thinking, it will be very difficult for us to get enough materials at low enough cost to maintain a growing economy, a rising standard of living and a strong military position."

The Paley Report, as summarized in *The Washington Post* of June 24, 1952, pointed out that, in just "a flash of geologic time . . . we have been devouring what it took Nature eons to deposit. In less than 40 years since the outbreak of World War I, the United States has used more of almost every metal and mineral fuel than the whole world used in all the centuries preceding."

79

This is the identical conclusion Baruch reached in the First World War, even before President Wilson appointed him, in October, 1916—seven months before the U. S. declared war—as one of seven members of the Advisory Commission of the Council of National Defense. The duties of these members were not officially established until after an authorizing vote of the Council on February 12, 1917. By that time, however, Baruch, voluntarily pushing through a study of steel, copper, and other metal industries, had qualified for the key position as Chairman of the Committee on Raw Materials. That committee inevitably evolved into the War Industries Board which mobilized production for victory, and Baruch inevitably became its Chairman.

The general principles of conservation, substitution, and development of new sources, which Baruch formulated and used in meeting World War I shortages, have not changed, and are emphasized in the Paley Report. The technological processes to make the principles work have, of course, changed radically with the necessity to utilize more low-grade ores, less productive oil sources and wood by-products to piece out timber stands, and with the need to develop plastics and synthetic fibers.

The Paley Report also recommended that the nation's stand-by operation on synthetic rubber—which Baruch's Rubber Report in World War II helped to establish on a sound basis—be retained and expanded. As Paley himself stated: "Our needs for rubber will probably double, and the needs of other free countries will probably triple. The free world now turns out about 2 million tons of natural and synthetic rubber a year, of which the United States manufactures about half—and uses about half. But with a possible demand for 5 million tons of new rubber in 1975—with the United States using about half of it—synthetic production would have to expand a lot to keep pace."

The President's Commission stressed the need for continued stockpiling of strategic materials and for maintaining in peace the skeleton industries essential for war production—two perennial recommendations of Baruch's. Paley himself declared: "If we are to have security in materials we have to have enough materials to support us in a 'hot' war on the basis of many foreign imports being cut off. In certain cases, we will take care of ourselves through stockpiling; in other cases, we will subsidize a domestic industry so as to keep a core that can be expanded if war comes; and in still other cases we can take care of it by developing resources in 'safe' areas outside of the country—areas which we can depend upon and from which transportation lanes can be kept open without too much difficulty.

"We have to apply the 'low-cost principle' to security, too, and choose that method, or combination of methods, that will give us the most security for the lowest cost."

The Paley Report raises a question as to the **net effect** of the defense program upon the materials position of **the Free World** during the next twenty-five years. It would appear that the short-term total consumption of many defense materials is exceeding new ore discoveries and technological advances. However, there may not be serious cause for alarm: current acceleration of exploration and technical research, coupled with concern over our materials position, should make the materials outlook for the Free World brighter than might otherwise be expected.

The Paley Report in some respects has provoked controversy, especially in its demand for the elimination of the last vestiges of American protectionist philosophy—that is, elimination of tariffs on materials, raw and processed, which the nation needs critically—and for the end of all "Buy American" and other restrictionist legislation. Another of its controversial aspects is the recommendation for a series of changes in the tax and other laws to encourage conservation at home and expansion

81

of resources here and abroad. *The Washington Post*, however, predicted that regardless of election returns in the next decade, the report of the Paley Commission—that is, of the President's Materials Policy Commission—was likely to become the "basic document of American economic policy" in that period.

Few Americans—and least of all, Baruch—have questioned one conclusion of the report which Paley himself has stated in these words: "We just haven't enough technologists. We traced the number that might come out of the colleges by 1956, and the number is wholly inadequate to take care of our needs. Also basic research hasn't been going ahead as fast as our technology. Most of the scientists and technologists had to turn to applied science during the war and afterward, and our basic research shelves haven't been replenished at a fast enough rate.

"We called attention to the need of spending more money in this field. The National Science Foundation, which was set up by Congress to stimulate activity in this field, has received an appropriation of only about 3½ million, although the Act authorized 15 million dollars. Vannevar Bush, who earlier made a recommendation for the creation of the Foundation, estimated that 122 million dollars a year was needed.

"A later study raised that figure to 250 million dollars. We recommended that the 15 million dollars authorized be appropriated soon. Further, we suggested that Congress re-examine the adequacy of the authorized amount."

President Truman ordered an active Federal inter-agency follow-up of the report of his Materials Policy Commission. The work was begun under the direction of the National Security Resources Board, headed by Jack Gorrie. By the fall of 1952 this agency had been reduced to a small staff of less than thirty full-time people.

In a speech in Boston on April 29, 1952, several months after he took over from W. Stuart Symington, Gorrie voiced some of the views that were reflected in the Materials Policy Commission report shortly to be published. He especially stressed that our "primary resource is experienced personnel who, without a moment's delay, can step into the key jobs of directing an expanded mobilization program. . . ." He was particularly concerned with the slowness with which we have been increasing our reservoir of scientific and technological skills.

Gorrie added that our scientists and engineers numbered less than 1% of our available manpower—in contrast to Russia's emphasis on the training of such specialists. "Only about 97,000 degrees were granted in 1951," he declared, "in all fields of science and engineering. For various reasons this number of graduates is already sharply on the down-grade."

Turning to another phase of our mobilization efforts, Gorrie again anticipated one of the points that was to be emphasized in the Paley Report. "Benefits from assistance we are giving other nations of the free world," he said, "are twofold. Every improvement in their standard of living not only creates new markets, but is a blow to Communism. The availability of essential materials to us and our allies increases our collective strength and security. More than half of our imports, including many of our strategic materials which are absolutely essential in the building of military defense, come from under-developed parts of the world. These areas supply virtually all of our natural rubber, manganese, and tin, as well as a fourth of our zinc and copper."

Baruch does not seem to have made any public statement on the Paley Report, but he probably considered it a step in the right direction—even if a little late. If he has not been too successful over the years in getting the Government to concentrate on mobilization planning, he certainly had tried. He realized that democracies work slowly and all too frequently without observable plan or pattern. It is the way of democracies—which must let the people's representatives have their say before legislation is passed—not to mention all kinds of organized pressure groups. Only dictatorships are likely to have a precise plan for possible future action filed neatly in secret archives. On the other hand, the United States did go ahead after the summer of 1950 with the rapid buildup of military production to equip our forces in Korea and other key points, as well as with the expansion of our forces at home.

This rapid buildup—as Henry H. Fowler, appointed Director of the Office of Defense Mobilization in September, 1952, declared before a New York group of editors and publishers in the same month — was the first of four great objectives of the mobilization program as it developed after the invasion of South Korea. "The second objective was the provision of a military mobilization base—productive facilities, including machine-tools, and other production equipment, particularly of a long lead-time character, specialized for weapon production, which would enable the nation to swing rapidly into an all-out military production of key items if the need should arise.

"The third objective was basic economic expansion—the building up of industrial and raw material capacity which our current mobilization required in increasing quantities and which total war would require in far greater amounts.

"Last, but certainly not least, we were to maintain a sound and prosperous economy—civilian economy. This meant keeping things at livable level."

These were our objectives immediately after the Korean war began. Just where did we stand on October 1, 1952? At that time about half of the three-year period set for the initial program "to achieve our plateau of minimal armed readiness" had passed. Yet we still had a long way to go to achieve our goals. Of the 129 billion dollars which had been appropriated since June, 1950 for military procurement and construction, only 41 billion dollars' worth of products and facilities had been delivered by the end of June, 1952. Some 58 billion dollars had been converted into procurement contracts with industry and into orders for Government arsenals and yards. Another 30 billion dollars of appropriated funds were still to be contracted for as of October 1.

Mr. Fowler expected that the rate of production would be accelerated in the last quarter of 1952 but a much greater effort was still needed, he cautioned. "We cannot attain security if we let success in our current achievements give rise to a false sense of optimism, security, and complacency," he noted in the Office of Defense Mobilization's Seventh Quarterly Report to the President, dated October 1, 1952. "History teaches that any lethargy in national preparedness in the face of hostile and ruthless power will be followed by disaster. The Nation has definite objectives, challenging in time and scope, for our future steps toward national security can and must hold to these objectives despite the alternating storms and lulls generated by an enemy who is master of the art of their use."

Would there be time? Mr. Fowler again underlined what the Chiefs of Staff had testified before the Senate Preparedness Committee: 1954 is still "the most dangerous year for the security of the United States in the foreseeable future." Baruch had said much the same thing in his testimony of May 28, 1952.

Meanwhile, Baruch has revised his own blueprint for national security many times to meet changing conditions. The revision of 1945—advocating a constructive agency to promote conservation of resources and scientific development—reflected all that he had learned from Dr. Karl T. Compton, President of the Massachusetts Institute of Technology, and from Dr. James B. Conant. The three had worked together in 1942 on the Baruch Rubber Report. Both Dr. Conant and Dr. Compton had a vital part, throughout the war, in defense undertakings headed by Dr. Vannevar Bush, President of the Carnegie Insti-

tution of Washington, and former Dean of Engineering at
M.I.T. These scientists were associated in the National Defense
Research Council, which initiated the atomic bomb project
in August, 1939. President Roosevelt, at the suggestion of Dr.
Bush, appointed that Council and later created its successor,
the Office of Scientific Research and Development. Each was
directed by Dr. Bush.

Baruch had referred to this scientific defense work and to
his own earlier blueprint in his testimony to the Senate Committee on Military Affairs in 1945. He said: "As a result of the
experience in the first war, there was recommended, as part
of the over-all national mobilization plan, a mobilization of
the various professions—scientific, medical, engineering, chemical, electrical, mechanical and mining. This plan never was
put into effect. . . .

"Finally, the President created the Office of Scientific Research
and Development, which brought into being many effective
instrumentalities for war and peace. . . ."

In creating the National Defense Research Council, President Roosevelt reverted to an authorization dating from the
Civil War—the same one by which President Wilson supported
Baruch's use in World War I of advisory scientific and industrial committees.

Harry Hopkins, Secretary of Commerce when Bush made the
defense research proposal, was especially interested in it. A
somewhat similar suggestion had reached him through Lawrence
Langner, patent attorney and director of the Theatre Guild.
Langner had proposed a National Inventors' Council to stimulate developments of new weapons and equipment, and this was
established. President Roosevelt had also appointed Dr. Lyman
J. Briggs, of the Bureau of Standards, Commerce Department,
as Chairman of what Roosevelt called "a special committee to

study into the possible relationship to national defense of recent discoveries in the field of atomistics, notably the fission of uranium."

A letter Roosevelt received from Albert Einstein on August 2, 1939, just a month before Hitler marched into Poland, had led to the appointment of the Briggs Committee. The day after the fall of Paris, Roosevelt directed that special committee to report directly to Dr. Vannevar Bush. In his authorizing letter, Roosevelt said, "This country is singularly fitted, by reason of the ingenuity of its people, the knowledge and skill of its scientists, and the flexibility of its industrial structure, to excel in the arts of peace and to excel in the arts of war if that be necessary."

It was the same conviction which had impelled Roosevelt much earlier to establish the National Resources Planning Board, an agency that was very dear to his heart. Robert E. Sherwood, in his biography of Harry Hopkins, tells of working with Roosevelt and Judge Samuel Rosenman at "Shangri-la" on a speech to save that Board "from death at the hands of Congress." News of Mussolini's downfall, on July 25, 1943, interrupted their writing. Among other contributions, this Board drew up the plan for the G. I. Bill of Rights, but "to the conservative majority on Capitol Hill," Sherwood added, "the very word 'plan' was considered a Communist invention and any planning board must be part of a plot to disrupt the capitalistic system of free enterprise."

The same prejudice against Federal planning repeatedly killed others of Baruch's more constructive proposals, though he was always a champion of free enterprise. Fortunately, such prejudice had not blocked action on his proposal, late in 1918, that the work of "planning and statistics" such as had been carried on under his supervision in the War Industries Board, be conducted during peacetime by the Department of Commerce. The National Resources Planning Board stemmed directly from the National Resources Committee and the Federal Employment Stabilization Office in the Department of Commerce, and from the Federal Statistics Board which President Hoover set up in the Bureau of the Budget when coordinated information was necessary to plan anti-depression measures. The National Resources Committee in turn had evolved from the National Planning Board of the Federal Emergency Administration of Public Works, an agency recommended by Baruch's disciple, Hugh S. Johnson.

Johnson also saw to it that Hoover's Statistics Board, crippled from the outset by inadequate funds and staff, was replaced by a Central Statistical Board which lived on after NRA until 1939. Then, in the sweeping governmental reorganization, it was abolished, but its functions were transferred to the Division of Statistical Standards, set up in the Bureau of the Budget. Later the Office of Government Reports, a means of centralizing questionnaires and circulars, was established. Both are branches of the Executive Office of the President.

Business and industrial management, complaining of the statistical jungle in Washington during the depression and in both World Wars, raised up a champion in 1942 in the Byrd Committee, and found another—to their surprise—in Harold Smith, Budget Director. Smith asked the Controller's Institute of America to form a helpful council with other business groups. As a result, such organizations as the National Association of Manufacturers and the United States Chamber of Commerce did work with Government officials to improve Federal questionnaire procedure. Their suggestions, plus Congressional orders in the Federal Reports Act of December 25, 1942, stimulated streamlined operations in the Office of Government Reports.

Baruch, always persistent in recommending such streamlining, has had no patience since 1916 with the attitude perennially expressed by a large part of management that the Federal gathering of economic data is a kind of non-essential snooping which, along with the wide publicizing of the data, adds to business costs. He learned the hard way in the First World War that organized, accurate information gathered from all over the nation and by official observers overseas is essential in mobilizing for national security. Baruch always has insisted that business itself benefits incalculably in peacetime and in war from receiving the flow of comprehensive, dependable economic data which is pieced together consistently and painstakingly in Washington.

Bernard M. Baruch was the sole Democrat appointed by President Wilson to the Advisory Commission of the Council of National Defense. Called Commissioners in the early defense emergency period, they were: Baruch; Daniel Willard, President of the Baltimore and Ohio Railroad; Howard E. Coffin, Vice President of the Hudson Motor Company; Julius Rosenwald, President of Sears Roebuck and Company; Dr. Hollis Godfrey, President of Drexel Institute of Philadelphia; Samuel Gompers, President of the American Federation of Labor; and Dr. Franklin Martin, Secretary General of the American College of Surgeons.

For more than three years, Wilson counted on Baruch and his associates to mobilize the nation's industrial resources, not for fighting in Europe but for defending the country against possible attack. In his staunch Calvinist soul the President saw mobilization for this purpose as an essential. Kaiser Wilhelm changed Wilson's mind—the Kaiser probably lost the war largely by initiating unrestricted submarine warfare. After Germany began this practice, the United States broke off diplomatic relations with her, and declared war two months later, on April 6. Then, at last, Wilson called for a draft and the Selective Military Conscription Bill became law on May 20, 1917.

During the period when Wilson was "waging neutrality" he was criticized as being weak both by pro-Ally citizens, led by Theodore Roosevelt, and by equally vocal pro-German groups in many parts of the country led by George Sylvester Viereck. These hostile factions declared a brief armistice in their verbal abuse late in 1915 when Wilson called for a Navy second to none. He wanted it to shield the national borders. One wing of his critics wanted it to aid the Triple Entente; the other wanted it to strengthen the Allies.

It was the Naval Building Program of 1916 that inspired the first preparedness organization, the Naval Consulting Board, headed by the inventor, Thomas Alva Edison, and composed of two members each from eleven of the principal scientific societies of America. This Board fathered the Industrial Preparedness Committee, under the chairmanship of the Detroit automobile manufacturer, Howard E. Coffin. This national voluntary committee, broadening its interest to include all military needs, enlisted members from five leading engineering bodies in every state, and by September, 1916 had collected data on the defense production capacity of some 20,000 manufacturing plants. Congress, pressed by this Committee, increased appropriations for both the Navy and Army.

Other highly useful preparedness work was being done by the National Advisory Committee on Aeronautics, created in March, 1915; by the National Committee of Physicians for Military Preparedness, authorized by Congress in April, 1916; and by the National Research Council, also authorized by Congress in 1916.

Most important of all, Dr. Hollis Godfrey of Drexel Institute, in May, 1916, introduced an idea he had been developing since 1906, when he met Sir Henry Campbell-Bannerman and Winston Churchill in England at the time they were working on "a council of imperial defense" for Great Britain. Their device of enlisting industrial management in preparedness plans became the core of his proposal for the Advisory Commission to which Baruch was named.

Dr. Godfrey won the interest of an eminent scientist, Dr. Henry E. Crampton, and of General Leonard Wood, who had promoted the "Plattsburgh plan" for training officers. General Wood agreed that, in organizing industrial management for defense, the nation would get "product and service at a minimum of cost and time." The Secretary of Commerce, W. C. Redfield, also agreed and took the idea to L. M. Garrison, then Secretary of War. Garrison declared, "This is the most amazing baby that was ever put on the War Department steps." Elihu Root, former Secretary of War, finding no statutory basis for creation of the Commission, outlined the authorizing legislation. So zealous were the proponents of this idea that they had it incorporated in three overlapping measures.

Root's draft became Section 120 of the National Defense Act of 1916, which gave the President the power to "place orders for war material directly with any source of supply," to commandeer plants if necessary, and to appoint an industrial mobilization board. This Section also directed the Secretary of War to build a complete list of all privately-owned plants equipped to manufacture arms or munitions. A separate Act gave a similar order to the Navy and similar authorization to the President. At the same session of Congress, the same provisions, as drafted by Major General E. H. Crowder, were included in the Military Appropriations Act of 1916.

The authorizing text, doubly significant in that it was evoked again in World War II by President Roosevelt, began:

"That a Council of National Defense is hereby established for the coordination of industries and resources for the national security and welfare, to consist of the Secretary of War, the Secretary of the Navy, the Secretary of the Interior, the Secretary of Agriculture, the Secretary of Commerce, and the Secretary of Labor.

"That the Council shall nominate to the President, and the President shall appoint, an Advisory Commission, consisting of not more than seven persons, each of whom shall have special knowledge of some industry, public utility, or the development of some natural resource, or be otherwise specially qualified, in the opinion of the Council, for the performance of the duties hereinafter provided."

The Act also empowered the Council to "supervise and direct investigations and make recommendations to the President and the heads of executive departments as to . . . railroads . . . so as to render possible expeditious concentration of troops and supplies to points of defense; the coordination of military, industrial and commercial purposes in the location of extensive highways and branch lines of railroad; the utilization of waterways; the mobilization of military and naval resources for defense; the increase of domestic production of articles and materials essential to the support of armies and of the people during the interruption of foreign commerce; the development of seagoing transportation; data as to the amounts, location, method, and means of production, and availability of military supplies; the giving of information to producers and manufacturers as to the class of supplies needed by the military and other services of the government, the requirements relating thereto, and the creation of relations which will render possible in time of need the immediate concentration and utilization of the resources of the Nation."

The idea for the Council of National Defense was anything but new. It had, in fact, been kicked around for nearly seven years. Richmond Pearson Hobson, who had served with great distinction in the Spanish-American War as a naval officer, first proposed it in 1910, when—as a member of the House Committee on Military Affairs—he introduced a bill to create the Council. He tried again and failed again in two other Sessions of Congress, but succeeded in having it nailed into the

Democratic national platform as an important plank in 1912. The proposal was widely discussed in newspapers and magazines that summer and in the two following years.

In 1915 its most ardent advocate in Washington was Franklin Delano Roosevelt, then Assistant Secretary of the Navy. In a letter of August 28 of that year he wrote to his wife: "In the afternoon, I had a long talk with the President about various routine matters, but especially about the Council of National Defense which I am trying to get started. It seems that I can accomplish little just now as the President does not want to 'rattle the sword' while Germany seems anxious to meet us more than half way, but he was interested and will, I think, really take it up soon."

"Soon" stretched out into a year while the idea won champions in Benjamin Strong, Governor of the Federal Reserve Bank in New York; Nicholas Murray Butler, President of Columbia University; Newton D. Baker, who had succeeded Garrison as Secretary of War; and Baruch's best friends in the Administration—Wilson's son-in-law, William G. McAdoo, Secretary of the Treasury, Joe Tumulty, Wilson's secretary, and Colonel E. M. House, then Wilson's favorite assistant—the Harry Hopkins of World War I.

Even more important—as later events proved—the Defense Council idea also had won an advocate in the shrewd young Congressman from South Carolina who had already gained much power over the nation's purse strings, James F. Byrnes, then a member of the House Appropriations Committee and its key deficiency subcommittee. Byrnes already was working in tandem with young F.D.R.

Wilson, a profound student of history and of human nature, knew how thoroughly the Germans had been integrating their industrial and economic resources with their military might, and how systematically they had been building this whole war machine since the turn of the century. Moreover, Wilson was

93

positive he knew why. Discussing the causes of the war with Walter Hines Page, a Tarheel whom he had appointed as Ambassador to England, he spoke—as Page later reported it— "of England's having the earth and Germany's wanting it." Of course, he said, the German system "was directly opposed to everything American." This conversation took place in 1916 when the ardently pro-British Page, coming home to impress his Chief with the righteousness of England's cause, found Wilson decidedly frigid. The President had not yet worked out the only kind of rationalization for war which he thought intelligent and compassionate human beings could ever find acceptable—a "war to make the world safe for democracy" and "a war to end war."

On the other hand, Wilson by that time had accepted all the implications of the phrase, "industrial preparedness," which had been publicized in the press, in schools, colleges, pulpits, and on billboards since the establishment of the Naval Consulting Board's Industrial Preparedness Committee. In essence, the phrase "industrial preparedness" meant the same thing to Wilson that Baruch's current phrase, "peace through strength," and Vannevar Bush's phrase, "modern arms and free men," meant to the American people in 1952.

Nevertheless, Wilson was still determined in the fall of 1916 not to "rattle the sword"—a determination that he manifested again when announcing the appointment both of the Council of National Defense, and of Baruch and the other six members of the Council's Advisory Commission. Here is the statement he made public on that occasion:

"The Council of National Defense has been created because the Congress has realized that the country is best prepared for war when thoroughly prepared for peace. From an economical point of view there is now very little difference between the machinery required for commercial efficiency and that required for military purposes. In both cases the whole industrial mechanism must be organized in the most effective way. Upon this conception of the national welfare, the Council is organized. . . .

"The organization of the Council likewise opens up a new and direct channel of communication and cooperation between business and scientific men and all departments of the Government, and it is hoped that it will, in addition, become a rallying point for civic bodies working for the national defense. The Council's chief functions are:

" '1. The coordination of all forms of transportation and the development of means of transportation to meet the military, industrial, and commercial needs of the Nation.

" '2. The extension of the industrial mobilization work of the Committee on Industrial Preparedness of the Naval Consulting Board. Complete information as to our present manufacturing and producing facilities adaptable to many-sided uses of modern warfare will be procured, analyzed, and made use of.'

"One of the objects of the Council will be to inform American manufacturers as to the part they can and must play in national emergency. It is empowered to establish at once and maintain through subordinate bodies of specially qualified persons an auxiliary organization composed of men of the best creative and administrative capacity, capable of mobilizing to the utmost the resources of the country.

"The personnel of the Council's advisory members, appointed without regard to party, marks the entrance of the non-partisan engineer and professional man into American governmental affairs on a wider scale than ever before. It is responsive to the increased demand for and need of business organization in public matters and for the presence there of the best specialists in their respective fields. In the present instance, the time of some of the members of the Advisory Board could not be purchased. They serve the Government without remuneration, efficiency being their sole object and Americanism their only motive."

Those seven "specialists" did their best, but the best of some of them was not equal to the task, and they fell back into less publicized, if not downright obscure, roles soon after America entered the war. Some of them, naturally, made serious mistakes. Baruch himself, as we shall see later in this chapter, was reported to have made a serious error in judgment less than three months after he was appointed to the Advisory Commission. But if the test of the metal is in the rebound, then Baruch in that period, too, must be rated very high. He did his utmost to retrieve the mistake, and in doing so he won Wilson's highest praise: "Some men swell—some grow. Bernie grew."

Bernard Baruch grew in other ways, too, while he served on the Advisory Commission—and the growth eventually qualified him in Wilson's view for the responsibility that Baruch's partisans thought he should have had from the outset—the direction of our war production.

The record, indeed, does not bear out the view, repeated so often in recent years, that America's economic and industrial strength was not really mobilized in the First World War until after Baruch was named Chairman of the War Industries Board. This notion was assiduously peddled by the gifted but undisciplined Hugh S. Johnson who, like many another facile writer, never let himself be embarrassed by mere facts. In his understandable hero-worship of Baruch, Johnson failed to see that the actual record would have served his purposes better. Let's look at the facts.

President Wilson, in reorganizing the War Industries Board by executive authority on March 4, 1918, appointed Baruch as Chairman. Statutory authority for this reorganization was provided by the Overman Act of May 20. But from the time when Baruch actually began to serve as Chairman in March, until Germany on October 20 accepted Wilson's peace terms and recalled submarines to their bases, just over eight months passed. This was much too short a period for many of the reforms that Baruch made in the late spring and summer to yield results overseas.

On the other hand, without the magnificent work which Baruch and his associates did in the fifteen months before March, 1918—work which kept supplies moving to the hard-pressed Allies—it is more than likely that the war would have ended sooner, but in a stalemate—if not in victory for Germany.

Critical observers in Washington early in 1917 declared that the Defense Council, even with its Advisory Commission, was "little more than a knitting society with no power." Actually, Baruch and his associates moved so quickly and so effectively during that period as to horrify the Select Committee on Expenditure in the War Department—the House Investigating Committee, headed by William J. Graham, which began hearings in July, 1919. Graham carefully studied the minutes of the Advisory Commission. They were turned over to him by Grosvenor B. Clarkson, who had been Secretary both of the Council and of the Advisory Commission, and who continued to serve in one emergency agency or another throughout the war. Clarkson screened some 700,000 words in official documents, plus hundreds of pages of notes he made in interviewing "the pivotal figures" in the war mobilization. These became the basis of his comprehensive history, *Industrial America in the World War,* which includes many sections of praise for Baruch. It also expresses resentment of Graham's charges that the Commission had "served as the secret government of the United States." Yet, giving the devil his due, Clarkson added, "Perhaps the most striking, concise account of the Advisory

Commission in the first three months of its existence was made by a partisan critic, the Honorable William J. Graham."

Here is Graham's summary, as made public in the printed record of the Committee hearings and as quoted in Clarkson's history:

"An examination of these minutes discloses the fact that a commission of seven men chosen by the President seem to have devised the entire system of purchasing war supplies, planned a press censorship, designed a system of food control and selected Herbert Hoover as its director, determined on a daylight-saving scheme, and in a word designed practically every war measure which the Congress subsequently enacted, and did all this behind closed doors, weeks and even months before the Congress of the United States declared war against Germany. . . .

"It appears from the minutes of the Advisory Commission and the Council, which were kept separately, that practically all of the measures which were afterwards considered as war measures were initiated by this Advisory Commission, adopted by the Council, and afterwards acted upon by Congress. In many cases, a considerable period before the actual declaration of war with Germany, this Advisory Commission was discussing matters which were thought to be new legislation by reason of the necessities of war. For instance, on March 3d, over a month before the war declaration, the Advisory Commission endorsed to the Council of National Defense a daylight-saving scheme and recommended a Federal censorship of the press.

"On February 15, about two months before the declaration of war, Commissioners Coffin and Gompers made a report as to the exclusion of labor from military service, and the draft was discussed; the draft was also discussed on other occasions before any one in this country except the Advisory Commission and those who were closely affiliated with the Administration knew that a declaration of war was to be later made. At a meeting on February 15th this same commission of seven men (none of whom had any official authority except as advisers) recommended that Herbert Hoover be employed by the Government in connection with food control. It was generally understood, as appears from the minutes, that Mr. Hoover was to be in control of the matter, although the war was two months in the future. . . .

"Almost the first thing the Commission did was to take up the matter of arranging an easy method of communication between the manufacturers and the Government.

"In several meetings long before the war was declared this Advisory Commission of seven men met with the representatives of the manufacturing industries and formed an organization of them for selling supplies to the Government, which organization was well perfected before the war was declared. This method consisted of having the representatives of the various businesses, producing goods which the Government would have to buy, form themselves into committees so that they might be able to sell to the Government the goods direct, which their industries produced. In almost every meeting that this Advisory Commission held before the declaration of war, they discussed and recommended to the Council (which consisted of six Cabinet members) these plans for fixing prices and selling to the Government. When war was declared on April 6th the machinery began to move, headed by the Advisory Commission of seven men, who were, in effect, as shown by these minutes, the active government of the United States so far as the purchase of supplies was concerned. So far as I can observe, there was not an act of the so-called war legislation afterwards enacted that had not before the actual declaration of war been discussed and settled upon by this Advisory Commission."

Though Clarkson points out "the bitterly depreciative tone" of this summary, he adds, "Broad as it is, it does not tell the whole story." The Commission met for the first time on December 7, 1916—just 25 years to a day before Pearl Harbor! Clarkson reports that at the second meeting, on January 8, 1917, two practical suggestions "destined to grow into great realities" were made. The first, by Daniel Willard, Commission Chairman, led to the establishment of the Government Railroad Administration. The second, by Baruch, "was really the first stirrings of life in what was to be the War Industries Board." Baruch told about his intensive, but voluntary, recent study—adding to knowledge he had acquired over many years—of steel, copper, and other metal industries, and politely asked for authority to reach some understanding with the "traders" concerned on "how to get their resources together."

Reporting progress at the February meeting of the Commission, Baruch was named Chairman of the Committee on Raw Materials. He had already enlisted his top assistants, Eugene Meyer, Jr. and Leland L. Summers. Meyer, later publisher of *The Washington Post* and a former Chairman of the Federal Reserve Board, was at that time known as an expert on copper and other non-ferrous metals. Summers, who had been identified with Allied war purchasing in America since 1914, knew at first-hand the relationship of synthetic chemistry to warfare, and especially how the Germans had harnessed their nitrogen-fixation and coal-tar industries to their war machine. Summers later headed the crucial Foreign Mission which Baruch sent to England.

As Clarkson saw it, Baruch's committee became the backbone of the War Industries Board chiefly because it proved very quickly that the fundamental economic problems of war are increased production, conservation, substitution, speedy procurement and allocation of the basic war materials—all of which require a system of priorities and price fixing. Furthermore, Baruch's committee, realizing that these problems can

be met effectively only through efficient and integrated administration, sought the necessary reorganizing machinery.

Baruch's insistence on these general principles eventually
impressed Wilson. The President had long appreciated Baruch's
knowledge of America's financial and industrial resources, and
in the fall of 1915 had named him "Dr. Facts." Baruch's greatest
strength, however, does not lie in innovation, but in appraising,
organizing and promoting the concepts that less dynamic men
formulate. It was largely by this process that he arrived at his
guiding principles for industrial mobilization.

With charm enough, in most cases, to win the reluctant
gratitude of the men whose brain children he adopted, Baruch
finally made a friend of even Arch Wilkinson Shaw, the initiator
in war-time Washington of orderly priority, conservation, simplification of styles, and substitution.

Shaw, the owner of varied enterprises in Chicago, was the
forerunner of such efficiency experts and management engineers
as Frank B. Gilbreth, his wife, Dr. Lillian M. Gilbreth, and
Charles E. Bedaux. The science of priority and conservation
of time, material and energy was Shaw's specialty. He had
learned that the systematic Germans had already stepped up
their efficiency in war-time through orderly priority, and—as
he put it—through methods of conservation, substitution, and
simplification, "stretching industry." It shocked him to learn
that, by contrast, civil and military needs in France and England
had long been left to compete with each other for capital, labor,
facilities and materials, and that "business as usual" plus the
failure to promote conservation and substitution had caused
those countries to force rationing upon the civilian population.

Like many patriotic citizens in the suspenseful weeks of early
1917, Shaw decided to come to Washington. Once there, he

outlined his ideas to D. H. Houston, then Secretary of Agriculture, and to Franklin K. Lane, then Secretary of the Interior. Those two members of the Council of National Defense submitted his plan to the Council, then directed by Walter S. Gifford, who was on leave as chief statistician of the American Telephone and Telegraph Company. The Council approved Shaw's plan and Gifford became the eager spokesman of "priority of delivery of materials and finished goods." A new agency was set up, the Commercial Economy Board, and Shaw was named its Chairman. It operated almost independently of the Advisory Commission for nearly a year. It was then absorbed by the War Industries Board and re-named the Conservation Division.

Shaw enlisted many able men, including E. F. Gay, Dean of Harvard's Graduate School of Business Administration. The Board first pushed through a wheat-saving measure by eliminating the return of bread by retailers to bakers. In addition to saving labor and handling costs, it saved enough bread daily, Shaw estimated, to supply 200,000 people.

Herbert Hoover, soon to take over as Food Administrator, popularized the slogan, "Food Will Win the War," and encouraged consumption of rye, graham, whole wheat, and corn bread, instead of white bread. Further, Hoover ordered the purchase of a pound of meal or cereal with every pound of white flour. When the Fuel Administration introduced heatless days, Hoover introduced meatless and sweetless days, and finally rationed sugar—the only commodity ever officially rationed to civilians in the First World War, although shortages in many lines became more and more severe.

Shaw's Economy Board and later his WIB Conservation Division introduced "buy and carry" purchases to save manpower and delivery costs, popularized cafeterias in sections that had known only restaurants before, and instituted a multi-

tude of substitutions and simplifications which later generations took for granted. These included paper cartons for wooden
boxes, corsets without steel, typewriter ribbons in five colors
instead of fifty, baby carriages without luxury linings or fad
gadgets, and coffins without metal linings or trim. The list
seemed endless in 1918, but was short, of course, measured
by the simplification standards that have been developed since
then.

Shaw, through J. J. Jusserand, the French Ambassador to
the United States, asked that the Parisian fashion designers save
material for war needs. The slim silhouette of 1918 resulted—
or so it was claimed. Mere shortages of cloth may have decided
the issue.

Baruch was very much taken with the idea of simplification
in models and style. Even before he was named WIB Chairman he encouraged such simplification in armament wherever
readily feasible, and to the utmost in civilian goods. He was
ready to order further drastic reductions in civilian wardrobes
when the Armistice came. "Had the war gone on another year,"
he testified in 1935 at the Nye Inquiry, "our whole population
would have emerged in cheap but serviceable uniforms. . . .
Types of shoes were to be reduced to two or three."

Baruch's unattractive "cheap but serviceable uniforms," if
commanded today even in "austerity" England, very likely
would promote a revolution. Before the outraged cries died
down, he made public an explanation that though "needs, not
wants" must be met, he really didn't mean to "goose-step" the
nation—an explanation offered by many officials in World
War I when complaints rose that regimentation for the sake
of regimentation seemed to be becoming the order of the day.
The complaints multiplied despite the morale-building propaganda of George Creel, and many were communicated through
the incredible duplicating machinery Clarkson reported of

"184,000 units of the state, county, community and municipal councils of defense," which, throughout the war "sent back to Washington the moods and aspirations of the people." But Baruch—never resigned to the fact that emotion is a more powerful human trait than logic—revived his proposal for similar drab clothing in World War II.

The practical applications Baruch made of all he was able to learn about the munitions industry in goose-stepping Germany proved of inestimable value, and especially the measures he devised to meet Army needs. Those, at first, were even more pressing than the needs of the Navy. "The Navy men," Grosvenor Clarkson reported, "had been forehanded and were proud of their success." Many historians, in agreeing, attribute much of that forehandedness to Franklin D. Roosevelt. The young Assistant Secretary of the Navy was pushing for a bigger and better-equipped fleet months before his Chief, Josephus Daniels, and President Wilson called for a strengthened sea arm. A story got around Washington later that every time the conservative Daniels left town or even turned his back for a couple of hours, F. D. R. cut some more red tape and placed another order.

Such purchases, at first, were necessarily made without legally executed contracts, for at that period the money to pay for them had not been appropriated. On this basis, manufacturers started work on $40,000,000 worth of depth charges, light ordnance including 3, 4, and 5-inch guns, and other supplies. Eliot Janeway is the authority for the statement that James F. Byrnes, on the Deficiency Subcommittee of the House Appropriations Committee, "covered Roosevelt's operations from the rear and saw his accounts balanced." Eventually, Wilson called Roosevelt to a conference with the Army Chief of Staff and said, "I'm very sorry, but you've cornered the market for supplies. You'll have to divide up with the army."

Roosevelt also had improved labor conditions for civilian personnel in the naval yards. Louis Howe, soon after he became Roosevelt's secretary in Washington in 1913, aroused his interest in the labor matter—a turning point in his life, as Eleanor Roosevelt reported in her book, *This I Remember*. One immediate result was her husband's effective service on the War Labor Policies Board.

Baruch, however, felt that the statistical information gathered by the Naval Industrial Preparedness Committee under Roosevelt's direction was inadequate, since it catalogued concerns by product, total output and expansion potential, but did not list equipment and processes. The extra data, Baruch thought, was required for speedy conversion to war production, and he saw that remedial fact-finding procedures were set up by the WIB in the Industrial Inventory Section.

He and his associates also were dissatisfied with the data which had been gathered for the War Department by the Kernan Board. That survey, they thought, seemed directed more at reform than at preparedness. The Board reflected the bitterness in Congress over the fact that war profits, especially of the steel industry and the munitions makers, had soared unconscionably in the mad scramble by the Allies for supplies in this country. Though the survey yielded less information on raw materials than on established facilities, the Kernan Board advocated that the Government stop block profiteering on armor plate by setting up its own plant in West Virginia. That plant, rushed to completion, was never operated until a Second World War loomed.

As for the Army, Baruch and his associates got no reliable information at all from that quarter for some time, so Clarkson reported. "It is of record," he added, "that the reports of our military observers with the armies of the belligerents in Europe lay unread in the archives of the General Staff up to the time of our own entry into the World War." The military intelligence service, he explained, lacked personnel to examine "what little it was able to collect."

"The so-called General Staff at that time was a purely military group," Clarkson continued. "It had no comprehension of the fact that in modern war the whole industrial activity of the nation becomes the commissariat of the military." Its procurement estimates and practices were unrealistic, he added, with "eight departments" in the Army buying the same class of supplies, and with "twenty-two spigots for the diffusion of emergency funds."

When the driving General Peyton C. Marsh became Chief of Staff, he made improvements but "was never in sympathy," Clarkson stated, "with the work of the War Industries Board," believing, as professional soldiers traditionally believe, that all war-making measures should be under military control. General Hugh S. Johnson abandoned that view quickly in association with Baruch in the work of the WIB Requirements Division. When General Palmer E. Pierce, Director of the Army's newly created Bureau of Purchase, Storage and Traffic, was sent to France, his post in Washington was taken over by General George W. Goethals, Panama Canal engineer, who was recalled to active duty. Though Goethals assigned General Johnson even greater responsibility in Army buying, he did not give him enough authority, Johnson reported later in his official biography, to eliminate the wasteful competitive procurement practices of the varied branches of the services. Because top officers in those branches kept bucking Baruch, Johnson charged, they impeded war-waging and added greatly to over-all war costs.

As just one sample of what Baruch faced in trying both to stimulate necessary production and to apply necessary priority in meeting military needs, Clarkson stated that "at one time the army actually called for twenty suits of underwear for each soldier in France." In that pre-DDT era of trench warfare, when the word "cootie" was too frequently heard, the Army theory, Clarkson charged, was that "the underwear would have to be thrown away at the end of a week's use." The knitting industry, Baruch realized, would be strained beyond capacity by such a huge underwear order. It was substantially reduced after the WIB recommended better "delousing apparatus."

Strong desire for authority to procure supplies characterized the Army after the Advisory Commission of the Council of National Defense, taking the initiative, had recommended early in 1917 that an Army of one million men be raised; that the Navy be brought to full strength; and that a central Purchasing Board be set up to establish priority in all military buying. This Board, soon re-named the General Munitions Board, virtually swallowed up an earlier agency, established on February 17, called the Munitions Standards Board.

It was widely believed at the time that Howard E. Coffin would be appointed head of the General Munitions Board, since to him "more than to any other individual," as Clarkson reported, was "due the evocation of the pre-war movement for industrial preparedness." Coffin, like Baruch, was made a member of this Board, but Frank A. Scott was called from Cleveland as its head.

President of the machine-tool manufacturing firm of Warner and Swasey, Scott had been a student of military matters since boyhood and of the industrial implications of war from the outset of his business career. As early as 1909 he had concluded that Germany was preparing for a war of conquest. On three trips to Europe before 1914, he studied the production of military material in England, Russia, Germany, France and Italy. The extraordinary development in Germany of by-product coke ovens, of the dye industry, of plants for the fixation of nitrate, and of turret lathes used in the production of shell fuses convinced him in 1913 that war would begin the next year.

Under Scott, the General Munitions Board soon began to duplicate undertakings already being carried on by Baruch's Committee on Raw Materials, and by Julius Rosenwald's

Committee on clothing and canned goods. There was one big difference. Scott paid insufficient attention to civilian needs, according to Clarkson who reported that Scott was "too respectful of the army . . . and did not fully grasp the need of civilian domination in supply matters." When both Gifford, Director of the Council, and Daniel Willard, Chairman of the Advisory Commission, agreed that "a central authority and decisive information" were essential, the Council on July 8, 1917 voted to set up the War Industries Board. Baruch, in this agency established on July 28, retained and extended his old responsibilities with respect to raw materials. Scott was named the Board Chairman, and Secretary of War Baker, Clarkson reported, continued "to let the army run wild through the supply pastures."

The pressure was too much for Scott. When he had a breakdown, Daniel Willard succeeded him as the WIB chairman. The Army steam-roller upset Willard. Credited with preventing the threatened railroad strike on the eve of the war, he went back to his own railroad, though he returned to Washington late in 1917 and for eight months served on the Railroads War Board.

For a month after his resignation from WIB, that agency was without a chairman. It was at this time that the so-called War Council was created—another debating society, actually. Acute observers predicted that the real power in war production would be torn at last from civilian hands by the War Department. Another attempt in this direction had been under way since January when Edward R. Stettinius, Sr., partner in the banking firm of J. P. Morgan and Company, was brought to Washington as the Surveyor General of Supply for the War Department. The plan, Clarkson reported, was to create "a munitions department within the army that would have left the War Industries Board a shell."

It was then that President Wilson decided to intervene—as President Roosevelt planned to do under similar circumstances in World War II, just before Donald Nelson fired Ferdinand Eberstadt from his War Production Board post. Both Presidents considered Baruch, but Wilson, unlike Roosevelt, held to his decision. By an Executive Order of March 5, 1918, he reorganized the War Industries Board, took it out from under the control of the Council of National Defense, and named Baruch its Chairman.

President Wilson is reported to have personally typed the Executive Order and wrote a letter to Baruch, making public a statement defining the duties of the re-constituted Board. The final sentence in this announcement said that the Board "will lodge responsibility for effective action as definitely as possible under existing law." The first section in the statement read:

"The Board will act as a clearing-house for the war-industry needs of the Government, determine the most effective ways of meeting them, and the best means and methods of increasing production, including the creation or extension of industries demanded by the emergency, the sequence and relative urgency of the needs of the different government services, and consider price factors and, in the first instance, the industrial and labor aspects of problems involved, and the general questions affecting the purchase of commodities.

"On this Board Mr. Baruch will give his attention particularly to raw materials, Mr. Bookings to finished products, and Mr. Lovett to matters of priority. These three members, in association with Mr. Hoover so far as foodstuffs are involved, will constitute a commission to arrange purchases in accordance with the general policies formulated and approved. . . . The sub-committees advising on particular industries and materials, both raw and finished, heretofore created, will also continue in existence and be available to furnish assistance to the War Industries Board.

"The purpose of this action is to expedite the work of the Government, to furnish needed assistance to the departments engaged in making war purchases . . . and to make clear that there is a total disassociation of the industrial committees from the actual arrangement of purchases on behalf of the Government."

The President's reference here to industrial committees was of especial significance, as we shall see.

According to Carter Field, Wilson, in his letter to Baruch, after first "outlining the functions, the constitution and action of the Board as I think they should now be established," defined Baruch's duties as follows:

" (1) To act for the joint and several benefit of all the supply departments of the government.

" (2) To let alone what is being successfully done and interfere as little as possible with the present normal process of purchase and delivery in the several departments.

" (3) To guide and assist wherever the need for guidance or assistance may be revealed; for example, in the allocation of contracts, in obtaining access to materials in any way preempted, or in the disclosure of sources of supply.

" (4) To determine what is to be done when there is any competitive or other conflict of interests between departments in the matter of supplies; for example, when there is not a sufficient immediate supply for all and there must be a decision as to priority of need or delivery, or when there is competition for the same source of manufacture or supply, or when contracts have not been placed in such a way as to get advantage of the full productive capacity of the country.

" (5) To see that contracts and deliveries are followed up where such assistance as is indicated under (3) and (4) above has proved to be necessary.

" (6) To anticipate the prospective needs of the several supply departments of the Government and their feasible adjustment to the industry of the country as far in advance as possible, in order that as definite an outlook and opportunity for planning as possible may be afforded the businessmen of the country.

"In brief, he should act as the general eye of all supply departments in the field of industry."

The press and the public, of course, immediately dubbed Baruch "General I." The appointment was a partial triumph over Secretary Baker who, according to Clarkson, had frankly told Baruch in January when they discussed reorganization of the Board, that "while he [Baruch] had done the best work of any of the civilian executives called into service by the emergency, he [the Secretary] did not consider that Baruch was fitted for the place of an executive in a large organization. It was the Secretary's idea to appoint to the headship of the new organization a great industrialist not then connected with the Board. Baruch was to be a sort of under-secretary to the new man, and the real power behind the throne."

In another sense, however, Baruch was disappointed. Instead of recommending the re-organization of the WIB, Baruch had, instead, submitted a plan to Baker for the appointment of a Director of War Industries and Raw Materials, with "the power, subject to the approval of the President, to commandeer plants, products, equipment, manufacturing facilities, mines and materials, and the additional power not now granted of reselling and distributing materials thus commandeered."

Baker sent Baruch a copy of the letter he wrote to Wilson in February: "We recognize that the present question is the appointment of a successor to Mr. Willard, and that the redistribution of power will have to be delayed until the President is empowered by legislation; but the immediate reorganization could begin and suitable distributions of power could then be made when the legislation is secured.

"Our suggestions, therefore, would be that a chairman of the

War Industries Board be appointed; that he be directed immed-iately to reorganize the institution. . . ."

Baruch reportedly protested to Baker, in a letter of February 5, 1918, that Baker's recommendation to the President "was not definite enough as to our thoughts that this *agency should be an individual who decentralizes the execution of his authority.* In this letter you speak of it as a body, which gives the impression that we thought it should be a board, whereas I understood we were both agreed that it should be one man."

This protest repeated the view Baruch had been expounding for more than a year. Even in his diary he had recorded it. An entry there of November, 1917 read, "No one wants to give the power to one man. This makes them less powerful, and they think it makes him too powerful. Fiddle while Rome burns. It will go, but time is the essence." Another entry read, "All these men get everybody's advice, and then take the wrong advice. . . . What is everybody's job is nobody's job." Another diary entry stated, "The greatest disorganization is going on, and grabbing right and left for men to strengthen themselves with no thought of the thing as a whole."

Grosvenor Clarkson thought Baruch's patience had been pushed too far. "Despite untold discouragements and humili-ating rebuffs," he wrote, "Baruch had steadily driven ahead with the work in hand, doing each task as it arose or as he created it." It was a shame, he thought, that President Wilson didn't realize that 'Director' has a more impressive sound than 'Chairman of the War Industries Board'. "It took some time," he added, "for all who were affected to understand that the chairman after March 4th was as little like the chairman before that day as a lion is like a lamb."

If the change of name had been made, Clarkson added, "the public would have perceived at once what was then only plain to close observers, that the instrumentality of industrial control for war purposes had been revolutionized, and that a tired and discouraged committee had been replaced with an industrial dictator, surrounded it is true, by a board, but by a board with no more real authority over the dictator than the Cabinet has over the President; in fact, designedly occupying precisely a similar relation."

The Board, headed by Baruch, was more compact and far more efficient than its predecessor. It included Alexander Legge, Vice President and General Manager of International Harvester Company, serving as the WIB Vice Chairman and Chairman of its key Requirements Division; Edwin P. Parker, of a Houston law firm, as Priorities Commissioner; R. S. Brookings, then President of Washington University, St. Louis, as Price-Fixing Committee Chairman; George N. Peek, Vice President of Deere and Company, Commissioner of Finished Products; J. Leonard Replogle, President of American Vanadium Company, Steel Administrator; Hugh Frayne, American Federation of Labor organizer, as Labor Commissioner; Leland L. Summers, Technical Adviser; Rear Admiral F. F. Fletcher and Major General George E. Goethals, representing the Navy and Army; and Harold P. Ingels, of the Youngstown Realty Guarantee and Trust Company, as Secretary.

In addition, Baruch as Chairman had four official assistants. They were Herbert Bayard Swope, who had been Executive Editor of the *New York World;* Clarence Dillon, of Dillon, Reed and Company, investment banking firm; Harrison Williams, director of numerous companies who also served as a member of WIB's Facilities Division; and Harold T. Clark, of a Cleveland law firm. A. W. Shaw, not given the title of Board Member, was Chairman of the important Conservation Division, and reported directly to Baruch.

113

General Pershing, in appreciation of the service rendered by Baruch and his associates, stated later, "I marvel at their success. They were reconnoitering an unknown country. No precedent in American industry or in government authority existed to guide them. . . . Until the spring of 1918, the flow of troops and supplies to France was not encouraging. There was evidence of lack of authority and proper organization. . . ." The great change then effected impressed Pershing with the wisdom of Baruch's appointment by President Wilson—as the General stated many times. He repeated his appraisal when war clouds were gathering again, in the preface he contributed to Baruch's book published in 1936.

Why was it "that the man who could certainly have done in the fall of 1917 what he did in the spring of 1918," to quote Grosvenor Clarkson again, "was passed over for many months after he had demonstrated to all close, unprejudiced observers that he was marked for leadership?

"There is some unwritten history here that has never been and may never be told," Clarkson added. "It is known that early in the war President Wilson had the intention of making Mr. Baruch general purchasing agent for the government."

Late in 1917, when Secretary Baker first proposed to bring Edward R. Stettinius, Sr. to Washington to develop an all-powerful Munitions Department, Baruch's warm friend Joe Tumulty wrote two letters to his chief opposing Stettinius and advocating Baruch. Those letters, of November 21 and December 7, 1917, are cited in an authoritative biography by John M. Blum, entitled *Joe Tumulty and the Wilson Era,* published in 1950.

Tumulty, who had great skill in public relations, believed that to give such power to a Morgan partner would revive all the horrified cries raised in the months immediately preceding America's declaration of war, that international bankers and industrialists were pushing the nation toward war largely to protect their heavy investments in Allied undertakings. Right or wrong, the feeling was widespread. The protests were summarized by the distinguished historians, Charles and Mary Beard, in their monumental study, *The Rise of American Civilization.* They pointed out that many citizens—still pacifist in 1916 and 1917, but still reputable—tried to combat a publicity campaign "by the selfish factions," a campaign "adequately financed, astutely managed, and effectively carried out." The counter-propaganda group, according to the Beards, argued that "American investors who had staked money on the Anglo-French side, munitions makers who had accepted the paper of London and Paris in return for supplies, merchants and manufacturers who had huge Entente credits on their books . . . were in danger of immense losses unless the United States government came to their rescue."

These charges would be revived, Tumulty advised Wilson, if a Morgan partner were given great war production power. The common man might be led to believe that it was not, after all, "a war to end war," but a capitalists' war. "One thing is certain," Tumulty added, "we know where Baruch stands. . . . We are sure of Baruch's vision, loyalty, and generous sympathies." Wilson still hesitated to name Baruch—for more than three months.

About this time, a hue and cry in the nation's press led to a Congressional investigation. The *New York Times Index* of early 1917 required two and one-half columns of agate type just to list the news stories on this matter. The irresponsible charges had one thing in common. They were all vicious.

The stories impugned the honor of Wilson's official family and Baruch's patriotism was questioned. As the accusations had it, either Tumulty or Secretary McAdoo, or the President himself or his wife, Edith Galt Wilson, or a combination of that quartet, had "leaked" the news of a new peace note the President was preparing to send to the Imperial German Government, and Baruch, taking advantage of this advance knowledge to sell steel short, had made millions of dollars on the transactions. It was also charged that Wilson's brother-in-law, R. W. Bolling, member of a Washington brokerage firm, and Tumulty, and Otto Kahn had also capitalized on the "peace note leak." In addition, it was charged that Baruch had bought his way into the Advisory Commission by contributing $35,000 to the Democratic national election campaign of 1916.

The opening blast was made by Thomas W. Lawson, author of *Frenzied Finance,* and a highly successful Wall Street operator. Two Republican Congressmen decided to exploit the charges. They were William S. Bennet, of New York, and William R. Wood, of Indiana. Lawson, testifying before the House Rules Committee, said Tumulty, meeting Baruch in the Biltmore Hotel in New York, had leaked the news. Tumulty, he added, received "his bit"—another piece of character assassination which was later traced to Mrs. Ruth Thomason Visconti. The political writer David Lawrence, coming to Baruch's and Tumulty's aid, had her lurid career unfolded by William J. Burns, head of a nation-wide detective agency. It included varied dealings with Bulgarian spies and Latin American millionaires.

The truth, as finally established, was that Tumulty knew no more about the peace note than every smart newspaper reporter had been able to surmise from the facts open to all the public. A new peace drive by distinguished Americans broke on the front page in November. This group included Jacob H. Schiff, David Starr Jordon, and Oswald Garrison Villard. European developments, too, had indicated renewed possibilities of peace.

Newspaper reporters predicted that Wilson, more interested in peace than profits, would send a decisive peace note in answer to a cautious peace feeler put forth on December 12, 1916 by the German Chancellor, Bethmann-Hollweg, and echoed several days later by Baron Sonning of Italy. Lloyd George, shortly after he became British Prime Minister, referred to those official peace feelers.

Baruch himself testified that it was the Prime Minister's speech of December 18 which had given him the only tip he needed to start selling steel short. He frankly admitted that, as a result, he had made $600,000 in one day alone. Hugh Johnson later said that Baruch actually made five million dollars in the period before "peace jitters" ended.

Many others acted on the same hunch, as was indicated by stories on the financial pages day after day. A characteristic headline in the *New York Times* on December 22 read: "Peace and War Talk Hit Stocks. Most Violent Slump Known in 15 Years. Some Issues Off 30 Points. Entire List Down 5 to 15 Points."

In any case, Baruch submitted to the House Committee all the complicated records of his transactions for the period and, making no claim to the more impressive titles of banker or financier, stated candidly that he was a speculator. Asked about that Democratic campaign contribution of $35,000, he stated that it was $50,000. In the end, of course, he was completely vindicated by the Committee. David Lawrence reported, "The only thing the Republicans sought to reveal was that Baruch had gambled and won."

Nevertheless, as the late Mark Sullivan, a life-long friend of Baruch, pointed out, "A large section of voters regard a money making career with distrust" and especially frowned upon successful Wall Street speculation. Baruch, of course, had done nothing illegal in selling steel short, even as a member of the Advisory Commission. But talk as to the impropriety of his transactions at that critical period in the Wilson Administration and in the nation died down slowly, and Baruch grew self-critical, as was reported by Alvin S. Johnson, later to be Director of the New School for Social Research, but then an economist for

117

the Council of National Defense. "What ground on Bernie," Johnson said, "was the fact that his career appeared to be essentially acquisitive. . . . He had nothing to impress on the public but his essential creative character."

Shortly before Baruch was named a member of the first War Industries Board, he told the President that he was selling his seat on the New York Stock Exchange, of which he had been a member since 1897. Financial pages carried the confirming news early in August, 1917.

Attacked once again eighteen years later, Baruch submitted a detailed statement to the Nye Committee as to his Government service in the First World War. This statement effectively answered all the ugly charges that he had made huge war profits while serving the WIB without salary. During that period, he said,—and he submitted his financial records and income tax reports to prove it—he "never had a dollar's worth of interest in any concern manufacturing munitions." He added, "I divested myself of all holdings that even remotely touched upon my official activities. I took this step freely and at a heavy cost to my fortune. I made absolutely no purchases of securities except bonds, mostly government. In buying these bonds I was, of course, under the necessity of selling some of the other securities I had in my box, which, as the records show, were sold at a loss. I was not a participant either directly or indirectly in any market transactions.

"I carried through the war three major investments in which I am still interested. They were, first, Alaska Juneau Gold Mining Company, in which I invested before the war and which for many years had no value; second, Texas Gulf Sulphur Company, in which I originally invested about twenty-five years ago and which never produced an ounce of sulphur during the entire war; and third, the Atolia Mining Company, a producer of tungsten. . . ."

118

He tried to sell that mine, he said, but found no buyers because of the fear that it had no ore reserve. "I did not resort to the subterfuge of a fake transfer," Baruch declared. "I informed certain officials in Washington, including the President of the United States, the Secretary of War, the Attorney General, the Secretary of the Interior, and my fellow members of this interest and also of a plan that I had devised. I ordered the segregation of every dollar that the mine paid me and directed that all the dividends should be paid to various charities. After this decision, from the end of 1917 to the close of the war I made contributions of approximately $400,000 to the Red Cross, the Knights of Columbus, the Y.M.C.A., the Y.M.H.A., the Salvation Army, and other relief agencies and also for other war purposes. In this period I had received Atolia dividends of approximately $300,000. Incidentally, the mine became practically worthless due to exhaustion of visible ore reserves, with an occasional trifling dividend since then. I still have the stock."

Convinced of Baruch's disinterest when he named him as a member of the original WIB, Wilson watched Baruch grow in other ways, too. He was especially pleased with the work he was doing in tandem with Leland Summers, utilizing all the specialized knowledge Summers had, and all Baruch's seasoned judgment, in obtaining strategic materials.

By late fall of 1917, however, there were public outcries against the commodity specialists in Washington operating, as the historian Clarkson said, largely "through the existing business mechanisms instead of through an artificial, superimposed, brand-new administrative machine." Baruch had recommended the device and Clarkson had called it his "faucet idea," but some caustic critics said that, " 'faucet' or not, it was all wet."

The charge in the First World War was that "dollar-a-year men," acting in a dual capacity, were promoting the interests of their own companies ahead of the interests of the nation. Some of the complaints were made by business and industrial executives themselves—those who were not invited to join the commodity sections as experts, and who were not made members of the advisory industry committees. Their firms, these disgruntled officials said, were being discriminated against in the allocation of materials and in the placement of war orders. Their competitors, with representatives in the commodity sections or in the pivotal industry committees, were not only getting an undue share of war profits, they claimed, but were strengthening their chances to dominate the respective fields after the war.

Certain improvements in the use of industry advisory committees were made by the original WIB, but complaints continued. Hence President Wilson's insistence on further safeguards when he authorized the reorganization of the War Industries Board. These safeguards, he said, must effect "total disassociation of the industrial committees from the actual arrangement of purchases on behalf of the government." In naming Baruch as Board Chairman, he had Baruch's assurance that this purpose would be fulfilled.

Soon after that, Mark Sullivan reported, "Baruch promises to be the whole works here in Washington"—He has yanked "the reins out of everybody's hands, and is flying down the road with his tail over the dashboard. When there isn't any money available, he uses his own. . . . With all his assumption of authority, he doesn't get anyone mad at him."

The result of Baruch's driving power was ruefully acknowledged by Von Hindenburg in his memoirs. He said of the United States: "Her brilliant, if pitiless, war industry had entered the service of patriotism and had not failed it. Under the compulsion of military necessity a ruthless autocracy was at work. . . . They understood war." It wasn't quite so easy, as we have seen.

Hugh Johnson in quoting Von Hindenburg's comments in the preface of books he edited for Baruch, also quoted the grateful words of Clemenceau, the Tiger, who said in 1922: "The United States declared war in April, 1917. It was only in March, 1918 [the month Baruch was put at the head of the War Industries Board], that their industrial mobilization found its final form. Even in the land of quick decisions, the routine of peace days struggled hard to live. But the High Command of Industry was created. It was a splendid company of men who at the call of their country had come from all parts of the United States. It had no congressional birth certificate; a mere decision of the President, and in a few weeks resources were perfectly adapted to needs, the whole coordinated by the War Industries Board, which was supreme in all matters of production, priority and distribution.

"The steel they sent us represented the raw material for a hundred and sixty million '75' shells. The foodstuffs they sent us fed twelve million Frenchmen for a year and a half. If this help had not been forthcoming, our army could not have held, the army of the United States could not have fought."

Baruch himself, though proud of the very real achievements of WIB, has often acknowledged some flaws in its record. He came to devise certain improvements over the WIB price-fixing procedures. He did not echo the justification of General Charles G. Dawes, later Vice President, who told a Congressional Committee investigating wasteful war expenditures, "The business of an army is to win the war, not to quibble around with a lot of cheap buying. Hell and Maria, we weren't trying to keep a set of books. We were trying to win the war."

With the coming of the Armistice, one great conviction seized Baruch. Only strength could keep the peace or win a war.

The country must never again be left unprepared. He became a lifelong crusader for preparedness—for peace through strength.

The Armistice brought the inevitable Monday morning quarterbacks and the usual arguments as to who had been most responsible for winning the war behind the lines. The final truth on this point was stated in straightforward terms by Samuel M. Vauclain, President of Baldwin Locomotive Works of Philadelphia.

As Chairman of a special advisory committee on plans and munitions, Vauclain had worked closely with Baruch since Baruch first had been named to the Advisory Commission. He had helped speed production of locomotives and railway cars even before the creation of the Railway Administration, and later had promoted production of British Enfield rifles, Springfield rifles, French artillery, railway mounts, and the 14-inch guns designed to snuff out the Germans' "Big Bertha" which shelled Paris at a 70-mile range.

Vauclain knew what had been achieved by the emergency agencies fathered by the Advisory Commission, including the Food and Fuel Administrations, the War Labor Administration, the Shipping Board, the Emergency Fleet Corporation, the War Trade Board, the Housing Corporation, the Railway Administration, the War Finance Corporation, and, most important of all, the War Industries Board. He also knew how President Wilson, flanked by his key Cabinet officers, Daniels, Baker and McAdoo, had pulled the whole undertaking together.

"You will go a hell of a long way," Vauclain said, "before you will find men like our Americans and the way they worked together in Washington. There was no other government that had such a crowd. . . . But the people who won this war are the common people you see walking around here and every-where."

Nevertheless, Woodrow Wilson had affirmed—and victory had borne him out, too—that "modern wars are not won by mere numbers. They are not won by mere enthusiasm. They are not won by mere national spirit. They are won by the scientific conduct of war, the scientific application of industrial forces."

Clemenceau, leader of fighting France, agreed. Later, in addition to the quote about Mr. Baruch cited above, he acknowl edged American help and expressed especial gratitude to "the organizers of industrial victory."

As one of those seven original organizers, Baruch had gained international stature. His accomplishments were so solid, and his prestige so great by the end of the war, that Wilson himself must have wondered why he had listened to criticisms of Baruch by leading conservatives. These criticisms were summarized by the staid publication, the *New York Analyst,* and by Clinton Gilbert, author of *Mirrors of Washington.* An *Analyst* item pointed out that Baruch was not in *Who's Who* and did not have a line in the *Directory of Directors.* He was "a big speculator in stocks; a gambler." As for Gilbert, though he greatly admired Baruch personally, he quoted the accepted view that Baruch came from "that part of Wall Street which is beyond the pale; he did not belong to the right moneyed set." Even Grosvenor Clarkson admitted that he, too, was unfavorably influenced at first by the talk that Baruch "was of Wall Street, but he was its Ishmael."

Yet, in the period when Wilson was by-passing Baruch in his search for some superman to head the reorganized WIB, he offered the post twice to other men. They were Homer Ferguson, President of Newport News Shipbuilding Company, and John D. Ryan, President of Anaconda Copper Company. Both men declined it.

Ironically, John D. Ryan had first come to Wilson's attention through Baruch and Eugene Meyer. At their urging, Ryan and Daniel Guggenheim, early in 1917, formed the Copper Cooperative Committee of the chief copper producers and Ryan became its head. He made a dramatic gesture on the eve of the country's entry in the war, offering the Council of National Defense 45,500,000 pounds of copper for the Army and Navy at nearly 17 cents a pound—about half the inflationary price the Allies were then being billed. That amount of copper was, of course, but a tiny fraction of American war production needs, and the Copper Committee hiked the asking price to 37 cents for the next orders. Months later Baruch negotiated a better deal—getting a compromise offer of 23½ cents a pound in September, 1917, but agreeing to 26 cents in the summer of 1918.

By the late spring of 1918, Baruch's importance in the "War Cabinet" was generally recognized. An official photograph of that Cabinet had been widely published showing Baruch with the President, Secretary Daniels, Secretary McAdoo, Benedict Crowell, Assistant Secretary of War and Director of Munitions representing Secretary Baker; Herbert Hoover, Food Administrator; Edward N. Hurley, Chairman of the Shipping Board; Vance McCormick, Chairman of the War Trade Board; and H. A. Garfield, Fuel Administrator.

One of the war-time contributions which influenced the President's eventual choice of Baruch as a top economic adviser at the Peace Conference was Baruch's part in fostering America's development of certain industries, formerly almost a world-wide German monopoly. These included the dye industry; its related chemical developments utilizing coal-tar derivatives essential for explosives and munitions; and the manufacture of precision optical glass.

The synthetic production of ammonium nitrate—essential for both fertilizer and munitions—through processes of nitrogen fixation from the atmosphere, also was undertaken for the first time in the United States in two plants built by the Government at Muscle Shoals. For that process, James Buchanan Duke, prior to the war, had obtained the American rights for use of the German patents. A former tobacco monopolist and a pioneer developer of hydroelectric power in the two Carolinas, the shrewd Tarheel had used the patent rights as a foundation for the American Cyanamid Company. Duke had known Baruch for many years. In fact, it was Baruch who was chosen in the late 90's by Thomas Fortune Ryan to lead the raid on stock in Duke's tobacco empire which—so Ryan is reported to have stated—would "send Buck Duke back down south to skin mules." Instead, the stock fight eventually brought Duke and Ryan together in a bigger tobacco monopoly—and a tighter one—until anti-trust action broke it up.

German patents for the production of synthetic dyes and related chemicals had been confiscated by the United States Government in 1916, and a protective tariff and other devices to encourage rapid growth of the new war babies were immediately established. Speeding their development, Baruch and his technical adviser, Leland L. Summers, called in another expert, E. R. Weidlein, then Acting Director of the Mellon Institute. Weidlein was later to be a World War II consultant also, aiding the Defense Plants Corporation in promoting synthetic rubber production. The chemical industries themselves created Chemical Alliance, Inc., to deal with the Government on the German patents, and this organization was supplemented by the National Fertilizer Association and related trade associations.

Even before that, Baruch had advised the du Ponts to obtain toluol, essential for T.N.T. and other high explosives. When Summers had given similar but still earlier advice at the first meeting of the General Munitions Board, Army and Navy representatives had said they were not interested. Within a few months, they had to order the extraction of toluol from the gas jets of kitchen stoves and "parlor gas lights." Subsequently, the Army's Ordnance Department erected 53 plants and spent some $350,000,000 in developing explosives.

Meanwhile, Baruch's Raw Materials Division late in 1917 arranged with the Allies to rig the nitrate market and obtain better prices and a greater supply of nitrate from Chile. Chilean nitrate deposits formerly had been controlled by Germany. Baruch exchanged part of this nitrate supply later with fertilizer-starved Spain for mules which Pershing's army desperately needed.

Certain developments stimulated by Baruch through the Chemical Division of WIB kept the country largely independent of that type of foreign supplies after the war. On the foundation he laid also rests a great part of today's astounding chemical developments in the United States.

Another related development in this country which Baruch encouraged through the Potash Section of WIB was wiped out by the Versailles Treaty. Before the war, Germany controlled the only commercially available sources of potash in the world—in Stassfurt and Alsace—which Germany had obtained after the Franco-Prussian War of 1870. These were ceded back to France at Versailles. France needed foreign exchange from the potash sources, which were cheaper than the sources that had been developed in the United States through the war-time cooperation of WIB, the Geological Survey, and private industry at a cost of $25,000,000. War-time potash was obtained by evaporating brine in certain alkaline lakes in the Nebraska sandhills, and from the Searles Lakes Deposits in California, kelp on the West Coast, and brines and alunite in Utah.

Eventually, every influential organ of business and industry acknowledged Baruch's important role both on the Advisory

Commission and in WIB as mobilizer of the country's production and resources. Many expressed gratification for his zeal during the war, and for his astuteness in devising safeguards for postwar business interests. *Business Week,* thirteen years after the war, in its issue of December 23, 1931, again marveled at that aspect of Baruch's work, stating, "When 'Win the War' was almost the only thought, Baruch's cool brain and foresight prevented one or another of our allies from setting up a situation which would mean that after the war that particular ally would have dominated a world industry." The article pointed out that Baruch had been an especially smart trader in handling some of the negotiations with the businessmen of Great Britain who, of course, were themselves looking far beyond the end of the war.

In part, it was Baruch's remarkable success in the negotiation for war purchases by all the Allies through the Allied Purchasing Commission in Washington, and through the Foreign Economic Mission he had sent to London, which—as we shall see presently—qualified him in President Wilson's view for service even more crucially related to national economic security and world peace.

Bernard M. Baruch, in testifying before the Senate Committee on Unemployment and Relief in 1938, maintained that Nazi, Fascist and Communist systems "disregarded human equations and economic laws as immutable as the multiplication tables." He warned the Senators to avoid that mistake in devising measures to combat "this depression." "Every action," he continued, "should be designed not to attempt to repeal natural economic laws, but to accommodate them to our uses and harness them to our needs. Every action should consider all human equations, and not attempt to force divergent humanity into the rigid molds of some social or economic thesis."

CHAPTER 4

"Human Equations and Natural Economic Laws"

NO UNELECTED OFFICIAL in American history before the First World War was ever delegated such immense powers over American resources as Baruch's wartime authority gave him. Testifying before the War Policies Commission, in March, 1931, he stated, "The total of our expenditures for the world war was thirty-nine and one-half billion dollars." This sum was more than the total cost of the Federal Government from the Revolutionary War to that time. Though Baruch, of course, signed no military contracts, his decisions were crucial in the allocation of about twenty billions of the entire amount expended for the nation's military needs. In addition, he and his associates helped the Allies spend substantial sums in this country from their own war chests, plus some ten billion dollars of the twelve billions they received in loans from the U. S. Government.

Congress voted the first five billions to the Allies just five days after it declared war. In the final months of fighting, the foreign missions established an Inter-Allied Munitions Council. This body, like earlier Allied purchasing representatives, dealt in Washington, after August, 1917, with the Inter-Allied Purchasing Commission set up within WIB. Baruch, in charge of Raw Materials, was from the outset its most powerful Commissioner. Robert S. Lovett, in charge of Priorities, and Robert S.

Brookings, in charge of Finished Products, had less responsibility after Baruch brought in Alexander Legge as General Manager of the Commission. Baruch soon replaced Brookings with George N. Peek, and James A. Carr, President of the American Seeding Machine Company, eventually succeeded Legge.

Through the Inter-Allied Purchasing Commission, Baruch negotiated with the High Commissioners of Great Britain, France and Italy. These were Lord Northcliffe and his successor, Sir Charles Gordon, André Tardieu, and General Tozzi. Baruch's warm friend, Secretary McAdoo, designed the Commission as an instrumentality of the Treasury, to synchronize disbursements of money to the Allies with available supplies of raw materials and manufactured products, including civilian goods. Later, its priority functions became intertwined with the all-important Requirements Division developed by Baruch in WIB. Every war agency and some old-line Government departments found it essential to buy through that Division after Baruch became Chairman of the War Industries Board.

To obtain from the Far East such strategic materials as rubber, tin and jute posed bargaining problems in reverse for Baruch and his associates. British businessmen, in fixing prices for products they sold the Allies, were not influenced notably at first by the enormous loans the American Government made to their country, which were siphoned to them through the Chancellor of the Exchequer. Maintaining lower prices for their own government, they kept living as long as possible by the old motto, "Let thy right hand know not what thy left hand doeth."

With traditional initiative, plus greater wartime opportunities to exercise it, American business came out of the war with an increase of eight thousand in the number of individuals reporting taxable incomes of from $30,000 to $40,000 annually, and a record number of millionaires. The results were, in Baruch's words, merely a question of "natural economic laws and human equations."

132

Messages sent from London by Austen Chamberlain, Minister without portfolio, and from Winston Churchill, Minister of Munitions, diplomatically expressed some sympathy with Baruch's position that such British-controlled materials as jute should be available to America at something less than steep prices. In rebuttal, British businessmen assumed an injured air. Had they quibbled when prices skyrocketed in America on everything the British needed? Granted, price-fixing as instituted by Baruch and his associates on selected commodities had somewhat lowered their bills.

Since neither negotiations with British purchasing representatives in Washington nor long-distance haggling could break that impasse, Baruch dispatched to London the Foreign Economic Mission headed by Leland L. Summers. There, Summers resorted to a Baruch-authorized threat that the U. S. would stop shipments of silver to the Indian mints, assail the Indian rupee in the markets, and buy jute in the resulting depreciated currency. His tactics were effective. The horse-trade went through on Baruch's terms.

A more complex deal forced the Dutch to take the American-offered price for tin which the British had found, under similar pressure, to be "pretty much all right." The new price meant a saving of some $75,000,000 a year to the United States alone, to say nothing of the other Allies, but the maneuver worked only once. The British and Dutch producers of crude rubber, seeing the punch coming before it was telegraphed, banded together and resisted effective price-fixing to the war's end. American imports of this strategic material fell to one-third, with necessary restrictions on manufactured rubber goods, including tires. The truth apparently was that the British and French themselves wanted most of the rubber then being harvested.

Baruch later took to the Peace Conference an urgent plea from the war service committee of this country's rubber industry for protection in the post-war world against the near-monopoly of crude rubber by the Dutch and British. The two governments, this plea ran, should officially guarantee access by American manufacturers to this raw material "upon as favorable terms as the manufacturers of any country."

Related services by the Foreign Economic Mission were summarized many years later by James F. Byrnes, then a Senator, in a statement he submitted to the Nye Committee in 1935. He based his statement on the facts set forth by Albert C. Ritchie, General Counsel of WIB and later Governor of Maryland. Ritchie had laid that information before the Deficiency Subcommittee of the House Appropriations Committee when Byrnes was a member.

"He told us," Byrnes said, "that it was necessary for a mission to be sent to Great Britain by our Government for several purposes. First, to see that the material that the United States was shipping to Great Britain and our allied nations was really being used for military purposes and not commercial purposes to advance their export trade; and, secondly, inasmuch as we had fixed prices upon commodities in this country, and our Allies were receiving the benefit resulting from the fixing of prices, that as to certain commodities, such as tin and jute, there should be a price fixed by Great Britain, so that this Government would not be paying an excessive price for such commodities.

"There were other purposes that I do not now recall. About the time that the mission was scheduled to leave, it was discovered that there were no funds to pay the expenses of this mission representing the Government of the United States. Mr. Baruch paid the expenses of that mission out of his pocket, and according to the statement of Mr. Ritchie and his associates in the War Industries Board, it amounted to something like $85,000."

The Economic Mission saved millions of dollars for the Government of the United States, Byrnes reported. "After the matter was presented to the subcommittee of the Appropriations Committee . . . we agreed that we would put into the appropriation bill an item reimbursing Mr. Baruch for this expenditure, and about two or three days later Mr. Ritchie again came to the committee to say that he had mentioned the matter to Mr. Baruch, who stated that under no circumstances would he accept the money, and, because of that fact, it was not included in the bill."

The facts Byrnes cited regarding the Foreign Economic Mission were first brought out while Baruch was with President Wilson in Paris. Ritchie, representing Baruch, was then questioned by a Congressional Committee in preparation for a full investigation of the conduct of the war. Other facts which Byrnes did not mention to the Nye Committee also had an important bearing on post-war economic conditions and on the measures which Baruch specifically recommended at the Peace Conference.

Through the President and the State Department, arrangements were made for the Foreign Mission to have such diplomatic status as would enable it to act with full authority in economic matters. Colonel E. M. House, then Wilson's chief adviser, officially headed the Mission, which also included General Tasker H. Bliss, then Chief of Staff and a member of the Supreme War Council. They attended several important Inter-Allied Councils.

Leland Summers was a kind of economic tactician for the Mission. Baruch had indoctrinated him for his wartime assignment much in the same way as—for nearly forty years—he has coached other men for public service. He worked on Summers at Hobcaw Barony, his South Carolina plantation, in the fall of 1916, and offered the chemical engineer, out of his own pocket, the same salary to come with him to Washington that he himself was then getting.

"How much is that?" asked Summers.

"Nothing—and pay my own expenses."

Summers agreed to join Baruch, and on the same terms. After a year of close association with him in the Capital, Summers was well-equipped to snip British red-tape, too. Taking the chair at the first meeting of the Mission with the group then being formed into the Allied Munitions Council, Summers overrode parliamentary formalities. Having nominated Paul Mackall, General Sales Manager of Bethlehem Steel, as permanent Chairman of the Council, he quickly added, "Hearing no objection, I declare him elected." The British were stunned, but Mackall stayed in the saddle.

Information of much use in American war production and also in the post-war plans of this country's steel industry, was unearthed by a small task force Mackall sent through British plants to see whether steel from America was being used for war needs. Much of it, they discovered, was being hoarded for post-war trade. Similar discoveries regarding copper were made both in France and England.

Other American experts in the Mission sought better supplies of such strategic materials as manganese, tungsten, platinum and vanadium, and obtained better prices than previously quoted. Arthur D. Whiteside, on leave as President of the National Credit Office, who was a member of Baruch's WIB Wool Section and later a Vice Chairman of the War Production Board in World War II, helped Summers obtain better prices on wool from South Africa and Australia. He chalked up a saving of some $45,000,000 on one wool order alone. In addition, a better bargain was made on flax imports.

A shoe specialist with Summers dug out facts which resulted in cancellation of an order to British firms for a million pairs of shoes for General Pershing's A.E.F. A new contract was awarded to American manufacturers and the leather previously earmarked for shipment to England was allocated to them instead.

Every one of these arrangements had some lasting effect in supplementing other and vaster war developments which diverted the old channels of commerce and finance to the United States. The soldiers America sent to the front from the two million men hastily fused into an army represented only 20 percent of the Allied fighting forces, but the nation's economic contribution to the cause represented the wealth and resources of half the world. Even before the end of 1918, when war was taking nine-tenths of America's tremendously expanded production, the economic balance of the world had been shifted to this country. With it, the political balance too began shifting. This process, halted by isolationism in the Twenties, was—optimists believed—completed early in World War II. Since then, Baruch's chief concern has been to help keep that balance from shifting to Russia.

Late in 1917, however, Baruch's need for reliable information in establishing priority for overseas shipping was another reason he advanced for the creation of the Foreign Economic Mission. Though the Allied Marine Council had able American representatives, including Dwight Morrow of the Morgan banking firm, ocean shipping was "the neck of the bottle." Unloaded shipments glutted the docks, hundreds of freight cars backed up on nearby tracks, and other shipments crazily piled up in open fields miles away. In the shipping crisis of May, 1918, the British charged that the United States, leaving too many ships in private trade, was not doing its share in the shipping pool.

Wilson recalled Morrow and his assistant, George Rublee, for an explanation at the White House, which Baruch also attended. The flow back to Baruch of information on shipping was increased, once the Foreign Mission tackled the job, and the flow of supplies overseas was speeded by drastic measures which General Hugh Johnson instituted. His assistant was Gerard Swope, then President of Western Electric, later President of General Electric. Baruch first sent "Ironpants" Johnson on an inspection trip to the nation's industrial centers, and then dispatched Swope, Peek and General Williams in a follow-up which broke the shipping bottleneck in this country.

The fresh economic data accumulated on European countries by the Foreign Mission was especially valuable to Baruch and Thomas Lamont, the leading Americans among the international experts who drafted the economic and reparations section of the Versailles Treaty.

When named by Wilson as a top economic adviser at the Peace Conference, Baruch called Alexander Legge back into service from his Chicago office, telling him to enlist specialists and screen war emergency agency files for all pertinent information. The best-organized material had been gathered by the WIB Statistical Division. The first fact-finding staff Baruch had called in was headed by Dr. Leonard P. Ayres, who later became an expert on Allied war debts.

After losing Ayres and most of that staff to the War Department, which offered Army commissions, Baruch built a second one. Colonel Ayres and his group also made their data available to Legge, who turned the whole collection over to Baruch's staff in Paris and immediately began accumulating first-hand information for Colonel House on the devastation in France and Belgium.

This material, of course, was essential in discussing reparations. Colonel House sided with the French and other Allied representatives who demanded huge indemnities for their countries. President Wilson opposed the reparations claims, but eventually had to give in to some. However, through Baruch and Herbert Hoover, also a member of the Supreme Economic Council, these eventually were scaled down somewhat.

Many well-informed observers predicted then that reparations claims would be the seeds of a new war. Baruch, testifying before a special Senate Committee 19 years later—just after

Hitler had swallowed Austria—declared, "Much of the Nazi and Fascist upheaval stems from the blunders of the Treaty of Versailles, particularly in its reparation clauses. To avoid facing grim realities, burdens were placed upon the vanquished which disregarded human equations and economic laws as immutable as the multiplication tables. Partly because of this impossible artificial forcing, both the Communist and Fascist systems also adopted measures equally inconsistent with the great natural laws of human and economic nature."

Baruch's responsibilities increased as the discussion at Versailles continued. He was a chief economic adviser to the American Commission to Negotiate Peace and a member of the Economic Drafting Committee. As the Reparation Commission, the Economic Commission, and the Supreme Economic Council were established, he was made a member of each of those, too. His lengthy book about those duties entitled *The Making of the Reparation and Economic Sections of the Treaty*—published in 1920—now seems very dry except for its Preface, which contains many illuminating phrases.

"It is singular but true," Baruch wrote, "that peace seemed very beautiful during the war, but almost hateful when the war ended." Many of the participants at the Peace Conference, he added, gave the impression that they "preferred war with all its horrors to any peace short of that which they demanded." The discussions were shot through with evidence of "ineradicable hatreds and insistent desire for self-protection against future danger. . . .

"Not a few among the Allies were so intent upon momentary gains as to imperil the entire structure of world peace, which after all was the real purpose of the Conference," and he found "the peace delegates individually able and high-minded, but bound to the wheel of their national aspirations. . . . In the reparation clauses, the Conference was not writing a mere contract of dollars and cents; it was dealing with blood-raw passions. . . . There are cross-currents in the tides of circumstances against which principles and men, no matter how strong they may be, are at times unable to make headway."

The Peace Conference had been over for more than a year when Baruch was preparing his book. From that perspective, he thought that the critics of the treaty had expected too much and had lost hope too soon. Wanting negotiations "free from enmity and vengeance," they looked for action "transcending human nature." Baruch himself was not yet ready to grant that a wholly Draconian peace treaty had been written.

"It was impossible," he pointed out, "to ignore the human factors, but provision was made whereby reparations could be reduced or eliminated later, and whereby the reparation Commission in the process of enforcement might become a flexible instrument of wisdom and justice. . . . It is a fundamental mistake to assume that the treaty ends where it really begins. The signing of the document on June 28, 1919 at Versailles did not complete its history; it really began it. *The measure of its worth lies in the processes of its execution and the spirit in which it is carried out by all of the parties to the contract.*"

Viewed in this light, the treaty, Baruch insisted, "embodied the best attainable at the time in justice and wisdom . . . and enables us to look forward with hope instead of backward with hate."

Baruch took considerable satisfaction in the fact that he had helped beat down some, at least, of the unreasonable demands made by representatives of the Allied and Associated Powers. One of these was that the war expenditures by their countries should be added to the amount Germany would be required to pay. Though President Wilson flatly rejected this demand as contrary to his proposal to Germany before the Armistice, it was brought up repeatedly, and most stubbornly by the representative from Australia.

"The American delegation," Baruch reported, "finally took the position that it could not consent to demanding any fixed sums from Germany unless satisfied of the damage to at least that amount. The Allies wouldn't introduce evidence of their own or accept American estimates."

Wholly fantastic sums were asked, although it hardly seemed possible to Baruch and his associates that Germany could pay more than fifteen billion dollars within the near future. For this view Baruch was openly accused of being pro-Boche. His position, however, was that a reasonable sum paid quickly would be of greater value then, when "the Allied peoples needed rehabilitation, readjustment and a new basis of credit," than a larger sum would be later.

Baruch added that the United States was "directly involved only to a relatively small amount" and was "chiefly interested in stabilizing world conditions." But President Wilson's advisers did not allow him to rise wholly above nationalism. When other Allies proposed that "all Germany's merchant marine be surrendered as part replacement of the losses" to submarines, the President "refused to give up any of the ships the United States had taken over by Act of Congress."

Wilson and his financial advisers, Baruch continued, "spent weeks vainly trying to persuade" representatives of other countries that even if Germany could pay the astronomical sums asked, "the Allied governments could not afford . . . to exact payments that would be made at the expense of their own trade." Germany could make the payments only by selling the Allies raw materials and manufactured products, it was argued.

The same logic was later used to influence forgiveness by the United States of part or all of the Allied war debts to this country. Not even Baruch ventured to make that proposal in 1919, however. On the contrary, he then sought renewed guarantees of those loans. In the same period he recommended that the Reparation Commission "should postpone the fixing of the German indemnity until it could be more scientifically estimated." But in signing the treaty, the Germans pledged their nation to pay 33 billion gold dollars.

By 1920, it was becoming plain that the sum must be scaled down, as Baruch indicated in concluding the Preface to his book on the Treaty. He pointed out that a conference with Germany had just begun at Spa, with John Foster Dulles there to emphasize, "We claim no penalty. . . . We ask for justice, not revenge."

It was in the map-making at Paris, however, that the future woes of humanity were most concretely forecast—and a lifetime job was outlined for Baruch and all other leaders concerned with building an enduring peace. Wilson had anticipated both the territorial grabs and the new schemes for commercial imperialism. Those who still worshipped him or damned him as an idealist—according to their own standards—underrated Wilson's realistic appraisal of human nature, which was rooted in the Calvinist training of his childhood: "All men are born sinful," yet, being created "a little lower than the angels," can be saved.

Moreover, Wilson grew up in the South, which had been impoverished by the Civil War and further maimed after the peace. A legalized blight miscalled "Reconstruction" had been forced upon the section by such vengeful Senators as Thaddeus Stevens and Charles Sumner, against all moderate public opinion in the North and West. It had continued to hold back political and economic recovery well past Baruch's childhood, too, in South Carolina. By word of mouth in boyhood, both he and Wilson had learned of the evils of sectionalism, personal vindictiveness and economic stupidity, and Wilson had made that knowledge the foundation of his early career as a professional historian.

Academic training and the rough and tumble of politics had further prepared Wilson for the attitudes they would encounter at the Peace Conference table. The descriptive text to fit the occasion might have been lifted from a sermon by Wilson's father: "Wherever the carcass is, there will be eagles gathered together."

But even if a miracle had not put Wilson in the White House, he still would have been prepared for the treaty-writing wrangle. As late as February 2, 1917—according to the testimony of Franklin K. Lane, Secretary of the Interior—Wilson told his Cabinet that "he didn't wish to see either side" win the war, "for both had been equally indifferent to the rights of neutrals, though Germany had been brutal in taking life [on ships] and England only in taking property."

Shortly after Wilson justified in his own mind America's entry into the war, Arthur J. Balfour, British Foreign Secretary, disclosed to Wilson certain information which renewed the President's distrust of Allied war aims. Balfour, coming to America as the champion of Zionism—for political as well as for moral reasons—reluctantly gave the President, on May 17, 1917, a report on the Sykes-Picot Treaty, the Treaty of London, and other "secret" agreements between Britain, France, Russia, Italy and Japan. They pledged in advance to divide the spoils of victory and write a peace governed by the ancient Roman principle of "Woe to the Vanquished." Broad hints concerning these treaties already had reached Wilson through American diplomatic channels and from Colonel House, his personal representative overseas.

The hints served as levers for obtaining Balfour's disclosures. Then Wilson's attitude hardened. America had not been a party to the agreements, and, under his leadership, America would not help write the jackal peace they required. Wilson hoped, it has been reported, that the existence of the secret agreements would not be exposed until the war's end. If they were, he doubtless wondered, would the American people still go on believing they were sweating and fighting and weeping to make the world safe for democracy?

Seven months later, in December, 1917, when Leon Trotsky and his Bolsheviki tore open the Czar's diplomatic archives in Petrograd, they flung the secret agreements in the face of mankind and raised up thousands of new cynics. Then in January, 1918 there came the harsh and opposing demands of the imperial governments of Germany and Austria at Brest-Litovsk. These terms again advertised how solid a bloc were the Central Powers and how ruthless their ambitions. To divide booty, they had no need to make secret treaties in advance.

Edgar Sisson, the representative of the American Committee on Public Information at Petrograd, cabled a plea to George Creel, his Director in Washington, that the President "restate the anti-imperialistic war aims and democratic peace requisitions of America" for propaganda use in Russia and in Germany.

Five days later Wilson went before Congress and proclaimed his Fourteen Points, the most important of which called again for an association of nations to build enduring world peace. These articles of faith were an expansion of proposals he had made twelve months earlier in a peace address to the Senate. As stated in his compact but less eloquent appeal of January, 1917, his concepts had been greeted with doubts and even laughter by political spokesmen at home and by influential publications overseas. The *London Daily Mail*, for example, had derided it as an "abstract pontifical statement of a future international morality."

The yeast in Wilson's Fourteen Points was potent, however, and has never yet stopped working, even though much of the original batch was thrown out at the Peace Conference. There Clemenceau, as Sir Philip Gibbs reported, "looked more like a walrus than a tiger, a poor old walrus in a traveling circus," but he was able to act "the indomitable Tiger of French victory." Lloyd George was just as fierce an antagonist of Wilson's, and for the same reason. Both were equally shortsighted, though they counted themselves astute in forcing compromises which, in the main, provided the boundaries and rewards proposed in the secret treaties.

General Jan Christian Smuts, summarizing the Peace Conference, said, "Not Wilson, but humanity failed in Paris." The context, however, gives a different emphasis to the result. Humanity was betrayed at Paris, and betrayed by the immemorial methods of representatives who know the price of everything, but few of the enduring values.

As a concession to Wilson, they agreed to incorporate the Covenant of the League of Nations in the Treaty. Even so, they remained contemptuous of his faith that through this institution peace could live.

Senator Henry Cabot Lodge, meanwhile, in his determined effort to keep America out of the League, introduced ten reservations to the treaty. If they were accepted, he would introduce more from the thirty he had prepared in reserve. By such rewriting, the treaty in the end would be his, not Wilson's. Baruch and other advisers, including Mrs. Wilson— not knowing then of the other reservations Lodge was holding back— advised the President to accept those the Senator did introduce. Wilson refused. The reservation to Article X alone, he declared, was designed to cut the very heart out of the League. Ironically, Henry Cabot Lodge, Jr., himself a Senator and the grandson of the man who led the Senate fight against the League, was appointed on November 29, 1952—thirty-three years later—to head the U. S. Mission to the United Nations!

Wilson left Washington on a nation-wide tour to combat the political propaganda that was playing upon every popular prejudice and misrepresenting all that he stood for, and all that he had embodied in the Covenant of the League. If he had not collapsed on September 25, 1919, could he have won out against the confidence men, as he believed them to be, who were offering the American people a gold brick in place of national security and world peace? That—as F.D.R. would have said— is indeed an "iffy" question. In any case, Wilson was brought back to the White House a completely incapacitated man.

Baruch became one of the group that made decisions during the President's illness—a disturbing period for its members and for the democratic nation. Called "the Regency Council" by Mark Sullivan and other newspaper men, the group included Rear Admiral Cary T. Grayson, Wilson's physician; Tumulty; and Baruch. From his sick-bed, Wilson dismissed Robert Lansing, Secretary of State, after he learned that Lansing had been calling Cabinet meetings on his own. Though he broke, eventually, with numerous associates, including Colonel House and Tumulty, Wilson clung to his trust in Baruch.

With the election of Warren Gamaliel Harding, a group simi- lar to the one that maneuvered into power on Grant's coattails after the Civil War took over the Government. They described their actions as a return to "Normalcy!"

As for accepting qualifications in order to get Senate rati- fication of the League of Nations, it took Baruch himself some years to realize—as he finally admitted—that "Wilson was right." It took the people even longer to catch up with the vision of the leader whose body was broken by the failure of that vision. Twenty-odd years later, as victory over Hitler drew near, the idea of the League was re-invoked by a man who believed that Wilson's faith had helped sustain his own courage after he was stricken by infantile paralysis. In *This I Remember,* Eleanor Roosevelt told how her husband, while first struggling to re- cover from his polio attack, had learned all he could about the way in which the League was functioning despite America's re- jection of idealism. Roosevelt's draft of measures to strengthen the League was submitted for the Edward Bok Peace Award

of 1923, and was entitled *A Plan to Preserve Peace*. President
Roosevelt later brought that draft up to date in the White
House, and renamed his concept "The United Nations."

President Wilson offered Baruch the post of Secretary of the
Treasury shortly after the Armistice. However, Baruch was
more concerned in 1919 with international issues, and wanted
to make his influence count in the peace decisions. He declined
the offer to be free to advise Wilson in Paris. While he was
abroad, Baruch's disciples Hugh Johnson and George Peek
worked hard in Washington to create a peacetime model of the
War Industries Board—something Johnson actually succeeded
in doing a decade later, after he was named to plan and head
the NRA.

In his autobiography, Johnson said that Baruch at first
poured cold water on the post-war industrial organization idea,
which had come to Johnson while he was getting the WIB
records together for Baruch's final report. "It's a dead cock in
the pit," Baruch said, according to Johnson. "Let's turn industry
absolutely free. Everything that made us possible is gone—the
spirit of cooperation and sacrifice—the vast purchasing power
of the government—the scant legal authority we have had—and
the support of public opinion."

Many of Baruch's war-time colleagues liked the idea, however,
and predicted that "a sudden post-war business paralysis could
be avoided by self-government in industry under Government
supervision." Though they had hurried back to their own
private jobs and wanted no responsibility for a proposed organization that would keep them in Washington, they especially
liked the idea of maintaining price agreements. Mark Requa,
the war-time Oil Administrator, was Johnson's first assistant
in promoting the plan. "The President," Johnson reported,
"actually appointed an Industrial Board of the Department of

147

Commerce. George Peek was literally drafted to head it, and I acted as his General Counsel. We began at once to consult steel and other industries. . . . We even got an agreement with the steel people which was preserved by them for years. But it suited my friend, Carter Glass, the Secretary of the Treasury . . . no better than its inheritor, NRA, suited him, and it blew up when the President agreed with him."

Wilson actually needed no great push from Glass to make this decision. By long training and sincere belief, Wilson was an economist of the Manchester School, and had agreed to centralized industrial power and to Federal operation of the railways only as war emergency measures. In peacetime, he believed in Federal regulation of private enterprise to assure the advantages of genuine competition to consumers. Before naming Glass as McAdoo's successor, Wilson rejected McAdoo's proposal to seek Congressional authority for continued Federal operation of the railroads, and the lines were returned to their owners by the Transportation Act of 1920. Though it took some time for several temporary agencies, including the Shipping Board, to work out decontrol problems, the Executive Department gave up its emergency powers before Congress had time to remove war-time measures from the books.

Wilson's hope for improved relations between capital and labor led him to schedule an Industrial Democracy Conference for October, 1919. He named Baruch as one of the key speakers, and called on Secretary Lane, William B. Wilson, Secretary of the Department of Labor, and Tumulty to set forth the Administration's policies at the sessions. Representatives of labor, business, industry, and the general public were invited.

A similar conference had been called at the start of the war "to establish a truce between the conflicting industrial interests." Samuel Gompers told the meeting—as was his custom in every possible speech—how he had come to this country and worked in sweatshops as a child, adding, "For this, I have never quite forgiven society." Numerous promises were exchanged by labor, company executives, and leaders of such organizations as the National Association of Manufacturers to the effect that no group would take advantage of the war to promote its own interest. The War Labor Board, under the co-chairmanship of former President William H. Taft and Frank P. Walsh, was created to devise means to prevent strikes and lockouts and to adjust industrial disputes.

Through this Board and the President's Mediation Commission, labor did make some gains during the war. Although the rights to organize, to bargain collectively, and to seek a minimum wage were not actually established by law, these principles were accepted in numerous industries, and wages rose. Other promises to labor included better housing, better working conditions, elimination of child labor in war industries, and measures to keep down the cost of living. Those pledges were not kept.

Additional dissatisfactions arose, as indicated in Clarkson's book. "As labor as a commodity began to reach the state of a known and controllable factor," he wrote, "the War Industries Board established in the fall of 1918 a Labor Priorities Section. . . . It led to great expansion of the power of the board. It now became the allocator of men not only between industries, but between military and civil life. . . . All America in all its material and human resources was subject to its command. It was an industrial dictatorship without parallel."

In the period of reaction, the phrase to emphasize in the postwar world became "industrial democracy." The Labor Priorities Section did not live long enough before the Armistice to magnify resentment greatly, however. It was established just after President Wilson's Labor Day address of 1918. He did not promise that price-fixing on selected commodities would be extended to consumer goods. Instead, he appealed for increased production to combat inflation.

Meanwhile, Tumulty began to think more deeply about the conflicts between labor and management. He sent a memorandum to the President recommending new post-war policies, which he entitled "The Revolt of the Underdog." War controls, he pointed out, "had left the thing sought to be regulated, stronger and more hateful in its influence." Tumulty predicted that the Democratic Party would "cease to live" after the war ended unless it paid renewed heed to the average man. While Wilson was in Paris, Tumulty sent him a stronger memorandum on the same subject, and in this he recommended that the Industrial Democracy Conference be called.

About this time, and at the instigation of Wilson and the liberals of other nations, peace treaty provisions were being drafted to set in motion the International Labor Organization. The ILO, which James T. Shotwell called one of the constructive accomplishments of the Conference, was aimed at bettering working conditions the world over. Reporting on this significant development, Harry Hansen pointed out that it had strong support from all the English-speaking nations "though their attitudes differed widely." The British wanted an international parliament of labor with power to make laws effective in all member nations. The Americans, led by Samuel Gompers, with William Green among the advisers, were strongly opposed to a "superstate" and held out for promotion of their aims through established national agencies.

Because the United States did not ratify the treaty, it did not become a member of the ILO until 1934, when Congress accepted a special invitation to this country to join, making ours one of the chief industrial states in the organization. Meanwhile, more progressive labor measures were being demanded in America early in the post-war years, and one was enacted. Others were recommended at the Industrial Democracy Conference of 1919 which Baruch helped lead and which, at the time, seemed to end in a fiasco. Tumulty had recommended that the Conference consider proposing to industry a profit-sharing plan for labor and "a plan to get labor representatives in the management of business." Such matters were discussed as the 8-hour day—which only railway workers had under the Adamson law—the 48-hour week, and protection for women and children in industry.

But the long-rankling resentment against Wilson on the part of important segments of business and industrial management also erupted. These groups had never forgiven him—to name only a few of their grievances—for instituting taxation on personal incomes and heavy taxes on corporate incomes; for the 1915 tariff revisions, and, in the same year, for the raising of the Labor Bureau to the position of a Cabinet Department; for the Adamson law and the La Follette Seamen's Act, permitting seamen to organize and bargain collectively; for agricultural loan legislation lowering the interest rate; and for the creation of the Federal Reserve System.

Almost hopeless divergence of opinion would have come out of the Industrial Democracy Conference even if fate had permitted a better timing. But shortly before it began, Wilson's illness had eliminated his leadership and eloquence, and three days before he collapsed, steel workers struck all over the United States. Staggering on, the Conference was thrown into even worse confusion by the threat of a soft coal strike—John L. Lewis had just become Acting President of the United Mine Workers —and it gave up when labor representatives walked out just before that strike began on October 31.

The coal walk-out, Tumulty biographer John M. Blum has stated, followed management's refusal "to agree to compromise the formula proposed by representatives of labor and the public." Tumulty, doing an about-face on his earlier labor championship, and Baruch "decided that the steel strikers deserved no government support." The result was that "Management won without government assistance."

Labor unrest and the general postwar economic debacle should have been foreseen and forestalled, Baruch decided, and to that end provisions for peacetime readjustment should be included in future preparedness plans. From that resolve and from his many recommendations for M-Day revisions over the years grew his *War and Postwar Adjustment Policies* of World War II, including recommendations for a "Work Director," published in 1944.

Broad aspects of the economic picture of management-labor relations after the First World War were summarized by Grosvenor Clarkson in 1923 in his book, *Industrial America in the World War*. His partisan phraseology, giving the true flavor of the period, makes his summary worth quoting. "It was thought," Clarkson wrote, "that the principles of the minimum wage, recognition of trade organizations and collective bargaining would be so firmly anchored during the war that the backwash of peace could not dislodge them.

"Four years after the armistice it is plain that these hopes are not to be realized. . . . Labor . . . feeling too fully its power, slowed up after the war to such an extent that for a long time it was not more than sixty per cent efficient. Employers felt that labor had taken advantage of the necessities of war to exact from them concessions that were unendurable, and they determined to even up the score when the circumstances should be favorable.

"Such circumstances arose when the inevitable industrial depression set in. But even before that, the program of the radical laborites—who were not content with the advances made during the war, but boldly sought to syndicalize industry—was crushingly defeated in the great steel strike of the fall of 1919, which was also a blow to conservative labor programs. The failure of this strike was the death-blow of bolshevism in America and stimulated chauvinism among employers.

"Since then, there has been a powerful campaign for the open shop, and virtually for the destruction of the power of labor organizations. The aggressiveness of employers, combined with the pressure of unemployment in 1920-21, resulted for a time in an apparent loss of most of the advantages gained by labor during the war."

Nevertheless, labor made a very definite gain in 1920 when Congress passed the Industrial Rehabilitation Act advocating community responsibility for industrial accidents, and offering Federal funds to the States for assistance in restoring to civil employment persons injured in industry or in any legitimate occupation. To benefit every class, the next session of Congress appropriated money to safeguard the welfare of mothers and infants at the time of childbirth, and three years later Congress made another attempt to outlaw child labor. Earlier attempts had been overruled by the Supreme Court. In 1924 Congress proposed an amendment to the Constitution empowering it to "direct, regulate, and prohibit the labor of persons under 18 years of age," and, by 1935, 28 States had ratified this amendment. Though this number was eight short of the total necessary for enactment, most of the 48 States have since adopted this type of state legislation.

Superficial observers of Baruch's part in the varied developments before the crash of 1929 are reported to have charged— unfairly—that he seemed to run with the hares and hunt with the hounds. That is, his general views on social concerns, when he made them public, were acceptable to liberals; but his many statements on specific economic problems were equally acceptable to conservatives.

Baruch's address at a reunion of the War Industries Board on December 10, 1920, was cited as such an example. He chided business and industry, in the war's aftermath, for rapidly descending "from heights of optimism and courage to depths of pessimism and fears of impending disaster. . . . It is a curious fact that capital is generally most fearful when prices of commodities and securities are low and safe, and boldest at the heights when there is danger."

Inviting businessmen to take an affirmative stand, Baruch said, "Let us look for the dawn of a great and enduring industrial renaissance, always bearing in mind the predominating fact that the economic, political and social elements are so interwoven that one cannot survive without the others."

Both capital and labor, he insisted, must content themselves "with returns more nearly commensurate than recently with the service performed. . . . We must look for profits from big production, not from limitation of production. We must see to it that the present mass readjustments of prices are carried through to the ultimate consumer."

Baruch also called for the revision of "our burdensome and paralyzing wartime taxation, which is no longer necessary." Shortly afterwards, Andrew Mellon, in some circles hailed as "the greatest Secretary of the Treasury since Alexander Hamilton," made the same recommendation, being especially insistent that the surtax on highest incomes should drop from 65 to 25 percent. Congress kept the surtax levy on top incomes at 50 percent.

It was the reparations problem to which Baruch addressed most of his attention at the WIB reunion, however. "We will not have peace in the fullest sense," he said, "until a revived Germany again takes her part in the economic system and reopens the sources of production and distribution. . . . The crux of the world industrial and commercial problem lies in the fixing of the reparations that Germany must pay. . . . Germany must work to produce the wealth with which to pay. In helping herself she will do what is more important—she will be helping us all."

Baruch then emphasized another specific aspect of the problem which already had troubled him for nearly a year. "If we are to dispose of our surplus products, Germany and the rest of Europe must resume commercial and industrial activity so they can be the customers of old."

An effective plan for the disposal of surplus farm products became one of Baruch's major concerns in the paradoxical years of Normalcy and "keeping cool with Cal." To this end, he became one of the most determined sponsors of the McNary-Haugen Bill. When he first discussed the idea, many who had watched his operations in New York and war-time Washington were aghast. Testifying during the hearings of a special Senate Committee on Unemployment and Relief, in 1938, he admitted that he had been told, "Baruch, you seem to be pretty sound on economics, but get cockeyed on agriculture." This Baruch denied. On the contrary, he pointed out, "I was one of the first advocates of the McNary-Haugen Bill when it was not so fashionable as it is now to talk about the inequality of agriculture."

When Senator Frazier remarked, "That is a mild proposition nowadays," Baruch agreed. "Now I think the people who fought it would be glad to have put it into effect instead of something else."

Senator Frazier's statement that the McNary-Haugen Bill was defeated by the business interests of the country and the Chambers of Commerce brought this answer from Baruch: "We got it passed twice in the House and the Senate."

"But they got it vetoed," Senator Frazier replied.

"I think they were very stupid," Baruch answered, "and I said so at the time."

Before this little set-to, Baruch had declared, "On the economic side our two principal problems are unemployment and agriculture. They are problems that must somehow be solved.

We cannot go along with a lopsided economy– half boom, half bust.

"I have been giving my attention and effort to the farm problem for 17 years, ever since 1921, because it was quite as clear then as it is now that there was too great a disparity between farm and other income to permit a sound, balanced national economy.

"We started the chain of events that upset that balance at our very beginning when we adopted a system of protective tariffs that was deliberately intended to subsidize our industry at the expense of our agriculture. At first, with virgin soil, free or very cheap, agriculture could stand the burden and perhaps it was the best system. But even before the war our chickens were coming home to this roost.

"We interfered with natural economic laws, when we started this disparity. There are only two possible solutions. One is to knock down the old artificiality of the tariff. The other is to build up a new artificiality to offset it. Under existing world conditions only the latter alternative is possible. That always happened when we begin to interpose man-made devices against natural laws. We have to interpose another new invention to save us from the effect of the old one.

"The necessity here is to give a boost to farm income to permit the 40 per cent of our market which is rural to consume the products of the cities. After studying many methods and even tentatively approving some, it seems to me that the best, simplest, fairest, and most logical way to do this is by a straight subsidy on the domestic consumption of farm products, leaving marketing and production free."

The devices Baruch here emphasized—maintenance of the tariff and the building up of "a new artificiality to offset it" —were important features, also, of the McNary-Haugen Bill. The measure was actually rooted in the efforts of two of Baruch's disciples, Hugh Johnson and George Peek. A third disciple, Alexander Legge, became Chairman of the Farm Board established by Hoover in a different approach to the problem of farm relief.

The Biblical words which so aptly characterize conversion from war to peace in every age—"They shall beat their swords into plowshares"—literally applied to the work of these disciples. Both Peek and Legge, before joining Baruch in the WIB, had been competitors in the manufacture of farm machinery. Legge returned to International Harvester Company, but Peek, deciding not to go back to Deere and Company, accepted an offer to reorganize the tottering Moline Plow Company, which had just been bought by John Willys, the automobile manufacturer. Johnson became Peek's assistant, but it was uphill work.

How could farmers then buy any new equipment? Farmers had suffered from the inflation-deflation cycle that began in 1915 more than had any other part of the nation. As Johnson put it in his autobiography, "To feed our Allies in the war, the federal government induced vast over-production in agriculture." In one chapter entitled "Swords and Plowshares," he tells how farmers over-extended their credit in buying greater acreage, more efficient machinery to replace the farm help they lost to the armed services, and more trucks and automobiles to speed their products to market. They could not keep up the payments when the prices of farm products plummeted, and even in recent years the nation's big insurance companies were the absentee landlords of vast tracts they took over from the bankrupt farmers in 1921.

"The resulting prostration of the whole rural forty per cent of our national economy," Johnson reported, "restricted the domestic market for industry and material, increasing and prolonging the depression." The farm machinery business in particular could not make a come-back until farmers were aided, and the countless other items of manufactured goods which debt-ridden farmers could not buy added to the nation's surplus, and to urban unemployment.

In their own interests, industrialists, bankers, and labor leaders eventually were obliged to consider the farmer's woes, and accordingly they gathered in a national conference called by President Harding and presided over by Representative Sidney Anderson, shortly after the Congressman had headed an extensive Congressional study of the agricultural depression. No immediate practical benefit resulted from either effort. Meanwhile, the varied enterprises of John Willys, which had mushroomed so quickly, fell into other hands, and Peek told Johnson, "There can't be any business for us until the farmer is on his feet. Let's find out what is the matter with agriculture." The results of their investigations went into a pamphlet called *Equality for Agriculture*, with some features similar to the proposals Baruch had put forth in two earlier pamphlets entitled *Putting Farming on a Modern Business Basis* and *Agricultural Finance*.

Baruch also advised the Kansas State Board of Agriculture during this period. He recommended scientific crop marketing, with more elevator space, built either privately or through loans at low interest rates, to farm cooperatives "getting low bulk prices just as big business does."

He approved the plan set forth by Johnson and Peek in their pamphlet, which Johnson described as a "proposal to remove the agricultural surplus from the domestic market, sell it abroad for what it would bring, thus permitting the tariff to protect American prices for domestic consumption, and then to spread the government loan on the surplus over the whole crop by means of an equalization fee, all of which would have elevated the average price considerably. It was based on the proposition to restore the prewar parity of farm purchasing powers. It was the essence of the McNary-Haugen Bill."

Johnson took the idea to the senior Henry Wallace, then Secretary of Agriculture, who called a conference of leading bankers and industrialists to consider it. Ogden Armour, Charles Dawes, and Otto Khan approved. But Julius Barnes, key man in the export grain trade who—according to Johnson—"controlled the conference," killed the idea. Barnes was influenced by Herbert Hoover, then Secretary of Commerce, Johnson charged. Hoover, he said, was "intent on building export trade and would consider nothing that would raise the cost of American industrial products." Next, a conference of economists was called. They approved, but Wallace and Hoover clashed and the idea went down again.

In somewhat modified form, nevertheless, the McNary-Haugen bill eventually was pushed through Congress. Coolidge then vetoed it. Like Baruch he believed in "natural economic laws," and, again like Baruch, he recognized no other school of economics than the one to which he belonged. Their schools overlapped in many ways, but in this instance they were miles apart. In vetoing the bill, the President dogmatically asserted that such Government intervention in "natural economy" could not be tolerated.

Baruch, Peek and Johnson won Al Smith's approval of the idea and Peek stumped the Republican states in the entire Mississippi Valley promising the farmers "Equality for Agriculture" if Smith went to the White House. John J. Raskob, a du Pont executive and a leading spokesman for the Democratic Party then, also added the farm surplus disposal plan in his speeches, though he emphasized that technology and mass methods had created an industrial surplus quite as threatening.

Johnson handed Smith a Baruch-approved statement on the same subject. When he looked it over, Smith is reported to have said, "Aw hell, General. I don't know anything about this kind

159

of stuff and if I tried to do it, everybody would say that at last Al's letting somebody write his speeches for him. They gotta take me the way I am or not at all."

The McNary-Haugen Bill was again introduced after Hoover's election. His veto was on the same general grounds as Coolidge's, although—following the crash of 1929—Hoover sponsored various measures using Federal funds in vain efforts to improve business conditions.

A very different plan to deal with the surplus of farm products was put through by the New Deal when Baruch was coaching the original Brain Trust, including Peek. Instead of dumping the surplus abroad, farmers were asked to eliminate it in return for payments from the Federal Treasury. "If anybody is entitled to be called the father of Farm Relief," Johnson quotes Franklin Roosevelt as saying, "George Peek is the man."

Conservatives in every walk of life denounced the plowing under of crops and the killing off of little pigs, but the AAA has since been credited as a success, and especially in the period when widespread drought helped eliminate the surplus.

Meanwhile, the nation was benefiting from the services of Eugene Meyer, Jr., appointed a member of the Federal Reserve Board by Hoover on Baruch's recommendation. Earlier that year, Baruch had played a leading role in aiding the confirmation of Charles Evans Hughes as Chief Justice of the Supreme Court. Hughes' magnificent contributions to the American people in that post might have been lost through partisan politics if Baruch had not persuaded his old friend, Joe Robinson—then Democratic leader of the Senate—that the plan to block the appointment was contemptible. Hughes, defeated by Wilson in the Presidential elections of 1912, had never lowered his party's banner, but more important, he had never once raised it above his sense of responsibility to all the people.

In the honeymoon period of the New Deal, Baruch approved Roosevelt's interpretation of the Constitutional provision making the Government not merely an umpire but the people's instrument to help effect their safety and welfare. The same provision had been the foundation of the liberal policies and the great achievements of President Wilson, too. But the power in that provision had not been evoked by the Republican Presidents of the intervening years. Indeed, many regulatory powers for the general welfare even went by the board.

The inevitable result was the depression. "The crash of 1929 and the lean years that followed it," Baruch said, "at last thoroughly awakened this nation and the world to the startling necessity to temper the raw doctrine of laissez faire with the age-old lesson of our race—that we must not lie down dumbly under the destructive effect of natural laws. We must stand up and apply human intelligence to their adaptation, as mankind did to the glacial age, to flood, fire, famine and pestilence—to storm and drought and earthquake."

This view, which he expressed in 1938 to the Senate Committee on Unemployment and Relief, again justified Wilson's old tribute to him: "Bernie grew." For the June, 1929, issue of *The American Magazine* carried an article entitled "Bernard M. Baruch Discusses the Future of American Business," and that future then seemed to him very bright indeed. There was the possibility, he admitted, of one upsetting factor. "A prohibitive tariff would inevitably force our best customers into defensive tariff agreements. Such a result I do not fear because I know Mr. Hoover to be too sound in his economics and too keenly aware of our necessity in this regard to permit such a thing. . . . He will use the protective principles to preserve the markets which are rightly ours, and I trust, to relieve agriculture in that very limited field where protection will be of benefit."

Baruch's article was, in general, a paean to progress, prosperity, and the genius of the American businessman and industrialist. He praised certain safeguards against depression "which never existed before: The Federal Reserve Bank; the better understanding and use of statistics by nations, by banks, by industries and by individuals; the coordination of the financial systems of all the leading nations; and the great increase of human wants and ambitions throughout the world, which, with occasional and temporary setbacks, ought to provide a huge volume of business for many years to come. . . . In broad and general terms, progress is on the march. The economic condition of the world seems on the verge of a great forward move ment. . . . Through higher wages we gave the people an opportunity to indulge their desire for better things and more of them, and then, by the development of more flexible credits through installment buying, we enlarged that opportunity. The basis of our prosperity is our own domestic market, which we have vastly enlarged by this simple process of increasing the power to consume."

The article was the record of an interview Baruch granted the famed advertising and publicity man, Bruce Barton, who was later elected to Congress where he became one of the triumvirate in Roosevelt's rhythmical mockery, "Martin, Barton, and Fish," in the 1936 election campaign. The article went to press, of course, a number of weeks before it appeared on the news stands. Even in June, however, very few people questioned Baruch's optimism.

Part of the folklore which has grown up since 1929 is a story to the effect that the ever-wise Baruch had long anticipated the crash late that year. If so, surely his sense of moral responsibility to the American people would have prevented him from encouraging further reckless rides on the roller coaster. If ever the people needed one of Baruch's famous warnings of disaster ahead, they needed it then.

162

It is a matter of record, however, that by late fall that year Baruch did advise four of his personal friends, Arthur Krock, Alexander Woollcott, Franklin P. Adams, and Harpo Marx, not to buy more stocks but instead to switch their money to bonds. By then, most of his own wealth was so invested.

Baruch, stating his theories as to the cause of the depression when he testified to the special Senate Committee in March, 1938, called the boom period one of mass delusion, along with the earlier Tulip Craze, the Mississippi Bubble, and the South Sea Bubble, and added, "In the great madness and delusion of 1929, people bought everything and anything. They did not care what it was. Some people did make a profit. I did not make as much as others because I knew that the boom was bound to break some time."

Hugh Johnson in his autobiography states that Baruch told him, in 1928, "Watch automobile sales and the construction figures. This whole false fabric is built on the unprecedented conjunction of these two big credit-inflated booms. When they slide the whole structure will collapse."

Johnson had gone to work for Baruch in New York in 1927, after seven heart-breaking years in the plow business. Of that period he later said, "I had done some specialized jobs for Baruch—examining companies in which he was asked to invest. Three had been highly propagandized." For several years, he added, "I was the only research staff Baruch permanently retained, but he gave me a free hand in consultation and use of such scientists and experts as I might need." After eighteen months of this association, according to Johnson, Baruch proposed, "Let's just get out of everything and begin studying the world and the domestic economic and political situation and see if there is any suggestion of a way out of this mess." They blueprinted ideas for the relief of the destitute, and again called for the abandonment of Prohibition, but their estimate of how much additional revenue could come from excise taxes on liquor got them into a little squabble with Ogden Mills, Hoover's Secretary of the Treasury.

Their assistance to the Brain Trust was better appreciated. Raymond Moley, who wore several New Deal hats—although his official title was Assistant Secretary of State—included numerous tributes to both men in his book, *After Seven Years*. Moley said he had originally suspected Baruch "as a fat cat" and resented his welcome by Roosevelt into the inner circle. "We gradually came to look upon his generous intellectual contributions with admiration, respect and gratitude," he added. Moley was especially grateful for Baruch's loan of Hugh Johnson to the battery of writers for Roosevelt's first campaign, and for "the magnificent draft speech" they had prepared blasting the economics of Hoover. He was also glad, in that early period, for Baruch's efforts to bring Senator Carter Glass into the Cabinet as Secretary of the Treasury—the same post Glass had held a decade earlier. Glass, however, declined and the appointment went to William Woodin, although Baruch also had been offered the position.

A detailed account of Baruch's services to the nation during the creative "First Hundred Days" of the New Deal is outside the province of this book, nor is it possible here to cite his equally valuable contributions as a critic of the Administration at a later period. He made his weight count not only through his own counsel to Roosevelt, the Cabinet members, other key officials and the Congress, but indirectly through the men he brought into public service in those years. His favorite recommendation for such individuals always was stated simply: "The fellow makes a noise like a dividend."

Baruch's two chief protégés in the New Deal, George Peek and Johnson, gradually lost favor. Peek's departure was influenced by his relations with Moley, whose disillusion began when he was unable to win his battle against Cordell Hull, Secretary of State, on tariff policies. After seven years, Moley left the government to pack his bitterness into a book and to write a column every seven days for *Newsweek,* usually expressing his irreverence for the latter-day Saints of the New Deal. Peek resigned his AAA job to campaign for Landon.

Baruch's own disillusion began even before Roosevelt took the nation off the gold standard, the ultimate heresy in his economic creed. Johnson wore out his enthusiasm and his welcome at about the same rate.

Though Johnson campaigned for Willkie, he never lost his confidence that the Blue Eagle he created in NRA was the best symbol of the New Deal's dynamic accomplishments. NRA, Johnson said in his autobiography, "created 2,785,000 jobs at a desperate time and added billions to the annual purchasing power of working people. It did more to create jobs than all the other emergency agencies put together and it did so without any draft on the Federal Treasury."

For the NRA plan, Johnson drew chiefly upon what he had learned through working with Baruch in the War Industries Board. He also utilized his experience with the Army in the housing and relief work for victims of the San Francisco earthquake of April, 1906. His basic idea, however, was, "If industry can act as a unit for the purposes of war, why cannot it do the same for the purposes of peace?"

Under NRA, industry committees, similar to those called in to advise the original WIB, adopted fair-price codes and agreed to pay minimum wages. Johnson had left the agency before the Supreme Court decision in the Schecter case. This ruling involved NRA's right to specify fair payment to a butcher in Brooklyn for killing chickens, and it became known as the "sick chicken case" that killed off the Blue Eagle. Johnson came back to Washington and appealed to several Congressional committees to introduce legislation which would pass the test of

165

the Supreme Court and enable NRA to survive. He made many appeals to private groups in support of the plan, and also wrote a pamphlet entitled *Where Do We Go From Here?* asking for a reborn NRA. But his pleading was to no avail.

Originally, Johnson had been slated for much greater power in Washington than he ever got. The NRA bill he helped draft was in two parts, Title I dealing with industrial codes and labor, and Title II embodying the public works program. Johnson expected to be the Administrator of both. Baruch, however, advised against the dual responsibility. Fond as he was of Johnson, and sincerely appreciative of his great drive and intelligence, he thought it was his duty to add a word of caution.

Speaking of Johnson, Baruch told Frances Perkins, Secretary of Labor, "He's been my number-three man for years. I think he's a good number-three man, maybe a number-two man, but he's not a number-one man. He's dangerous and unstable. He gets nervous and sometimes goes away for days without notice. I'm fond of him, but do tell the President to be careful. Hugh needs a firm hand." At that time, Baruch was not seeing President Roosevelt because of their differences over economic policies, and especially over the gold policy.

"Honest Harold" Ickes, Secretary of the Interior, got the additional responsibility as Public Works Administrator, though Harry Hopkins was the boss of the operating agency, WPA. Madame Perkins, consoling Johnson for his loss of that responsibility, rode around the Tidal Basin and other Washington parks with him in a taxicab for several hours before he became resigned to his disappointment. Later, she found it necessary to set up safeguards against Johnson's drive for power. She grew wary, she said, when he gave her a copy of *The Corporate State* by Rafaello Viglione to read. In this book "the neat Italian system of dictatorship for the benefit of the people was glowingly described."

Others in Washington had feared the same tendency in Johnson since reading a pamphlet he wrote with the caption, *By Muscleinny, Dictator Pro Tem, a Proclamation,* and beginning, "The undersigned has temporarily assumed dictatorship of the Republic." The pamphlet was circulated in 1932 among a small group. "It pretty accurately diagnosed the situation," Johnson declared later, "and anticipated much of the Recovery Program." The Muscleinny caption, of course, was just a gag, but not a welcome one to people who cherished democracy and who were already shuddering at the possibility which Sinclair Lewis later described in his novel, entitled *It Can Happen Here.*

The danger of too much Federal control was a main theme of Baruch's testimony to the Senate Committee on Unemployment and Relief. Citing his own record in behalf of the wise use of Government power, he said: "I have been among the first to urge that the lag of our economic and political systems behind the developing complexities and social necessities of modern life must be eliminated. I think that I was as early as any to urge economic equality for agriculture, a floor under wages and a ceiling over hours, Federal assumption of a share of the cost of relief, especially by public works, the elimination of unfair trade practices, the principles of social security and, in general, a point of view best expressed by Woodrow Wilson many years ago."

After reading a quotation indicating Wilson's belief that capitalism should be corrected, Baruch added:

"I agree that our system needs revision, but I do not believe that it needs revolution, peaceful or otherwise, and I think there are a few fundamental general principles that should guide us in everything we do.

"In the past fifteen years," he continued, "we have had an opportunity to study the workings of the Russian plan to do away with the profits system. We have also seen the Nazi and Fascist experiments. We have observed the backwash of these ideas flooding against the shores of the democracies—France, England and America.

"So much of the peace and trade of the world as ever rested on good faith and solemn international agreement is gone. Much of the commerce among nations, where not dwindling, is stimulated by artificial uneconomic devices. Peace hangs by a thread. . . . Both international and private morale are at low ebb. . . .

"Have we not yet learned that we cannot free ourselves from the ultimate workings of natural economic forces or the inevitable human equations which govern mankind?

"I think these experiments show the fundamental principle that should lie at the bottom of everything that we plan to do in combatting this depression. Every action should be designed not to attempt to repeal natural economic laws but to accommodate them to our uses and harness them to our needs. Every action should consider all human equations and not attempt to force divergent humanity into the rigid mold of some social or economic thesis.

"From the time man appeared from primordial obscurity to become the commanding figure among living things his existence has depended upon his ability to accommodate natural laws—to prevail against animals and insects, starvation and disease, war and weather—and above all—his own incredible folly. The lesson that shrieks for recognition throughout all history is that in solving this problem of existence, we do not oppose these laws. We apply them. We do not make them our enemies, but our allies. . . .

"Savages crouched in terror before lightning. Benjamin Franklin harnessed it. We have wisely used and adapted the laws of chemistry and physics but not so wisely have we managed laws governing economics and human nature."

Conceding that man had made much progress in social relations, he added:

"Savages destroyed the weak and the aged. We have progressed from that. But until a recent day, society was concerned with no more than mere alms for the unfortunate. We have made great strides away from this 'little mercy of man.' We recognize a responsibility of our national community for all its members. There are some who go much further and say that community responsibility is everything—individual responsibility nothing. That doctrine, I think, ignored the economic law that there is a limit to the burden a community can carry and the human rule that when relieved of individual responsibility man ceases maximum effort.

"These are not limits of selfishness. They are limits of natural effectiveness—limits beyond which the lack of responsibility among non-producers plus the burden on producers slows down all production and makes the real state of the whole community, including the less fortunate, much worse than it was before. I fear that in trying to amend our system we have attempted too much too hastily to keep within these natural limits.

"In the field of business economics, I sometimes wonder whether we have even stopped to discover what the true natural governing law is. We are blundering among three separate and diverse ideas: (1) complete government operation of business as in Fascist states; (2) a recognition that our economy has fallen naturally into great groupings and a determination to use them to our maximum advantage, regulating them to protect the public from exploitation and to prevent abuses; and (3) unlimited competition."

If Baruch had been leading a filibuster, he could hardly have talked at greater length, reviewing long periods of economic history; generalizing on past remedies that had succeeded and failed, and touching on some current world problems. No speech of any prominent man, of course, is ever aimed exclusively at a small immediate audience even when that audience is an influential Senate Committee. On this occasion Baruch's speech seemed designed more to sway public opinion and to influence the forthcoming off-year elections than to influence any immediate legislation. It was an especially ingenious blend of lip-service to broad New Deal social objectives, and skepticism regarding the few New Deal methods which he did not denounce. Every now and then he resorted to scathing ridicule. He said, for example:

"We have produced in the past four years some far-reaching prescriptions on particular fronts but have we done so wisely. Few indeed are the adaptations by man of natural laws that have sprung into being full-fledged. The skepticism of medicine to any new nostrum may, at times, have been too conservative but the scientist's approach is surely better than the witch doctor's.

Naturally, the anti-Administration papers played up Baruch's comments, along with his demand for lowered taxes, for revision or abandonment of anti-trust laws, and for greater encouragement in every way to business and industry.

"There is one general principle," Baruch emphasized. "The moving forces of mankind are acquisitiveness, the urge to function as an individual, a yearning for freedom in mind and body, and above all the constant quest of opportunity to advance. These are the attributes of individualism. . . . These have ever been, and ever will remain, the dynamos of all our progress. Recently we have taken too little care for this principle.

"For what is the alternative to the incentive of the hope of individual gain and advancement? Clearly it is the fear of punishment—compulsion by the state. . . . It cannot possibly create the type and quality of service and production that we must have. . . .

"To every ability, every investment, every effort we can say 'Yes, you can go ahead and do your best to earn,' but the state by regulation, restriction, administration or taxation is going to take the fruit of your labors to give to others who through whatever cause—weakness, sloth or misfortune—have lost the hope of gain. When we have done that, there will be less effort and hence less output. There will be less to go round. The poor will be poorer and the rich less rich. I believe our whole system will collapse in political and economic ruin because we shall have destroyed its dynamo through failure to recognize the economic and human laws that govern it.

"In stating these principles I do not mean to convey any idea that I am not in sympathy with most of the great social objectives for which I have myself argued for many years. I believe they can be attained within these principles. I think, however, that we must cut the coat to suit the cloth. . . ."

Hoover had been good at that kind of tailoring, New Dealers were quick to point out, when the speech was reported next day.

"I do not believe there has been a proper or even a wise cooperation," Baruch continued. . . . Approaches to a solution should be more sympathetically considered by those experienced in business who know what the practical workings and results would be. Furthermore, industry must help to eradicate its own abuses in the field of finance, public utilities, speculation and relations with labor and the consuming public. It has not done its full share there. If it does not help cooperatively, the job will have to be done by the government alone and far less well. . . .

"Above all, we must work and will work to meet the emergency and the needs of our unemployed. About $20,000,000,000 has been spent. This is a large sum. Yet important as it is, after all, it is wealth that can be remade and replaced. It will sink into insignificance if we have preserved to our people the morale and will to fend for themselves. It is that which has put America in the foreground of the world,

and it is that, and that alone, that can now pull America out of
this new morass."

When Senator Byrnes asked for Baruch's views on taxation
as it affected unemployment, Baruch began: "I want to make
it clear at the outset that I am not arguing for lower taxation
until the budget is balanced. But that is quite a different matter
from saying that I believe that rates and forms of taxation
cannot be reduced and readjusted with the greatest benefit to
all. As I have suggested there is such a thing as the 'law of
diminishing returns' and I believe we have given it far too
little thought in our tax structure. . . ."

It was particularly important, Baruch said, to modify the
capital gains and undistributed profits tax. "Instead of encouraging expansion and activity, which make for increased revenues,"
he said, "they have greatly repressed both. They are the
outstanding instance of failure to apply the law of diminishing
returns to our problems of revenue and taxation.

"I would not completely repeal either tax. . . .

"I agree completely with so much of the principle of the
undistributed profits tax as prevents tax avoidance through the
unproductive accumulation of surplus or the accumulation of
surplus beyond the needs of prudent business administration.
But that can easily be attacked without paralyzing the expansion
of old business and the creation of new industries. . . . I think we
should exempt small industries during development and also
exempt all expenditures of any corporation for expansion of
capital facilities or development of new products or for payment
of debt incurred for the same.

"The regular income tax structure should also be given a
thorough overhauling to discover its maximum revenue-pro-
ducing efficiency under the law of diminishing returns. . . .

"In our great need for revenue, the tax laws should be

172

designed for increasing employment and revenue and not for revenge, punishment, hatred, regulation, or advancement of any social theory. It is my belief that if they were scientifically revised for the two purposes I mentioned—maximum revenue and maximum recovery—we could make a very great advance."

When questioned by Senator Hatch as to whether the tax revision he recommended would result in "sufficient expansion in industry and business to reemploy the vast numbers now unemployed," Baruch hedged a bit, stating "Other factors may come into the situation." He emphasized, "Of course, we cannot stop relief until business has taken up the slack in employment. I hope nobody will understand me differently. We must continue relief until we see what business does. . . ."

For the Government to continue to build hydroelectric power developments, however, struck Baruch as unwise. Steam generators and diesel engines at "a much cheaper price may make unit power and light installations cheaper for every factory and household than great hydroelectric installations."

Baruch charged that the Administration was tipping the scales to benefit labor at the expense of capital, and in that period when Howard Scott's Technocracy was still the fad, he even proposed a tax on machines to replace Social Security taxes. That last recommendation stated:

"Take the Social Security payroll tax of upwards of a billion dollars on payrolls. In addition to deducting a tremendous sum from the direct purchasing power of the poorest classes, that tax is a powerful incentive to employers to replace men with machines wherever ingenuity can devise a way, and modern ingenuity is particularly good at that. There can be no doubt of the effect of that to increase technological unemployment. I suggest that the whole social security setup be restudied and that a tax on machine hours or even on gross sales (of machines) rather than on payrolls would be more logical. . . ."

"As for New Deal accomplishments," he declared, "after

173

almost four years we are not as well off as we were after the truly remarkable 1933 recovery as it stood on July 1 of that year . . .

"I say it with regret, but I would be less than candid if I failed to express my opinion that unemployment is now traceable more directly to government policy that to anything that business could or should do and that if those policies are not changed, neither business nor government can ever solve this most terrible of all our problems."

When queried as to the administration of unemployment relief, Baruch declared, "I don't think I could qualify as an expert and I wouldn't want to do so." He said, however, that more ought to be done by local communities, "because the men in the local communities know better than anybody else whether the man needs relief, and how much relief, rather than the central authorities."

Many of Baruch's comments at this hearing were headlined as a savage attack on the New Deal—an interpretation which disturbed the Committee Chairman, Senator Byrnes. At the next session, Byrnes read a newspaper headline, "New Deal in Democratic Administration is Responsible for the Unemployment Situation of the Country." Byrnes declared, "I recall nothing justifying a headline of that kind. Did you make such a statement or did you intend to create such an impression?"

Baruch quickly responded, "I do not think you will find in my testimony of yesterday one single word about a repeal of one single act upon the statute books."

He had, he insisted, asked for a modification of the tax laws. Senator Byrnes then pointed out that the House had reported a bill modifying the existing tax laws. Senator Hatch added that Baruch's proposal for a floor under wages and a ceiling over hours was another objective which the Administration had sought to achieve. Senator Hatch also pointed out that Baruch had made no definite criticisms of the relief administration at all, but did recognize the responsibility of the National Government.

Senator Byrnes said to Baruch, "One newspaper I saw quoted you as opposing the Social Security Law. Are you opposed to that? Did you say anything about that?"

"I did not advocate a repeal," Baruch replied, "only a restudy of it."

It troubled Senator Byrnes that the testimony had revived an old criticism of Baruch's career, best expressed in the folk-saying: "You can get a man out of Wall Street, but you can't get Wall Street out of the man." He provided Baruch with another good opportunity to answer the doubting Thomases who persisted in questioning his good faith, disinterestedness, and foresight. He pointed out that Baruch's wealth was discussed in Ferdinand Lundberg's book on the sixty most economically powerful American families, and asked him if "even unconsciously your views as to the results of high taxes would be affected by your own interests."

Baruch replied, "I don't think so, Senator. I think that I am inclined rather to lean backward. It doesn't make any difference who says a thing or what the position of the man may be, the great question is, Is he right, or is he wrong? . . . I have too much pride as a workman in anything that I may say or do to make here a prejudiced statement. I want to be right. I would like to have the future justify me. I think it will."

Events in Europe supplied the verdict. Eleven days later Hitler and his troops crossed into Austria, and Baruch was soon back in the White House advising Roosevelt that taxes in such an emergency period must be raised, that greater power must be concentrated in the Federal Government and centralized in one man at the head of an industrial mobilization, and that more plants must be built in the Tennessee Valley and on the West Coast to utilize the power of the great government-built hydroelectric power developments in the coming struggle for survival.

"I do not believe that you can treat price control as a separate effort. It must be intimately tied up with and move in step with all other war controls —wage and rent control, priorities, conservation, commandeering, war trade, war finance. . . . They are like the fingers of a hand. Without all together, the job cannot be done satisfactorily."

— From the statement on total defense by Bernard M. Baruch before the House Committee on Banking and Currency, September 19, 1941.

CHAPTER 5

"Like the Fingers
of a Hand"

"WE SHOULD THINK PEACE, talk peace, and act peace, but if war comes, we should be prepared to fight it, to win it, and to survive it."

When Baruch again voiced that stubbornly held conviction in *The American Legion Monthly* for January, 1936, Hitler's military might was growing and Mussolini had already become an aggressor. "Italy's African adventure, which may set the world on fire," Baruch declared, "should be the final warning" against America's lack of preparedness for both military and industrial mobilization. He urged the utmost help from veterans to push the necessary legislation through at that session of Congress.

At that time, he had been a crusader for industrial preparedness for more than seventeen years. "With the coming of peace in 1918," he continued, "one of my principal aims in life was to see that our country should never be caught again as it was in 1917, devoid of a plan for industrial preparedness without which all the military preparedness plans in the world are not worth the paper they are written on. . . . Year after year I have stated my views at the public hearings brought about through the zeal of your national officers. Year after year I have spent weeks and months in private consultation and study seeking the best legislation."

His first official proposal on this subject was written on Christmas Eve of 1918. It was the final section of his preliminary report as Chairman of the War Industries Board. That report to President Wilson recommended a skeleton peace-time organization which could be expanded quickly, when necessary, for effective mobilization of industry.

Baruch also recommended that pertinent information on industry, business and natural resources be accumulated consistently, and that the production of certain essential minerals and products be encouraged. How fruitful this recommendation proved has already been set forth in an earlier chapter.

Finally, he urged that private industries be encouraged, under proper government supervision, to maintain a skeleton organization for rapid production, when necessary, of armaments and munitions.

These important recommendations, looking to the future security of the nation, were stated in these words:

"It would be impossible in any statement of the activities of the War Industries Board . . . not to conclude with definite recommendations based upon the lessons learned. A similar emergency may arise in the future and it can more easily be coped with if the experiences of the last two years are profited by. The writer believes:

" 'First. There should be created a peace-time skeleton organization based on the experience of the war-making agencies. It should be headed by a chairman, who, when the emergency arises, should be granted the powers necessary to coordinate and synchronize the economic resources of the country. With him should be associated the representatives of the Army and the Navy or any other department vitally interested, as the Shipping Board, who should have centralized under them the various purchasing branches of their departments.

" 'There also should be in the skeletonized organization a vice chairman, a secretary, a counsel, and members in charge of raw materials, finished products, facilities, prices, labor, planning and statistics (during peace under the Department of Commerce), priority and conservation. Under these there should be also the various section or commodity heads. The peace-time organization would meet at least once a year to discuss and outline plans and to keep in touch with the general world situation and with one another. Each sectional head would name committees in each industry in order that, in the event of an impending crisis, it would be possible within a few days to create an organization which immediately would mobilize all of the industries of the nation and quickly make available for the government all of its resources. These men, with the exception of the Secretary, who would keep the records, would serve without compensation and the actual expense of maintaining such an organization would be small. I would recommend that all priorities, including those of shipping, should be centralized in the chairman.

" 'Second. Through a system of stimulation by a protective tariff, a bonus, an exemption from taxation for a limited period, licensing, or any other effective means, every possible effort should be made to develop production of manganese, chrome, tungsten, dyestuff, by-products of coal, and all such raw materials usually imported but which can be produced in quantity in this country. Above all, immediate and persistent effort must be made to develop production of nitrogen and its substitutes, not alone for war but for agricultural purposes.

" 'Third. Under the supervision of the proper departments of the Government some industries must be given encouragement to maintain a skeleton organization through which can be developed the rapid manufacture of guns, munitions, airplanes, etc. Some facilities already developed might be kept alive through outright purchase or by small orders for munitions and airplanes while at all times there must be kept on hand the necessary dies, jigs, fixtures, etc., needed for the manufacture of

181

munitions. The expert personnel of the War and Navy Departments in addition to keeping abreast of the times in new war-making agencies should keep the industries of the Nation attuned in a skeleton form to meet immediately that enlarged demand which would come through war."

Baruch re-emphasized these proposals in his final report which was published in book form in 1921, and told the comprehensive story of America's successful industrial mobilization in the First World War. He never altered certain basic features of these recommendations, including his advocacy of industrial committees, but as he kept brooding over the idea seeking improvements, he began to give much more thought to the need for an effective method of price control—a subject which in the preliminary report at the war's end received bare mention in the single word, "prices."

He had realized, even before he got the reins as Chairman of the War Industries Board in 1918, that the public was justified in its clamor over the high cost of living. Admitting that the price-fixing policies of the earlier war agencies did not protect civilian consumers—though they did save the government and taxpayers many millions on military purchases—Baruch devised certain corrective measures, as we have seen in an earlier chapter. But Armistice Day came before the public noticed much relief in its pocketbook.

When a post-war inflation quickly set in and brought prices topping even those of the war, complaints against "war millionaires" and profiteering were renewed. They were reflected in the 1919 hearings of the House Committee on Expenditures in the War Department. Its Chairman, Representative William J. Graham, was especially critical of the policies of the Council of National Defense and the Defense Advisory Commission which preceded organization of the War Industries Board. Resentment aired then against war profiteering was kept alive when the first post-war recession developed.

Baruch analyzed those economic problems at a reunion of the War Industries Board, December 10, 1920. Briefly referring, also, to the achievements of the Board, he said, "we met the situation by continually broadening price-fixing, and by restriction of the use of materials and services to needs and not to wants."

Now, he added, Americans must content themselves "with returns more nearly commensurate than recently with the service performed—and that applies equally to capital and labor. . . . We must see to it that the present mass re-adjustments of prices are carried through to the ultimate consumer."

Two years later, the American Legion demanded stand-by legislation to provide price protection in all critical periods of defense and of war. It was voiced again at the Legion Convention in 1932 when soldiers and sailors were still nursing their just grievance that while they had served their country for $1.10 a day their families at home suffered from high living costs. "Your position" then, Baruch reminded them, "was that every person, every dollar, and every thing should participate in defense of the nation, share and share alike."

More than thirteen years had passed, he continued, and the nation still had no such law. He admitted that there was some excuse for delay in the Twenties. "When the subject was first broached the nation and the world were war-weary. It fled from contemplation of . . . preparedness, seeking security in arms limitation agreements and the League of Nations. Before the futility of such designs became apparent, a tremendous inflation of credit . . . brought about a fool's paradise of fictitious prosperity . . . as unsound and unreal as the prosperity . . . induced by wartime wages and values. This collapsed in 1929, and then followed the lean years of readjustment" and "strenuous measures" to combat the depression.

Baruch was sure, however—as he told the Legionnaires—that the nation would benefit from their "exploratory activity" for

183

preparedness and from the varied resulting "discussions, studies and investigation." But the time had come to stop revising details of the plan and embody its essentials in law. That law, he added, "will not cost a cent and will be more of a protection to this country than a standing army of a million men. . . ." Providing for speedy industrial mobilization, it would also "conserve natural resources, and preserve the morale of the people to such an extent that we would be able to outlive any antagonist in any long-drawn struggle. . . . Profiteering would be prevented and burdens equalized. . . . It would be the best national peace insurance policy that any country ever had."

One definite law to help promote mobilization planning was enacted in that illusory decade of international agreements without effective enforcement provisions—of Locarno, the Washington Naval Conference, the Kellogg-Briand pacts and the debating at Geneva—and Baruch was influential in getting that law passed in 1920. Congress, in revising the National Defense Act of 1916, authorized the Assistant Secretary of War to institute and take active charge of Mobilization-Day planning. He was empowered to carry on the work through an M-Day planning branch which would make studies and plans for wartime industrial mobilization, and through the Army and Navy Joint Munitions Board. That Board would study and co-ordinate the needs of the two services so as to prevent the disastrous competition in procuring supplies which had crippled both services in the last war. Such efficiency in procurement was still being promised in 1952.

Baruch was also influential in the later establishment of the Army Industrial College to supplement the planning work of the Army War College. He and his War Industries Board associates—especially John M. Hancock and General Hugh Johnson —frequently lectured at both these colleges, and they brought the subject to a wider public each year in news stories of their annual WIB reunions. In addition, Baruch financed courses of lectures on preparedness at the Walter Hines Page School of International Relations at Johns Hopkins University, and later at the School of International Relations at Williamstown, Massachusetts. The world's leading statesmen and economists were brought to both schools.

Three Republican Presidents expressed their approval of Baruch's ideas on industrial preparedness—Harding, in the obliging words that came so easily to his tongue, Coolidge at the 1925 American Legion Convention in Omaha, and Hoover, who as Food Administrator in the First World War had favored more effective price control than was then achieved, and who, as Secretary of Commerce, had continued the statistical research begun by the WIB and developed its "industrial committee" feature by encouraging the growth of trade associations and agreements.

Baruch, naturally, emphasized different facets of the plan for different audiences, but in the era of voluble pacifists and isolationists, it was good public relations always to refer to it as a plan to take the profit out of war. The phrase and the measures proposed to that end had wide appeal. Both were heavily accented for the first time in a definitely quality magazine by the distinguished British author, Sisley Huddleston. His laudatory article in the February, 1925 issue of *The Atlantic Monthly* was entitled "An American Plan for Peace."

Notably enthusiastic reader response prompted the editors to invite Baruch to give more details. His article, "Taking the Profit out of War," appeared in the January, 1926 issue. Though here, too, he explained the usefulness of "committees representative of each industry," he was chiefly concerned with the problems of price-control and war supply priorities. Since he modified these concepts very little in later official testimony before Commissions and Congressional Committees, his foresighted statements in 1926 are of especial interest.

If his plan were embodied in a law, he said, the nation could start "in the event of another war at the place where we were industrially when the last war ended. The President, acting through an agency similar to the War Industries Board, would have the right to fix the prices of all things of a date previous to the declaration of war when there was a fair peace-time relationship among the various activities of the nation. It would be illegal to buy, sell, serve, or rent at any other than these prices. Brakes would be applied to every agency of inflation before the hurtful process started.

"An intelligent control of the flow of men, money and materials would be imposed instead of having the blind panic" previously brought on by the first "frantic demands of war. The Draft Board could more intelligently decide, with the advice of the Priority Committee, many of the problems with which it would be faced. There would be no sending of men to the trenches who were needed for expert industrial war-work and then bringing them back again." Businesses and industries "not necessary to the winning of the war would be curtailed but never destroyed.

"The use of money should be controlled and directed. . . . A man should no more be permitted to use his money as he wishes than he should be permitted to use the production of his mind, mill or factory except through the general supervising agency. . . . During the final phase of the World War, no man or corporation or institution could raise money without the approval of the Capital Issues Committee of the Treasury Department, which committee in turn would not permit the borrowing of money unless the War Industries Board approved the use to which it was put. . . .

"Standardization in every industry" and reduction in widely assorted styles of items would also be ordered. The fighting

186

forces would receive "those things that they need and no more" and "whatever was not actually required at the front would be left to civilian purposes."

Baruch next turned his attention to the critics who called the plan an "impetus to Socialism, or Communism, or Sovietism." These said, "If you show it can be done in wartime, there will be a demand that it be done in peacetime." This talk seemed nonsense to Baruch. "It cannot be done in peacetime," he declared. "There can be no great undertaking without a strong moving cause. In peacetime the moving cause is personal initiative and payment for services performed. The substitute for that in wartime is the common danger."

Not even Baruch, of course, could then foresee that he and his disciple, Hugh Johnson, would later find "the common danger" in the peacetime depression. Johnson did use some of the essentials of the Baruch mobilization plan when he conceived NRA—as an earlier chapter has indicated—and especially when he encouraged price-fixing through industry committees. The Fair Labor Standards Act embodied something that strikingly resembled another essential of the plan when it established minimum wages.

Though Baruch's entire article was a fertile seed-bed, the peace-loving nation liked best of all its reassuring promise that "to take the profits out of war is to take a long step toward creating economic detestation of war." Newspaper editorials, sermons, speeches, college lectures, articles and books by those who read *The Atlantic Monthly* brought this heartening promise to millions of people who had never even turned the pages of that magazine. Popular sentiment for this phase of Baruch's plan was partly responsible for the introduction in the Senate of the Capper-Johnson bill to give a statutory basis to most of the plan and to additional provisions. It proposed war-time power for price regulation, control of industry and resources, and the draft of men for military service.

That bill had been drafted even before Baruch appeared before the War Policies Commission during its extensive hearings on the problems of M-Day planning. He was influential in obtaining the joint resolution of Congress, approved June 27, 1930, that created this joint commission. Its hearings opened March 5, 1931, and continued through May. Its Chairman was Secretary of War Patrick J. Hurley. At Baruch's prompting, Hurley had initiated agitation for its establishment while serving for nearly a year as Assistant Secretary of War before his appointment as Secretary in December, 1929. It was the function of the Commission, which included certain Cabinet members, Senators and Representatives, to review the M-Day planning already attempted and to make further recommendations. As Hurley and Baruch then conceived it, any future war emergency was likely to require "all-out" efforts. This actual phrase, however, and the phrases "total war" and "total defense" were not Baruch's but were invented later by others.

Baruch's testimony before the Commission began the second day of the hearings. In appealing for a statute that embodied his plan, he emphasized the difficulty the War Industries Board had encountered because it never had specific legal authority for commandeering, nor even for its piece-meal price-fixing.

Army opposition to several aspects of the plan, and especially to over-all price control, was soon made all too plain by General Douglas MacArthur, then Chief of Staff. To bolster his arguments, he called upon Newton D. Baker, who had been Wilson's Secretary of War. He also brought in Leonard P. Ayres, Cleveland economist and former colonel, who had headed the Facilities (Research) Division, and later the Statistical Division of the Council of Defense before America's entry into the First World War. All three praised Baruch's work in that war and thought it absurd to try to improve methods that in their view had worked perfectly.

As Baker recalled those days, business and industry in a fever of patriotism accepted the suggested prices—the steel industry, especially. The fact that he had been counsel in 1930 to the Bethlehem Steel Corporation may have stimulated his memory. In any case, Baruch asked the Commission to take another look at the record.

"My recollection," he said, "is of a long and tedious period of bickering" before agreement on prices was reached. He cited the "bitter controversy" in June, 1917, between the Chairman of the Shipping Board and the steel and iron industry. "I remember also," he continued, "what I am now free to relate since Judge Gary has said in effect that he kept the steel industry from being nationalized." The steel magnate, he added, delayed agreement so long that "I was compelled to—and did—secure authority from President Wilson to commandeer certain companies in that industry." The threat of using that authority finally worked in August, 1917, when the price of steel was more than triple that of 1915.

Desiring to be fair to Baker and other witnesses, Baruch explained their differences of opinion as to the 1917-18 record in this way: their high responsibility in the war program was centered in their particular departments. "The furious effort to which they were driven left them neither time nor opportunity to know or to understand what was going on" in the next department. "How much less informed and more bewildered would a hastily assembled war organization or a new war Congress be when presented with this problem in the panic of a world upheaval?" he asked—and in World War II he got the answer.

General MacArthur maintained that "industry should have a voice in the determination of price" but even so, such agreement was advisable only for certain basic commodities. "So many factors are involved in general price stabilization," he added, "that injustice would follow, and attempts at enforce-

189

ment would likely create antagonism and the government would lose good-will. Without complete and unstinted popular support, no nation can hope to fight to victory."

To that Baruch replied again from his own experience. Nothing could antagonize so many people, he declared, as high living costs resulting from futile efforts to obtain voluntary fair prices for selected commodities. "No industrial leader," he added, "no matter how generous, could afford to restrict his own price unless all the prices affecting him were restricted, or unless his price was already so high that his profits were exorbitant."

He recalled that in many WIB conferences the Government had "the enthusiastic support of some producers and in some conferences the unanimous support of all, but, as a practical matter, there was no alternative to such acceptance. . . . I bore the heat and burden of nearly every one of the principal price determinations except food, and I am speaking from intense experience when I say that in most cases those prices . . . were not unconstrained free-will offerings of all by any manner of means.

"We used a good many euphemisms during the war for the sake of national morale and this one of 'price fixing by agreement' is a good deal like calling conscription 'Selective Service' and referring to registrants for the draft as 'mass volunteers.' Let us make no mistake about it; we fixed prices with the aid of potential Federal compulsion, and we could not have obtained unanimous compliance otherwise."

To make voluntary agreements stick, he continued, the Government must have "sanctions—some control with actual teeth, or some disciplinary power." The agreements the War Industries Board had achieved, he re-emphasized, were induced without statutory authority and the Federal judiciary since then had ruled that the "agreements were induced by duress and were not binding and such a method was invalid."

The truth of the matter, he added with wry humor, was that the WIB had got away with "a more or less truncated flush", but after public exposure of that hand by the law courts, "price control through such leadership alone will never again be possible. We must have statutory authority. . . ."

Former Secretary of War Baker greatly shocked Baruch by his contention that such a statute might prove a downright hindrance in time of war. "Modern war," Baker said, "is essentially a process of improvision. . . . As war progresses under modern conditions, the inventive faculty . . . is stimulated. . . . I think this is also true about the economic situation. . . . There is only a limited amount of preparatory economic legislation that can be done. . . . We of the War Department found ourselves perhaps more embarrassed by laws that had been passed than by absence of law. We were happiest when the laws that provided us power were more elastic, and least in detail."

Now how could any responsible man ask the nation to cherish the old custom of muddling through war—and mechanized war at that? Baruch could hardly hold back his indignation. "We improvised in 1917," he said, "but only because we had to. I know of no benefit that came from our total lack of prevision and the consequent necessity for improvisation of fundamental war measures. And I know of no burden that came from broad statutes which were enacted in advance . . . for the purpose of better administration in war."

He did not favor "an involved statute" anticipating the specific requirements of another war, Baruch emphasized. What he wanted was one law "in the broadest conceivable language" so as to permit necessary adjustments to whatever "kind of emergency we may encounter." Such a law authorizing necessary powers for the President would save the country from make-shift legislation "in the white heat and confusion of a war emergency."

"I think plans should be made and revised yearly," he added. "I think some steps should be taken to keep selected industrial leaders informed of these plans so that when the principal actors in the 1918 mobilization pass from the scene there will be a nucleus of personnel to take their places. I do not believe that we can go further."

Nor did Baruch agree with Baker that excess profit taxes in the First World War were sufficient protection. Such taxes are essential, Baruch said, but these "standing alone have no effect whatever to check inflation." On the contrary, they increased it when producers were left free to raise their prices so as to absorb the taxes. "Even with a fixed price structure and high excess profit tax," he admitted, "there will be huge war profits."

But Baruch lost the round to General MacArthur. "It is conceivable," the General said, "that a war might be conducted with such great regard for . . . justice and administrative efficiency" as Mr. Baruch advocated. "It is also conceivable that the outcome of such a war would be defeat."

The law that Baruch advocated was not passed and the three volumes of the Commission proceedings were filed away in the Archives! However, the War Policies Commission did approve an industrial mobilization plan in 1931. It included Baruch's provision for centralized authority—a provision that was retained in the subsequent drastic revisions of 1935, 1936, and 1939.

Meanwhile, British, French and German leaders, impressed by America's mobilization of industry in 1917, had been adapting the plan to their systems—and the Nazis most zealously. By 1934 there were alarming clues that Hitler was concerned with far more than the defense of Germany.

It was then that Senator Gerald P. Nye, of North Dakota, and Senator Lynn J. Frazier, inveterate critic of the Navy, set out to prove "the simple theory"—as Baruch's close friend, Senator

James F. Byrnes phrased it—"that war was the result of munitions makers' thirst for profits," that producers of all military supplies were "merchants of death" and that international bankers created the markets for those merchants. Accordingly, the Senate Munitions Committee launched an investigation of America's participation in World War I — its chief counsel was Alger Hiss. The many witnesses called to testify in the Nye Hearings of early 1935 included Lammot du Pont, among leading American industrialists, J. P. Morgan, among leading bankers, and Baruch.

A circus agent introduced one farcical element. The midget he sneaked into the hearing plopped on the lap of the sedate Morgan. The whole nation laughed then, but too few realized that most of the painstaking efforts of the earnest committee members at that particular period in history were just about as irresponsible as the story of Nero's fiddling while Rome burned.

Baruch and General Hugh Johnson had been under vicious attack by Senator Huey Long and Father Coughlin. The Kingfish and the radio priest were building their own kind of sinister power as they, too, roared against "merchants of death." But Baruch had better things to do with his time before the Nye Committee than either to answer questions about his personal fortune and affairs, or to defend his record as President Wilson's good right arm. He voluntarily submitted a full statement to the Committee several days before he went in person. That account, including financial records, and an impressive tribute voiced by Senator Byrnes completely demolished the charges made by Long and Coughlin.

Baruch was free then to renew his old crusade for preparedness, and as he talked the Committee listened with more and more respect. At the end *Time* Magazine reported that Baruch "met the Senators and departed not only with all his hair but with a Congressional wreath upon it." Leading newspaper editors throughout the country agreed.

The "wreath" was approval of Baruch's statement that a price control system and a pay-as-you-fight heavy tax program should be provided for war in time of peace; and that it is "essential for this government because of the present disturbed condition of the world to define clearly our neutrality . . . to establish contraband; to explain the limitation on travel which we may wish to impose; to treat thoroughly the whole question of shipping exports, imports and the related subjects."

Some members of the Committee took this carefully worded statement as an assurance that U. S. neutrality could be preserved by denying U. S. citizens and goods protection in war zones. They especially liked his emphatic comment, "The most important thing before this Committee today is the establishment of our neutrality laws in review, so that every American citizen should know exactly what they are, and so that he cannot involve his country. . . . No national has the right to go into a trouble zone and get into trouble, and expect his country to get him out."

Senator Homer Bone was delighted. "The nation," he said, "should have had sense enough to do that in 1917," and furthermore, it should not have "let them ship munitions." Baruch wasn't so certain that such a shield would have been enough. "If our neutrality rights had been clearly defined," he said, "we would have been less likely to have been drawn in and might not have been drawn in."

In brief, it was 1935, when there was popular trust in isolationism. Not even Baruch felt free then to affirm that the modern world is one world.

Some members of the Committee were not so pleased by Baruch's recommendation that it is essential "to regulate the flow of munitions," nor by his warning: "In eliminating profits, we must not eliminate munitions. There is such a thing as taking the profits out of war at the cost of losing the war." But his explanation of this view *did* succeed in killing a previously popular proposal advanced by John T. Flynn for conscripting virtually all wealth in the event of war. That policy, Baruch contended, "might defeat every purpose it asserts, and it would probably imperil the defensive power of the United States. . . .

"It is my deliberate and considered judgment that the Flynn plan would insure an exaggerated inflation far greater than if there were no plan at all. It would paralyze war production and render the nation practically helpless against a major attack by any enemy possessing an economic and industrial system fairly comparable with our own.

"Much as it may be decried," Baruch concluded, "the cold fact remains that ours is an economy actuated by profits. A certain return on money is necessary to make our system work." But a fair return for capital was never to be interpreted as a free pass to profiteering.

Gerald Nye beamed. But Baruch, by then Chairman of the President's Committee on Preparedness, still didn't get his heart's desire. While the Nye Committee rushed off on varied tangents, the legislation sought so long remained off the statute books. The War Department's M-Day plan, however, was revised again in 1936—and this time the proposal for strict control over propaganda and censorship was knocked out by the Nye Committee.

Late that summer Baruch returned from his annual trip to Europe deeply concerned by what he had observed and confirmed in talk with his old friend, Winston Churchill. The Nazi threat was greater, and Mussolini was dropping to second place as a menace. Yet England was deaf to Churchill, France was trusting to her Maginot Line, and the smaller European states were an invitation to aggression.

Baruch went to Washington and poured out his views to his most influential friends. Some of them understood and agreed.

But how could the people be made to listen? *They* were still resolved against authorizing increased armaments and a larger Army and Navy which they figured just might come in too handy in case warmongers started a push to send "our boys into another foreign war." *They* were still saying that every nation but little Finland had welched on debts they owed us for the last war. "Lord'll mighty! Wasn't *that* enough," the folks still asked, "to prove we had better mind our own business forevermore?"

It was then that Baruch made the appeal—as already set forth —to the American Legion. The veterans understood, but the long-sought preparedness bill was still not enacted.

Baruch then gathered together all his warnings through 1935 and published them privately in a book entitled, *Taking the Profit Out of War.* He dedicated it to all "who so efficiently, faithfully and unselfishly worked with me on the U. S. War Industries Board in the service of their country." Adding an explanatory note, he called the book "a compilation of some of the many thousands of words I have written and spoken on the subject of taking the profits out of war and of industrial mobilization." Arranging for and paying for wide distribution of the book, Baruch sent it out hopefully. Somehow, the defenses of America had to be rebuilt. Here was one important part of the necessary blueprint.

The foreword by General John J. Pershing was a plea for Americans to take these words of wisdom to heart. They didn't —not till after the fall of France in 1940.

Edmund Burke long ago put it this way: "The only thing necessary for the triumph of evil is that good men do nothing."

That triumph of evil seemed to be more surely on the way at the Annual Congress of the Nazi Party held at Nurnberg in September, 1937. Senator Byrnes, after attending the Inter-

Parliamentary Union in Paris as an official delegate, saw the frenzied crowds in Nurnberg and the display of might. He interpreted the Nazi vauntings not as joy over remarkable steps toward economic recovery but over a program for aggression. Hindsight has shown that it was launched the moment the German Reichstag passed the Enabling Act putting absolute power in the hands of Chancellor Adolf Hitler at midnight—as it happened—after President Roosevelt's inaugural on March 4, 1933.

Reporting at once to President Roosevelt on his return, Byrnes said, "We must immediately give serious thought to the nation's defense"—an echo of Baruch's words to the President somewhat earlier that fall.

It was Byrnes' job, however, to estimate votes in Congress on proposed legislation, and he sadly told Roosevelt that it would be very difficult to obtain increased appropriations for the Army and Navy. The President valiantly set out to make the danger clear to the people, but their reaction to his famous "Quarantine Speech" in Chicago on October 5, was a bitter blow.

Our Army then, with only 115,000 men, ranked eighteenth among the standing armies of the world. The President got authority to increase its enlisted strength to 165,000 men, and he also allotted funds appropriated for public works to naval construction projects. He then sent a special message to Congress on January 29, 1938, pointing out the dangerous implications in the fact that "one fourth the world's population is involved in merciless, devastating conflict." He asked for $20,000,000 for Army supplies, and a twenty percent increase in the naval building program with the construction of two battleships, two cruisers, and some smaller experimental vessels. Byrnes began the uphill fight to push the bill through Congress.

The annexation of Austria in March 1938, the Munich agreement, and the consequent dismemberment of Czechoslovakia in September put the world in a state of shock but failed to

197

bring the requested appropriation from Congress. Early in 1939, the President sent another special message to Congress on defense problems, asking them for a half-billion dollars largely for Army and Navy air arms. On July 14 he sent a third appeal— and again in vain.

Meanwhile, the House and Senate had an urgent request, on May 29, from Secretary of State Cordell Hull for repeal of the act placing an embargo on the shipment of arms to nations at war. The Senate Foreign Relations Committee waited till July to vote, 12 to 11, to postpone consideration of that repeal bill. Not long after Congress adjourned, Hitler and the Soviet Union concluded their pact, on August 23, and nine days later the Nazi blitzkrieg hit Poland.

Congress, called back into session, finally repealed the arms embargo provisions a week before Armistice Day, but the legislation Baruch had crusaded for, almost since the *first* Armistice Day, was still in limbo.

Baruch, however, had found many other ways to make his influence count in the critical months since early fall, 1938, when he had frankly told White House reporters that the United States was unprepared to defend even its own borders. That briefing served notice that once more he had a latch key to Roosevelt's confidence.

Almost obsessed by the evidence of the nation's peril, Baruch sought out business and industrial leaders—and especially those who had bitterly opposed "that man in the White House." He made many of them understand the need to close ranks in the common danger. President Roosevelt's secretary, Grace Tully, later reported, "The Boss . . . was particularly grateful for the missionary work Bernie did among industrialists . . . to awaken them to the threat of war in Europe and its effects on America."

The same kind of "missionary work" with Harry Hopkins, F.D.R.'s devoted assistant, was another vitally important contribution. For this, Baruch invited Hopkins to his South Carolina plantation, Hobcaw, late in March, 1939, when Hopkins was convalescing from influenza. Harry didn't have any of the good long dialogues he had hoped for about politics and liberal New Deal programs. Instead, Baruch kept emphasizing the Anschluss and Munich and Neville Chamberlain's umbrella and baseless optimism for international tranquillity; and the braggart, Mussolini, the Spanish Civil War, and the Sino-Japanese War. He related what he had observed and learned in Europe the previous summer and had reported confidentially to the President. He re-hashed conversations with Winston Churchill and quoted Churchill's words. "War is coming very soon. We will be in it and you will be in it. You will be running the show over there, but I will be on the sidelines over here."

Years later, Baruch said, "Harry didn't much want to listen to me, but I kept at him. And once he realized how greatly our security was threatened by aggressors in Europe and Asia, he was all-out for total preparedness."

Sure that the Secretary of War would soon have the most important post in the Cabinet, Baruch urged Hopkins to aim for that appointment. Not even Robert E. Sherwood, Hopkins' official biographer, knows for sure whether Hopkins tried to act on this advice, but the whole nation eventually learned that he—no less than his chief, F.D.R.—literally sacrificed his life in trying to speed preparedness and to lay the ground work for enduring world peace.

Not long after Hopkins returned from Hobcaw to the White House that spring of 1939, Congress finally enacted another important preparedness measure which Baruch had long advocated. This was the Strategic Raw Materials Act, with an appropriation of $100,000,000 to build up stockpiles, over a period of five years, of such essentials as rubber. The orders moved out with tragic slowness, with only $13,000,000 spent by

May of 1940, even though our rubber reserve at the beginning of that year was only about 126,000 tons.

As early as 1934, in testimony before the House Foreign Affairs Committee, Baruch had advised that rubber and tin be bought from debtor nations, and the costs charged off their war debts to us. He had pointed out that if war broke out—whether the United States was able to maintain neutrality or not—sufficient shipping space to meet our constant need of those materials would not be available for the necessary long haulage.

Very little came of this advice until 1937, when he and his associate, John Hancock, went to see Louis A. Johnson, then Acting Secretary of War. Johnson agreed that the need for strategic stockpiles was growing acute. He admitted, also, that the Army even lacked machinery for making smokeless powder, and he doubted if he could get the necessary appropriation of $3,000,000. Baruch offered to foot the bill, but somehow Johnson eventually got the money from Congress.

Soon afterwards, Johnson formed the War Resources Board with Edward R. Stettinius, Jr. as Chairman, and named John Hancock as head of the Raw Materials and Manufacturers Division. Hancock made a report to the Board on the eve of Hitler's march into Poland, and Johnson, thoroughly briefed for some months by Baruch, addressed that meeting on industrial mobilization. The Board held a number of conferences, the first on August 7, the last on October 12. Six weeks later, Board members received the written thanks of President Roosevelt for their report which included the comprehensive report Baruch had submitted to the Board. This combined report was never made public, however, perhaps because President Roosevelt felt that the public was not yet prepared to take such strong medicine. Eliot Janeway in his trenchant book, *The Struggle for Survival,* stated that the suppressed Baruch report was held so tightly that not even the War Department had a copy in its files. The result, Janeway declared, was that the

President was free to follow its recommendations whenever he chose without mentioning Stettinius or crediting Baruch.

The conferences of the War Resources Board, however, were of great value in preparing its members for other responsibilities soon afterwards in building our defenses. This Board and its successor, the National Resources Planning Board, stem originally from Baruch's recommendation in his 1918 report to President Wilson. The drastic revision of M-Day plans in 1939 authorized such work.

Baruch's advice carried great weight in that revision. Other influential men joined him in bringing pressure for the elimination at long last of the Army-favored proposal for strict control over labor in a period of national emergency. This responsible group said they had never seen any proof that the Army could plan with fairness toward labor, and added that while it was only just to expect Americans to work or fight, it would be slavery to order them to particular jobs.

Baruch at this period was already preaching the need for a two-ocean Navy, increased Army, greater air power, more tanks, and heavier taxes, but talk of the "phony war" that winter, and "blitz by pamphlet", revived a false feeling of security among the American people. That lasted till the Nazi Army—as fluid, swift and inexorable as volcanic lava—swept around the Maginot Line to envelop France. Roosevelt promptly pledged America as the great "Arsenal of Democracy," and Senator Byrnes, whose job it was to steer the Naval Appropriations Bill through the Senate, knew that the hour had come at last for favorable action. He promptly introduced it, and it was passed in three hours.

Yet across the nation there were all too many signs that the will of all the people was by no means committed even to the necessary steps for defending our own shores.

A national committee, formed the previous September under the leadership of William Allen White and including various members of the League of Nations Association, had helped bring about the repeal of the arms embargo. In May it was re-organized as the Committee to Defend America by Aiding the Allies. But it could risk no smearing editorials in the still tragically influential *Social Justice* of Father Coughlin. So this Committee stipulated that it would accept no contributions from munitions makers, international bankers, and steel interests—the group Coughlin was still attacking as "gold-protected, government-protected, foreign-protected" thieves and fifth columnists.

Both of these committees were a counter front to the isolationist organization, America First, to Roosevelt-haters, and to propaganda groups evidencing Nazi financing and direction.

In this climate of disunity—even after Dunkirk and the fall of France—the Republican Party at its convention in Philadelphia on June 24 declared its firm opposition "to involving the nation in foreign war," and the Democratic platform stated, "We will not send our armies, navies, or air forces to fight in foreign lands outside the Americas except in case of attack." The last five words were added by Senator Byrnes, who was so close to Baruch that it was sometimes impossible to tell which one of the two originated the view that both expressed. In this case, both Baruch and Byrnes feared that the statements of the two political parties would strengthen Hitler's hope that "the decadent democracy"—as he called the United States—would not fight and that he would act accordingly.

In November, the *Fortune* Management Poll reported that 75.6 percent of the nation's business and industrial management still believed that the Democratic Administration was using the national emergency as a pretext for pushing familiar New Deal social and economic gains. It was obviously up to Baruch to do some more missionary work—and he did.

He appealed for rapid industrial mobilization before the National Industrial Conference on December 10, 1940, and made another appeal in the next issue of *The Harvard Business Review*.

The article, entitled "Priorities, the Synchronizing Force," discussed such necessities as expansion of plant facilities, conservation, the search for substitutes, commandeering, and which defense demand among a multitude of competing ones should get first attention. "The priorities system," he said, "cannot work alone. It is the heart of industrial mobilization, but it needs other organs. Above all, it must have the assistance of price control, which is actually a means of short-circuiting the laws of supply and demand."

"Priority and price controls are completely interdependent," he emphasized. The rise in prices already under way, he noted, would be apt to add two and one-half billion dollars to the original estimated cost of the national defense program during its first year.

He asked for strict control of the money supply, proposed "something like the liberty bond campaign" of the First World War, and insisted upon heavier taxes not only as a safeguard against inflation but so that the Government could "pay as it goes." Including another cherished recommendation, of course—industrial committees—he suggested their advantages.

Baruch also asked for the establishment of some agency similar to the War Trade Board in the First World War, to license all transactions in foreign trade with due regard for preferential treatment lists, and for the formation of a Price Adjustment Committee to correct whatever inequities might creep into the control system. Data presented by the industry in question should, of course, get just consideration.

Several of these points were fairly persuasive, but Baruch didn't rest his case with them. Instead, he concluded with this reminder, "The power to take over plants that are essential to national defense has been given the President in the Selective Military Service Act, while the right to commandeer stocks of commodities could also be granted to him under the war powers."

"Now, boys," he seemed to say, "will you get in there and start pitching?"

Baruch's advice was sought more frequently by top defense officials the next year. Harry Hopkins, in particular, sent a stream of inquiries to him. After acting on the information, Hopkins saved the notes for the book he hoped to write. Here are characteristic excerpts:

"We are improperly organized. It has cost us 20 percent more in money (which is comparatively unimportant) but also 33⅓ percent more in time which cannot be measured. . . . I am sorry I can not be more encouraging, but . . . no one knows better than you that we must look realities in the face."

A later note read, "Any trouble in the Pacific will change our whole defense production. Aluminum is the most outstanding example of incompetency and procrastination, but there are other situations almost as bad."

Baruch felt more hopeful, however, when hearings began at last on a Price Control bill. Enactment of an effective one, he told the House Committee on Banking and Currency, is "the greatest single necessity of our present crisis—I think we have to do it not only to win the war but also to win the peace, and above all in both peace and war, to protect our people from unnecessary suffering and our American economic system from dissolution. This I have preached in season and out of season for more than two decades. I am here to be as helpful as I can.

Baruch was distressed that the bill under discussion did not propose over-all economic control, and bluntly said, "I do not believe in piece-meal price fixing. I think you have first to put a ceiling over the whole structure, including wages, rents and farm prices up to the parity level, and no higher—then to adjust price schedules upward separately, if necessary, where justice or governmental policy so require."

Experience in the last war, he emphasized, proved that it was not wise "just to fix a few basic prices and let the others go free.

"Piecemeal price fixing will not halt inflation. . . . It is like commanding a moving regiment, 'Regiment, halt!' but all soldiers except that fellow—No. 4 in the first rank keep marching.

"As inflation occurs the prices that are fixed soon become out of date and must be adjusted upward. Irregular rises in prices destroy the relationships between various costs, requiring even greater adjustments. . . .

"Why permit the 'norm', when the law of supply and demand was working, to be disrupted and then scramble wildly to recapture piecemeal what we had in the first place? The question is, shall prices be determined by an administrator working under every conceivable pressure, or whether Congress, by placing a ceiling as of a given date, shall keep prices at a level earlier established by supply and demand?

"Under the over-all ceiling, the price level is treated as an organic whole, with only exceptional adjustments here and there. That method stops a runaway and keeps the whole team in line. The piecemeal method submits to the runaway and then tries to keep some of the horses from running faster than the rest."

Baruch was equally distressed by the fact that the bill under discussion proposed partial price-control apart from the total defense undertaking. Here, if ever, was an emergency requiring the long-sought legislation for centralized authority to mobilize the nation's industries effectively. He launched this familiar plea by stating, "I do not believe that you can treat price control as a separate effort. It must be intimately tied up with and move in step with all other war controls—wage and rent control, priorities, conservation, commandeering, war trade, war finance. . . . They are like the fingers of a hand. Without all together, the job cannot be done satisfactorily."

Baruch then proceeded to outline the magnitude of the undertaking which faced the nation. Only through preparing for total defense could the United States be ready "to fight, to win and, above all, to survive war." All the nation's resources must be mobilized, he urged—"men, money, materials, morale," yet mobilized without exploitation and with the least dislocation of civilians. The needs of the Army and the Navy and other war agencies of our country and of those nations we desire to help through the Lease-Lend Act change and expand overnight. . . . A general formula of action must be evolved to coordinate and synchronize the multiplicity of national and international efforts . . . with the least injury to the industrial fabric of the nation. . . ."

Above all, Baruch demanded "one man as administrator—not a board. Then we will know where the responsibility is and look there for results. Whatever the risk is involved in such control must be taken, with provision for the ending of those risks when the emergency is over. . . .

"If we are to keep the war from reaching these shores or win any war into which we are thrust, it will not be done by 'business as usual'. . . . Full mobilization means transforming American industry from a highly competitive economy to a practically single unitary system under which all producers will cooperate, sharing trade secrets, pooling patents, resources, and facilities. Production must be speeded up to disgorge unprecedented volumes of supplies, military and civilian, with the fullest use made of every factory, worker, machine, dollar, tool, and material. This means regional organization to discover untapped sources of supply and plants which can be converted to defense needs.

"It also means special emphasis on subcontracting, using small businesses. . . ."

Baruch lamented the fact that conversion to war production was not begun soon enough. "We now face . . . widespread dislocation, temporary unemployment, possible business failures. What this postponement has cost the country is impossible to reckon." He felt grateful, however, that the seriousness of the problem was at last being realized.

"An adequate flow of materials," he continued, "must be maintained." Greater stockpiles of strategic materials must be accumulated. We can develop substitutes for many things we now buy. . . . That means there must be a driving and constant search for new sources of materials within our borders and in nearby countries. . . . Inventors must be put to work to find substitutes in every field of activity. Research should be unlimited. . . . The things we have plenty of must be used for the things that are scarce; wasteful manufacturing practices must be eliminated; patterns and styles simplified; materials salvaged and all deferrable uses postponed. . . ."

In spite of the utmost efforts in conservation and substitution, Baruch pointed out, shortages would occur. A Priority Authority should see that materials go not to the longest purse but to the most essential use.

"If some industry must suffer temporary deprivation, all producers in that industry should bear the burden proportionately," he said. With ample notice of impending shortages and priorities, plants would not be compelled to shut down, with workers thrown out of jobs. This is particularly important, he pointed out, for the average small businessman who may be forced into bankruptcy before he awakens to what has hit him. "Such bankruptcies impair production and have an adverse effect upon morale."

Priorities, Baruch emphasized, mean price control for this reason: "If the total supply is not sufficient to go around, a business man will bid a higher price to get what he wants at the time he can use it. Manufacturers naturally seek to give preference to such high-priced orders and so, in effect, you build up a private priority system that competes with and impairs the system of government priorities. . . .

"Under conditions of war production, there is no such thing as competitive price. There is more business than all the producers in the nation can possibly handle. It is unthinkable that the Government or the people should become victims of what the 'traffic will bear' or of runaway markets. . . ."

Baruch warned that inflation was already imminent and declared, "Except for human slaughter and maiming and all that goes with them, inflation is the most destructive of the consequences of war. It might double or more the cost of the war. It imposes the severest hardships on our people and, through inevitable deflation that follows, burdens the future with a constantly increasing debt and a long period of painful and bitter readjustment destroying the confidence of people in themselves and their government. . . .

"Much of the waste and confusion of our defense efforts today can be traced to the fact that priorities were instituted without doing the things that must go with priorities, finding out what we must supply and what resources are available for the job, controlling prices, increasing supply, conserving materials, converting plants, cutting down on demand. What was done was like sending a body of infantry into battle without proper reconnaissance, without the support of artillery, tanks, airplanes, quartermastering, and ambulances. . . .

"Because of the lag, these things will now have to be done under far more adverse conditions and with much greater hardships than should have been necessary. . . ."

Baruch quoted a German official: "The German economic mobilization system was conscientiously built in imitation of the similar American system." It must have hurt him to add, "Only at long last after repeating many of the errors we committed in the first war do we seem to be about to copy from

208

ourselves, but only in part. Once American industry has been mobilized in all its potency and terrible military might, America can still be the dominating influence for war and peace."

The Congressmen, however, were not ready yet to act on Baruch's advice. Their proposal to leave wages and farm prices free from control seemed to him downright perversity. He wrote Representative Albert Gore on November 18, that this plan "would be as abortive as to try to cure a sick man of all his ailments except the one that is most dangerous—the one that is likely to be fatal to him." Wages, he pointed out, "form the biggest component of all price structures." But he did not oppose adjustments in the wage ceiling to cover increases in the cost of living.

"Too much latitude toward the schedule of farm prices," he declared, "would distort the picture. . . . As one of those who fought for many years for farm parity, I do not want to jeopardize it be demanding too much now. . . ." Three days later Baruch emphasized the same points before the House Rules Committee. Again he mentioned his long championship of the farmers. "We have substantially attained agricultural parity; that is a proper relationship between what the farmer is paid for his product and what he has to pay for the stuff he uses."

As for labor, he added, "I have always opposed the old idea that labor is a commodity to be bought at the lowest possible price. I believe the worker is entitled to a thoroughly fair share of the wealth he helps to create. Perhaps even a little more, since he has been so long ground down by conditions that are now slowly changing. But I am opposed to an inflationary wage scale, and I agree completely with the President that no advantage should be taken of the present emergency."

But not even Pearl Harbor ended piecemeal efforts.

"Everything was extemporized in the time of crisis. The result was demoralization in getting industry on a war basis and then, after the war, getting it off; the needless expenditure of billions of dollars, and a great inequality in the distribution of burdens which were very hard upon many and made profiteers of others. Not until we were nearing the close of hostilities was the machine commencing to work towards its goal."

— From an article by Bernard Baruch in the *American Legion Monthly*, January, 1936.

CHAPTER 6

"The Needless Expenditure of Billions of Dollars"

S ABURO KURUSU signed the pact taking Japan into the Axis on September 27, 1940, but military extremists did not come into fully acknowledged power in Japan for more than a year. It was during the interval between Baruch's appearances before two House Committees in the fall of 1941 that General Hideki Tojo ousted the more moderate Prince Fumimaro Konoye as Premier on October 17, 1941. A secret coded message from Tojo to Ambassador Kichisaburo Nomura in Washington was intercepted the very day after Baruch appealed, on November 21, 1941, to the House Rules Committee for the emergency control measure which would put the good of all Americans before the special advantage of pressure groups.

Tojo's message was—in his own words—"an absolutely final proposal . . . a last effort to prevent something from happening," with a deadline set for November 29. Beating that deadline by four days, the Japanese task force set sail for Pearl Harbor on November 25, while the two Japanese "peace envoys," Nomura and Kurusu, continued their deceptive talks with Secretary of State Cordell Hull.

When the Japanese planes took off from their carriers for Pearl Harbor on that "day that will live in infamy"—as President Roosevelt called it in his special message to Congress on

December 8—the American people were no more awake to their peril than were their soldiers and sailors at Pearl Harbor.

Dr. John D. Morgan, Jr., Director of the Materials Review Division of the Defense Production Administration, aptly underlined the nation's apathy in his exhaustive study of economic mobilization of the mineral base of our natonal power, entitled *The Domestic Mining Industry of The United States in World War II.* Dr. Morgan stated, in reviewing the impact of the savage Japanese attack on December 7, 1941, that "had the American people not been shocked from their lethargy by the demonstrated efficiency of the enemy, we might have been the eventual losers of World War II."

The extension of Selective Service, as requested by the President, had been obtained in August by only a one-vote margin in the House of Representatives. The vote came on the final day of the Atlantic Conference at which Roosevelt and Prime Minister Churchill reached agreement on the Atlantic Charter.

The British people were puzzled by this paradox. An American radio commentator quoted a characteristic remark he heard in London: "The American people are a curious people. I can't make them out. One day they're announcing they'll guarantee freedom and fair play for everybody everywhere in the world. The next day they're deciding by only one vote that they'll go on having an Army."

After Dunkirk, when haste was of the essence, every day of delay in heeding Baruch's advice to establish over-all price control and a centralized defense mobilization agency added to the nation's peril. Yet Roosevelt, who lacked the necessarily drastic stand-by legislation, was advised that year by such realistic political leaders of his own party as Senator Byrnes not to jeopardize the main issue then by asking Congress to enact that law. Putting first things first, Roosevelt therefore sought draft legislation and measures to buy time by providing aid to the Allies. Pushed through with great difficulty, these included repeal of the Arms Embargo, which has already been discussed, passage of the Lend-Lease Bill, enactment of Selective Service, and extension of the period of training. "Not one of these would be law," the *New York Times* said editorially in August, 1941, "if the decision had been left to the Republicans in Congress." The editorial, which included a tally of the heavy opposition vote on each of the four measures, added, "Crisis or no crisis, the Republicans in Congress are still 'fighting Roosevelt.'"

That opposition had continued to invite disaster long after Roosevelt's attempt to win bi-partisan support by the appointment in mid-June, 1940 of two Republicans to the Cabinet— Frank Knox as Secretary of the Navy, and Henry L. Stimson as Secretary of War. Consequently, to avoid the heat on Capitol Hill, Roosevelt revived the power first granted to President Wilson in the National Defense Act of 1916 to establish a Council of National Defense for the co-ordination of industries and resources for our security. The Council consisted of the Secretaries of War, Navy, Interior, Commerce and Labor.

"Had it not been for that Act of 1916," Baruch had said in his testimony to the War Policies Commission in 1931, "I shudder to think what might have happened (in World War I). . . . The Council of National Defense provided by that Act literally produced, one after the other, the great war-time industrial mobilization agencies much as a hen lays eggs. I think it not too much to say that but for that . . . statutory provision we could not have made our contribution in time to avert allied defeat in 1918."

But in May, 1940, when Roosevelt, with the approval of his Council, took the next step and appointed a National Defense Advisory Commission, Baruch must have shuddered to see the pattern of successive agencies once more being adopted. By this time, the phrase "to lay an egg"—synonymous with failure, in the jargon of the theater—was well-established national slang, and Baruch doubtless realized that was what the Advisory Commission was going to do. Why should the nation repeat the wasteful fumbling of the First World War? Why try half-way measures through one ineffectual agency after another instead of creating at once the only kind that could do the job right?

Well, no man knows better than Baruch that "priorities are the synchronizing force" of defense production or war production. But this, too, seems evident: few men of his great influence in American history have ever been more impatient of the kind of priorities in legislation which democratic processes oblige any Administration—Republican or Democratic—to establish. Perhaps this impatience can be attributed to the fact that Baruch has never run for public office, and so has never had to make even praiseworthy political compromises, not on principle, but in details and method. Perhaps it is an impatience born of his respect for efficiency. Most likely, it is rooted in his genuine concern lest the slower traditional processes prove a straight-jacket in time of crisis. In any case, his testimony over the years contains many phrases indicating his belief that somehow political factors can be ruled out—phrases such as this from his speech of November 21, 1941, to the House Rules Committee: "We must be realistic, not political."

"That's idealism in this country, Bernie—not realism," his good friend Byrnes might have reminded him. "What can possibly be more realistic than to consider the temper of the people and of their elected representatives?" But Byrnes was too practical to waste his time and Bernie's in arguing that point again. Bernie was stubborn. He would, Byrnes knew, keep on complaining about stupid and costly delay. Yet Bernie also would keep on accepting responsibility for trying to speed the necessary action by the people's representatives and by the successive defense agencies.

Baruch did meet at once with members of the NDAC (National Defense Advisory Commission)—with what good

216

effect in one quarter, we shall see later. On the whole, however, as Donald M. Nelson in his book *Arsenal of Democracy* reported in 1946, "NDAC went on its own way and made little or no use of the available information." Nelson meant the advice of the War Resources Board, whose brief tenure in 1939 has already been discussed; the often-revised Industrial Mobilization Plan, which those board members became familiar with before it was suppressed; and the recommendations Baruch had made in person. "I believe," Nelson added, "most of the members thought that contemporary problems were so much more intricate that new and fancier remedies would have to be sought."

In any case, when NDAC went to work, the news was coming too fast to be digested—and most of it was bad. Scornful of the old war of position fought from trenches, the Nazis' motorized Panzer divisions were sweeping forward. On July 8, 1940 they added the Channel Islands of Guernsey and Jersey as stepping stones to Great Britain from their conquered continental domain, and their air blitz of that nation already had begun.

NDAC had been created on May 29 of that year and was placed in what Robert E. Sherwood called "that limboesque area known as the Office of Emergency Management," a division under the Executive Office of the President. Set up four days earlier than NDAC, OEM was actually the parent organization for all the civilian mobilization agencies that were to follow. They were called defense agencies, not war agencies, in the euphemistic days before Pearl Harbor.

The NDAC members and the special fields for their almost wholly advisory roles were: William S. Knudsen, called from the Presidency of General Motors to head the Industrial Production Division; Sidney Hillman, from his post as head of the Amalgamated Clothing Workers, to the Labor Division; Edward R. Stettinius, Jr., who had been Vice President of General Motors and Chairman of the United States Steel Corporation, the Industrial Materials Division; Leon Henderson, long a New

Deal economist, Price Control Division; Ralph Budd, President of the Burlington Railroad, the Transportation Division; Chester C. Davis of the Federal Reserve Board, an early champion of agriculture, the Farm Products Division; Dr. Harriet Elliott, Consumer Protection; William H. McReynolds, Secretary. Later, Donald M. Nelson was associated with the Commission as Co-Ordinator of National Defense Purchases.

The duties and powers of the Commission were about as clearly outlined as a black cat in a dark alley. Even if its job and authority had been clearly defined, it still would have labored under the downright inexcusable handicap of being leaderless. President Roosevelt never got around to naming its Chairman—and legislative priorities could not explain *that* failure. Moreover, the functions of some of the members overlapped. It was obvious, for example, almost from the outset, that Leon Henderson was not to allow Dr. Elliott much leeway for "consumer protection." In the contest between the requirements of the civilians and the needs arising for military security, Henderson invariably leaned heavily in the latter direction. She was criticized by some as not equipped by experience for that undertaking though she was a sincere patriot, widely informed, and a genuinely able woman in the field of university education. Later she returned as Director of the Women's Division of the Treasury War Bond sales, and her strenuous efforts undoubtedly contributed to her early death.

Unlike the Treasury, and unlike both peacetime and wartime national drives in the public interest—including Community Chest and health organization campaigns—NDAC did not try to organize the support of voluntary citizens' committees in every community. Baruch repeatedly recommended this kind of mobilization on a state and local basis, urging it before two House Committees in 1941. The pattern had been used during World War I in George Creel's propaganda efforts, Hoover's Food Administration appeals for cooperation on heatless, meatless and wheatless days, and the War Chest campaign of 1918 for the Salvation Army, the Y.M.C.A., and allied war relief.

Voluntary community committees of housewives enlisted to check on price ceilings in retail outlets could have provided the kind of effective policing of price regulations at the consumer level which no nation-wide hired staff, however large, could possibly supply. But NDAC had no legal authority to establish price controls and had to rely upon what newspaper reporters of the period called the "jawbone" method of persuading price agreement—and what Baruch in 1931 had called the "truncated flush" of his WIB. Yet when the necessary legal authority was finally given the successor price-control agencies —OPA in the war and the OPS later—housewives' committees still were not tried.

The name first given to Henderson's division of NDAC was very quickly switched from Price Control to Price Stabilization—another euphemistic concession to the divided public opinion of mid-summer, 1940. Donald Nelson later stated that, since there was then "little price stabilizing to look after," Henderson tackled more pressing problems as "an all-outer for production." He and Nelson also devised the "five-year tax amortization plan" to encourage the building of defense plants; though they won over NDAC, they didn't then get the support of Secretary of the Treasury Henry Morgenthau, Jr. and his staff. Knudsen, however, took the idea to the Finance Committee of the Senate, which approved it by a margin of one vote. It finally became the "Amortization Deduction" Title III in the income-tax law, and, incidentally, was re-applied after Korea.

Both Henderson and Nelson had been greatly impressed by Baruch's text when he addressed NDAC members on the subject of "Priorities, the synchronizing force of any defense system." They organized a study of this problem, drawing heavily upon Baruch's WIB reports, and eventually got the first Priorities Board established with Knudsen as Chairman. It was Nelson's view that the priorities method then adopted proved inadequate because "we had patterned it upon the system which had been satisfactory in 1917-1918," whereas the scope of the World War II job was must vaster.

Henderson became free at last to direct most of his attention to price regulation after OPACS was split in two parts. The portion concerned with material requirements for the various civilian programs was established as a Division of Civilian Supply in OPM. Henderson continued as head of both, however. By then, he had studied the latest data on the British experiments with controls. He was convinced that the line against inflation could not really be held without rationing authority—a view that was shared by his able assistants in OPA: J. K. Galbraith, who subsequently became editor of *Fortune* magazine; Seymour Harris, economics professor on leave from Harvard; and the dynamic spark-plug of the Civilian Supply Division, Joseph L. Weiner. Of particular note, because of his unflagging efforts and able assistance to Henderson during this period, was his legal counsel in OPA, David Ginsburg.

Henderson recognized at this time that price-fixing of "key-commodities" along with rationing and certain fiscal controls would be effective. He advocated the tightening of consumer credit, and especially restrictions on installment selling; a more rugged tax program; and the promotion of consumer savings through defense bonds.

When he realized that it would be possible at last to obtain statutory authority to replace his "jawbone" authority, Henderson still was not convinced that over-all controls were necessary. Baruch repeatedly had led him to water, but couldn't make him drink. The two appeals Baruch made to House Committees in the fall of 1941 were cases in point.

Baruch tried again in what was called the "Debate of the Month." The *Rotarian Magazine* for December, 1941 presented both sides of this controversy. Part of Baruch's complaint was that his advice as to priorities had been misinterpreted.

"Because priorities were put into effect without realizing what would follow," he said, "critical shortages have developed, serious temporary unemployment is threatened, businesses may have to shut down. It has cost the country time, production, hardship and money."

Baruch pointed out that SPAB had recently imposed drastic restrictions on defense building. "Many landlords will seize upon this curtailment to raise rents," he predicted. "Since rents are not under control the public will be unprotected against such profiteering. That is happening all around us. Everywhere the demands of total defense have suspended the normal workings of our free competitive economy. Because we have not brought prices and profits under control, the country is left at the mercies of runaway markets, speculators, hoarders and profiteers. . . .

Again emphasizing that he did not object to higher wages, he added, "If the real incomes of workers are slashed by rising prices, they are entitled to increases—for some workers such increases are already overdue. What the ceiling plan does is to tie wages and prices together so they can move together as the cost of living changes. That is the just way. It asks no special sacrifices of any group; it grants no special privileges.

"I cannot believe that the farmers and workers in this country want more than this—to be treated equally and not profit at the expense of the rest of the country.

"In effect, the over-all ceiling applies the principle of the Selective Service Act to price control. The obviously fair way to conscript the youth of our country was to bring everyone in the designated age groups under the draft and then make exceptions. That is what the ceiling does; it brings all prices under control and then allows whatever individual adjustments are necessary. . . .

"In contrast, piecemeal, partial price controls invite every pressure group, politician, lobbyist, trade association, and 'interest' to descend upon Washington and seek exemption. Since the general price level will continue to rise, the price administrator will have to make adjustments and inevitably he will yield where the pressure—not necessarily justice—is greatest. The little fellows who cannot make themselves felt will be forgotten."

Henderson was not one to cry out, "Oh, that mine adversary had written a book," but if he had had the time and inclination to leaf through Baruch's articles and books seeking substantiation for any part of the policy he had pursued at OPACS, he could have cited Baruch's own words. There was, for example, Baruch's cautious paragraph on over-all controls in an article on priorities which was published in the spring, 1941 issue of *The Harvard Business Review*.

"There is no need for such a thorough-going plan," Baruch then wrote, "until a general rise in the price level is threatening. If industry is working below capacity and the price level is resting fairly stable, it will be sufficient to attack the prices of individual commodities where scarcity is causing the price to be bid up above all equitable cost relationships." Baruch did not express in that article the opinion that such a general rise in the price level was then threatening. He did, however, commit himself on the subject of rationing. He said, "The situation never became so critical in the last war that such a drastic system as the ration-card became necessary, nor does it seem likely in any emergency of the near future."

Baruch also had repeatedly expressed the view, in the decades between wars, that "without a great surge of popular and patriotic inspiration neither the selective draft nor price-fixing, nor any other sacrificial statute can be enforced." These were his words before the War Policies Commission in 1931.

Henderson had evidence every day until Pearl Harbor

that there certainly was no "great surge of popular inspiration" for enforcing over-all controls. Congress, indeed, in pushing through the Emergency Price Control Act shortly after Pearl Harbor, was not willing even then to authorize more than piecemeal controls.

In any case, as events and demands crowded upon NDAC, it soon became clear that the Commission had been obliged to bite off more than it could chew. Its personnel mushroomed, but so did its problems. It let the Army-Navy Munitions Board run away with part of the NDAC job. It lacked the power to do the follow-up work on its own recommendations, and most of those recommendations, though arrived at almost independently of Baruch, had long been included in his blueprint for industrial mobilization. It made little more than a bare start on the crucial task of stockpiling strategic materials. Yet even its harshest critics had to admit that somehow in seven months NDAC did manage to come up with some definite achievements. But it was superseded in December, 1940 by OPM (Office of Production Management). As Baruch had predicted nearly twenty years earlier to the War Policies Commission, the first "hastily assembled organization . . . in the panic of world upheaval" proved unequal to its task.

Other ineffectual agencies followed, repeating the mistakes of the First World War—mistakes which Baruch had summarized in January, 1936 in the *American Legion Monthly*. "Everything was extemporized in the time of crisis. The result was demoralization in getting industry on a war basis, and then, after the war, getting it off; the needless expenditure of billions of dollars, and a great inequality in the distribution of burdens which were very hard upon many and made profiteers of others. Not until we were nearing the close of hostilities was the machine commencing to work toward its goal."

The mushroom agencies were set up for the most part outside the permanent Government structure, just as were Baruch's

WIB, its subsidiaries, and the cooperating emergency units in the First World War—and probably for the same reasons. First of all, personnel in the oldline departments were not geared for the bold and speedy action of war-time. Second, a cat with nine lives is one of the few creatures harder to exterminate than a Federal office, once it is integrated as an established unit of a powerful Department. Roosevelt, like President Wilson before him, felt that Congress would be more likely to support highly unpopular measures if administered by segregated agencies whose lease on life would expire with the emergency.

Roosevelt, however, was less wary of Congressional and Cabinet opposition when he decided that the directors of emergency agencies should report not to Cabinet heads but to him. Many of his critics are still decrying that decision.

Reproached for setting up a headless NDAC, he went to the other extreme in creating its successor on December 20, 1940, with William Knudsen as Director General and Sidney Hillman as Associate Director General. OPM was promptly dubbed a two-headed monstrosity by such caustic wits as Baruch's disciple, Hugh Johnson. George Creel said that after Baruch learned of this divided authority "it took two pulmotors to revive him."

Established mainly for conversion to defense production, the new agency had one big division called OPACS (Office of Price Administration and Civilian Supply) . OPM, like NDAC, lacked real power. Moreover, the hard-working men who moved over to it from NDAC took along the quarrels started there. Much worse, ever-accelerating developments in Europe and Asia continually increased the production problems inherited from the earlier agency. The result was that OPM soon began to wallow like a harpooned whale.

An attempt to re-invigorate it was made on June 24, 1941, after Hitler's invasion of Russia. Industry Advisory Committees and commodity sections, as repeatedly advised by Baruch, were then added to its three key divisions of Production, Priorities and Purchasing.

The death throes of the agency, however, became generally evident on July 20 when the Economic Defense Board was established under the chairmanship of the Vice President, Henry A. Wallace. About a month later, OPM and OPACS issued a limitation order which curtailed passenger car production by 26 percent as of November 30, and by 50 percent as of July, 1942. The automobile industry, of course, objected violently, but later developments tended to confirm Nelson's judgment that this order was the "most important single step toward conversion." A week later OPM expired. It had lived just one month longer than its predecessor.

OPACS, however, was divided and re-baptized under the name of OPA (Office of Price Administration), and a supposedly new "war baby"—as Baruch had called such emergency agencies in 1917—was christened SPAB (Supply, Priorities and Allocations Board). SPAB turned out to be not a new creation after all, but was actually an enlargement of the OPM Board with Wallace as Chairman and Nelson as Executive Director. Wallace continued to be Chairman, also, of the Economic Defense Board, which was later re-named the Board of Economic Warfare.

Nelson, who had been Director of Purchases for OPM, was named Director of Priorities for SPAB. Judge Samuel Rosenman, one of Roosevelt's trusted advisers, drew up the preliminary plan for SPAB, charging it with the duty of allocating available supplies to meet military needs, defense needs, and total civilian needs.

Baruch called SPAB "a faltering step forward," and later handed it the tiny bouquet already cited in the discussion of his testimony to the House Committees that fall. The weakness he pointed out then—that it was a general staff for industrial mobilization without a chief of staff—was the weakness he continued to emphasize.

225

Though metropolitan newspapers usually carried full reports of his testimony, and though his criticism generally inspired wide favorable comment in editorial pages and on the air, Baruch decided again to enlarge his audience. He was especially anxious for his recommendations to reach emergency agency officials and thoughtful readers who could influence action in Washington. Accordingly, he and his staff compiled a comprehensive volume on the original War Industries Board entitled *American Industry in the War.*

Baruch, in his foreword to the thick volume, said that the documents it contained "will show what should be done and what should be avoided. The War Industries Board Plan contemplated getting ahead and keeping ahead—avoiding bottlenecks rather than breaking them. It was arrived at by trial and error" in 1917 and 1918.

"It is regrettable," Baruch continued, "that we have to re-travel any of that road." Again he summarized the guiding principles he had so often explained, with special stress on the following needs: "Control of imports with a world-wide economic strategy to insure supplies to our friends and to withhold them from our enemies.

"Wise location of plants and new facilities having special reference to housing, transportation and labor, spreading to all communities the opportunity to take part in defense work. Not too many eggs in one basket or too much work in one place.

"Regional organization with special emphasis upon subcontracting, using small business for making parts to be assembled in larger units.

"The avoidance [by dollar-a-year men] of even any appearance of acting in a dual capacity for the government, themselves, or the businesses in which they have an interest."

And price control? Why, naturally—and it must, of course, be over-all price control!

"Methods proved for all this and more," he continued, "are outlined in this volume. At times the reader will have to raise his eyes from these pages to wonder whether he is reading what took place a quarter of a century ago or what is unfolding before us daily.

"All must be done without losing sight of our condition after the war—not merely to fight and win the war, but also to survive it economically, with a low price structure and an industrial system dislocated to a minimum degree, well prepared for post-war conditions in the international markets."

The book, running to 498 pages and with chapters devoted to a full exposition of each guiding principle for effective industrial mobilization, was published late in 1941. A great part of it reviewed WIB undertakings in 1918. Yet by the time the volume was available, it is doubtful if prominent officials could make much use of it. The attack on Pearl Harbor had overwhelmed them with day-to-day demands, leaving them no heart or time to study long-past mistakes and triumphs. The book, however, is a permanent part of Baruch's blueprint for security, and as such is an invaluable contribution.

If the text itself did not become required reading early in 1942, one part of the book had extraordinary immediacy and appeal. This was the conclusion to his foreword:

"America has the resources and the brains, and with the will to do so, it will be able to say again: 'It can't be done—but here it is.'"

Later, when the Commander-in-Chief made the final decision in January 1942, to centralize power in a new agency, the War Production Board, Donald M. Nelson was named as Chairman. Though Baruch is reported to have been keenly disappointed, he did his gracious best to fall in line. He and Nelson had dinner together at the end of Nelson's first day on the new job. It was a kind of love-feast, according to Nelson's later account of Baruch's congratulatory words and helpful suggestions, and of his own expressions of gratitude for Baruch's encouragement and previous good advice.

Though it is clear there was mutual respect between the two men, a comparable relationship never quite developed between Baruch and Leon Henderson, the boss of OPA. He had been a New Deal stalwart with NRA, WPA, TNEC, and SEC. Dubbed a wheelhorse because of his almost boundless energy, Henderson had the vigor and the gusto of the Biblical war horse who "saith among the trumpets, ha ha, and he smelleth the battle afar off, the thunder of the captains and the shouting." The President had come to value Henderson highly when he called the count on the recession of 1937, after others had pronounced the depression wholly routed. Like all born pragmatists, Henderson was ready to question any man's dogma or theories, including Baruch's concepts of "natural economic laws." On the other hand, he also was ready to seize upon any suggestion that looked workable, whoever presented it.

Meanwhile, Judge Rosenman had worked out the general outlines of a plan to establish the Office of Economic Stabilization. Roosevelt believed that this agency must have more than "jawbone" authority, but he feared it would take months to get the necessary legislation through the Congress. Byrnes, then an Associate Justice of the U. S. Supreme Court, agreed. He warned, however, that without Congressional authorization OES, too, would fail. Even with statutory basis, he went on to say, "This regulation of wages and prices is so controversial, it touches so many people so directly, that enforcement will be difficult."

OPA's original price control system under its General Maximum Price Regulation—familiarly known as "General Max"—created some critical situations on a spotty regional scale. By authorizing retailers to freeze their prices at the highest levels existing during a specified period, it froze the disparities between cash-and-carry chain stores and specialized credit stores. Available supplies, naturally, tended to flow to retailers with the biggest mark-up, and shortages became acute wherever mark-ups were smallest. This was one disadvantage in using the "normal" pattern of price-relationships as the basis for price ceilings. Had Henderson misunderstood Baruch's advice on this point? In any case, unscrambling this particular difficulty required much time and effort. For a while, indeed—as Baruch had predicted that any hastily devised price control system would demonstrate—"General Max" looked to the critics very much "like a dog trying to catch himself by running around a tree."

Henderson believed that Baruch failed to appreciate the vast scope of the administrative problems involved in price control, especially in his insistence to the House Rules Committee in November, 1941: "I would have the final price schedule submitted directly to the President of the United States for his approval as was done in the last war. I would take this step not because I desire to saddle him with extra responsibilities but, were he to give his official endorsement to the pronouncement, the public would accept it."

There was full agreement, however, between Baruch and Henderson on one important aspect of price control. They both insisted that farm prices must be regulated. Claude R. Wickard, Secretary of Agriculture, anticipated that a separate food authority, such as Hoover's Food Administration in World War I, might eventually be set up. If so, he was ready to step into Hoover's shoes, but he also hoped to remain the boss of his own Department. His fight with Henderson during consideration of the public control bill eventually led to his downfall. Henderson, of course, insisted that OPA should regulate all food prices—farm products along with all processed foods.

While Congress bitterly debated the issue, Baruch resorted

once again to his old practice of publishing all his relevant advice. This anthology was entitled *Preventing Inflation,* a title he had substituted, once war became imminent, for the long-useful phrase, "Taking the Profit Out of War." It was sub-titled, "Statements and Writings on Controlling Living Costs and Preventing Inflation, Sept. 1941–Dec. 1941." In the foreword, written on September 25, 1942, Baruch stated, "This booklet is gotten up to make one point:

" 'There are certain fundamental principles for controlling living costs and preventing inflation. . . . They are the same . . . that I have been preaching for more than 20 years. . . . As long as they are ignored, no effective control over the forces of inflation is possible.' "

Largely because of the needling by Baruch and Henderson, President Roosevelt issued his ultimatum to Congress on Labor Day of 1942 demanding a price control bill which would also stabilize farm prices. In effect, his ultimatum was: "Either you act before October first, or I will."

Eight months earlier, in February, the Second War Powers Act had given the President authority to stabilize wages and prices by Executive Order without reference to Congress. Byrnes, for reasons already cited, had advised him not to use that power. Many Congressmen—including those who had so often accused the President of dictatorial ambitions—hoped he would. They kept postponing action on this controversial issue in order to escape both the responsibility and the blame. Roosevelt's speech of September 7 gave them less than three weeks to act. The Stabilization Act became law on October 2, 1942. The President signed it as soon as it reached his desk, just one day past the deadline he had set—and just one week, as it happened, after Baruch wrote the foreword to the booklet re-capitulating his advice on the issue.

Many of Baruch's friends, at this time, did not pay him the compliment of reading past the headlines on reports of his official testimony. They persisted in their disservice by claiming that his advice was altogether ignored in the Stabilization Act. Actually, that Act incorporated many of his recommendations. Authorizing the stabilization of prices, wages, salaries and rents, the Act also empowered the President to correct inequities. This provision was interpreted in line with Baruch's specific advice, already cited earlier in this account, to tie "wages and prices together so that they can move together as the cost of living changes." Under this formula, in the language peculiar to agriculture, farm prices, as Baruch also had advised, were tied to parity—that is, to the production and living costs of the farmer.

Byrnes resigned from the Supreme Court to become Director of the Office of Economic Stabilization shortly after the Stabilization Act was signed. He became, in fact, a kind of "Assistant President," according to political observers. Writing of this period later, Byrnes stated, "From October 15, 1942, when the office began operating, until April, 1943, the cost of living index increased by 4.3 percent." Byrnes then drafted, and the President issued, what became known as the Hold-the-Line Order on controls.

Soon afterwards, Byrnes decided that the job of mobilizing resources was so big that he could not give sufficient time to it and to economic stabilization problems as well. He drafted the order establishing the Office of War Mobilization and became its head. Meanwhile, at his suggestion, Roosevelt asked Judge Fred M. Vinson to resign from the Circuit Court of Appeals, and take over OES as its Director. "From April, 1943," Byrnes stated, "until his [Vinson's] resignation in April, 1945, the cost of living index rose only 3.2 percent. In twenty-two months following his resignation and the abandonment of the Hold-the-Line Order, the increase was 20.2 percent."

It took many more months for Government officials, pressure groups, and unorganized civilian consumers to accept the unpalatable fact which Baruch has so often phrased this way: "The

price of anything is simply the resultant price of everything."
While that learning process was in its early stage, resentment
against the Democratic Administration was well organized and
well financed. The result was that Roosevelt in the 1942 elections only barely escaped the same kind of overturn which in
1918 was inflicted on President Wilson. Roosevelt's popular
vote was cut down to the narrowest margin of his entire Presidential career. The Republicans gained forty-seven votes in
the House—only one short of a majority—and ten votes in the
Senate. Not long thereafter, Leon Henderson left OPA.

When Byrnes became known as the "Assistant President,"
White House reporters correctly anticipated that Baruch would
soon be called in to treat some of the production sore spots.
How vital these problems were we shall see presently.

Byrnes also attempted to persuade Roosevelt not to set up
another board for the greatly expanded job after Pearl Harbor,
but, as he later reported, "to appoint one man charged with
the duty of supervising and expediting procurement." This
was, of course, exactly what Baruch had advised frequently both
during and after World War I. Byrnes made the suggestion in
a memo he sent on January 2, 1942, to Harry Hopkins, then
Chairman of the Munitions Assignment Board.

There is no record that Byrnes at that time urged Roosevelt
to name Baruch to the post. Indeed, he explicitly stated that he
had suggested no favorite nominee. But it is clear that Byrnes
was one of several who later advised supplanting Nelson with
Baruch, as Chairman of the War Production Board.

Writing of his own appointment as WPB Chairman, Nelson
has said, "One of the first men I made it a point to see was Mr.
Baruch." At the dinner after his first day in his new post, Nelson
reported that Baruch "told me that he had remarked to President Roosevelt a few weeks earlier: 'That fellow make a noise

like a dividend—I don't know how big a dividend, but I do think there is a dividend there.' "

Byrnes was called to the White House on January 12, saw Hopkins and learned that his memo recommending Baruch for Nelson's post had not been presented to the President, although the general idea had been discussed. Byrnes picked up the memo and took it in to Roosevelt who read it and said, "If I had to make a selection this morning, I would pick Donald Nelson." The previous evening, he explained, Nelson had been at a White House dinner honoring Lord Beaverbrook, the British Supply Minister. Roosevelt added that he hadn't known Nelson too well before then, but was much impressed by his discussion of the "sugar situation and a number of production problems."

Harry Hopkins was delighted to learn that Roosevelt was at last seeing the light—*his* light. The President had considered numerous men for the War Production Board job, including William O. Douglas, Associate Justice of the Supreme Court, but Hopkins had insisted right along that Nelson "was the best of the lot." To his diary Hopkins confided: "Everybody was a candidate. Wallace, I am sure, hoped the President would ask him. Bernie Baruch was in a hotel room in Washington spreading propaganda for himself. A great many of my friends were pushing Bill Douglas, Morgenthau wanted it worse than anything in the world. So did Jesse Jones, and, of course, Knudsen."

Hopkins wanted quick action. Perhaps he somewhat uneasily recalled Churchill's words to Baruch, "You will be running the show over there." Hopkins told Byrnes, "The first thing we know, somebody will be in here trying to change Roosevelt's mind." An Executive Order was prepared abolishing the Economic Defense Board, of which Wallace was Chairman, and establishing the new War Production Board with Nelson as Chairman. After Wallace was informed, the press announcement was released. Knudsen, whose critics had charged that he "didn't know the difference between a Chevrolet and a war," was commissioned a Lieutenant General in the Army, in charge of production, to work with Robert Patterson, the Under Secretary of War.

Nelson was a popular choice for head of WPB. Many papers reprinted Berryman's cartoon showing F.D.R. as a beaming Little Jack Horner pulling Nelson from a pie marked with the initials of all the previous ineffectual agencies. Nelson had had a relationship by remote control with Baruch's WIB through Julius Rosenwald, member of that Board and President of Sears, Roebuck and Company. Between wars, Nelson had worked in Washington for a short while with Clay Williams, who succeeded Hugh Johnson as Administrator of NRA.

Nelson had come back to Washington early in May, 1940 to work for "two months" with Henry Morgenthau, Secretary of the Treasury, who was then organizing airplane procurement for the British and French. Named Acting Director of Procurement for the Allies, whose military purchases then had to be placed through the Treasury, Nelson did so well that his two months continued indefinitely. His reputation grew as he moved on from one emergency agency to another.

A full recital of the responsibilities and accomplishments of the War Production Board is neither possible nor appropriate within the limits of this book. However, the influence of Bernard Baruch and his War Industries Board had considerable effect on its organization and policies. A brief account of some of the highlights, therefore, is in order.

The War Production Board was established within the Office for Emergency Management by an Executive Order of January 16, 1942, "for the purpose of assuring the most effective prosecution of war procurement and production." It inherited the functions, powers, personnel, and records of the Office of Production Management and the Supply, Priorities and Allocations Board. WPB became the chief instrument for mobilizing the industrial strength of the United States against its enemies.

Most of the intricate technical and administrative barriers preventing the full mobilization of our industrial resources were broken by WPB. The economy was converted to war production: supplies and resources were multiplied many times over and a tremendous expansion of facilities was effected. Large improvements in planning were achieved, effective distribution of materials was evolved, and efficient production scheduling techniques were developed.

By the end of 1942 the industrial mobilization crisis was largely resolved. Under WPB the value of war production in that year was over three and one-half times that of 1941. Munitions output totaled $32.5 billion, Government-financed war construction $14.1 billion, making a total of $46.6 billion. About one-third of the nation's production was then being devoted to the war program. Although output fell short of the production goals President Roosevelt had set, it was nonetheless high enough to confirm his convicition that our industrial capacity had vast, untapped productive potentialities. If proof was needed, it was supplied and underlined later in the production record for 1944 and again in approximately the same total of $64.4 billion in the so-called Two-Front Munitions Production Program for 1945.

The United States produced about 40 percent of the world's total munitions during the crucial years of 1943 and 1944. Combined with the 31 percent of world output produced by the other Allies, this gave Allied forces in the field the weapons and materiel to surpass those of the enemy. Factors other than supply were, of course, important in bringing ultimate victory, but the preponderance of Allied munitions, provided in large measure by American industry, was a decisive factor in the final outcome.

The significance of WPB's tangible contribution to ultimate

victory is beyond question. The true measure of WPB's achievement, however, lay not alone in its successful direction of the nation's economy during a global war, but also in the method by which it had maintained this direction. The Board had faced the problem of organizing the private and public resources of a free nation with its only precedent that of the War Industries Board of World War I. In a comparison of the two Boards, Donald Nelson has said in his *Arsenal of Democracy:* "The War Industries Board of World War II—our organization, of course —was ten times as large, just as our war needs were many times greater. Perhaps the closest parallel lay in the industry committees of the two Boards." The latter point undoubtedly resulted from the urgings of Mr. Baruch during the intervening years.

Although the WPB necessarily exercised sweeping controls, it maintained flexibility of structure and democratic procedures. Industry, labor, the civilian economy, and the Armed Services each participated in the formulation of policy.

The Chairman of the War Production Board was empowered to exercise general direction over the nation's war procurement and production program and to determine the policies, plans, procedures, and methods of Government agencies in such matters as purchasing, contracting, specifications, construction, conversion, requisitioning, plant expansion, and financing. It is noteworthy that another of Baruch's oft-repeated recommendations for one-man direction of the production program was achieved with the designation of Donald Nelson as Chairman with full powers to act, and his Board merely serving in an advisory role. In making this decision, the President sided against a suggestion made by Lord Beaverbrook in the closing days of 1941 that a committee of production be established under Harry Hopkins "with full powers and entire authority. Such a committee would not only dispose of the production requirements but would also be responsible for mobilizing and distributing the necessary raw materials."

A closer look at the Chairman of the War Production Board himself—a man whose role in World War II most nearly approximated that of Bernard Baruch in World War I—is appropriate at this point.

Donald M. Nelson stepped into the chairmanship of the War Production Board from the position of Executive Director of SPAB. The President had relied most heavily on Nelson, rather than on Knudsen or Hillman, in the weeks following Pearl Harbor for assistance in planning the all-out war production program for 1942 and 1943. As WPB Chairman, Nelson faced an extraordinarily difficult task in mobilizing resources in a manner that would secure maximum production while preserving the vitality of the basic economy. The record industrial output under his leadership entitles him to recognition as one of the most important contributors to the winning of the war.

There were a number of significant factors which affected Nelson's handling of the mobilization job, among the most important of which were: One, he stressed that it was essential to get action "in the democratic way without dictatorial tactics." Two, despite his vast powers on paper, in reality these powers had to command the support of other Federal agencies—notably the War and Navy Departments—since he was dependent upon them for execution of many of his major decisions. Three, he stated that he "purposely set up the War Production Board so that there are all shades of opinion in it"—it was this perspective gained from diversity of opinion which aided him in formulating policy. This worthy purpose contributed as well, to occasional delays in decision-making—a point his critics often liked to emphasize. Four, he had a grasp of the economy as an institution, an understanding of the part played by various public and private groups, and a feeling for political aspects and hurdles—an ability which enabled him to sense what the country would accept in terms of controls.

The first speech prepared by Donald Nelson after his appointment as Chairman of WPB showed a clear grasp of his mobilization responsibilities. "We are going to have to rely on our great mass production industries for the bulk of our increase under this war program," Nelson said. "Wherever we can we must convert them to war production, and convert them quickly. The only gauge we can apply to this process is: What method will most quickly give us the greatest volume of war production in this particular industry?

"The answer to that question may be hard to swallow, at times. . . . But what of it? The one thing that counts is to get the stuff out and get it out quickly. We cannot waste three months— or three weeks, for that matter—in wrangling and discussion; we cannot compromise this demand for all-out production, or accept a formula which gives us anything less than the absolute maximum of production, just because someone's toes are going to be stepped on."

Could this have been an echo of Bernard Baruch in World War I?

This discussion of the War Production Board and its Chairman would be incomplete without mentioning at least two of the principal aides to Donald Nelson—Charles E. Wilson and Robert R. Nathan. Both were exponents of Baruch's principles of all-out, rather than piecemeal, methods—Wilson in production, Nathan in planning.

Donald Nelson wrote in his book *Arsenal of Democracy*: "It seemed to me that the one man in the United States who could aid us most in that job was Charles E. Wilson, President of the General Electric Company." He was referring to the vital need for scheduling components properly to coordinate conflicting WPB programs. Nelson added that WPB had to devise some means of insuring to each competitor each month the precise number of critical items which he needed immediately, *and no more.* "Devising and executing such a scheduling operation, however, would call for some uncommon talents.

"President Roosevelt, at my request, asked Charley to come to Washington and, to all intents and purposes, drafted him.... He resigned his job, gave up his salary, which ran into six figures, and came to work for WPB. . . . Charley felt, as I had felt, that if he were going to work for the government he should have no connection with private industry, and he deserves all the credit that can be given to a man for making the decision he did at the time he made it. He joined WPB September 18, 1942, as Production Vice Chairman, and went to work immediately; first, to increase the supply of critical components, and second, to set up an orderly scheduling program."

Nelson summed up his opinion of Wilson's performance at WPB in these words: "Charley Wilson's drive and stamina were astonishing, and I unhesitatingly give him the full measure of credit due him for the grand job he did in making possible the production peaks we reached in 1943 and 1944."

With respect to Robert Nathan, he was a close adviser to Nelson in his capacity as Chairman of the WPB Planning Committee. This Committee played a cardinal role in spotlighting trouble areas and in recommending remedial action. Promptly after Pearl Harbor it was Nathan, then with OPM, who blocked out a production potential utilizing America's tremendous industrial resources. About that time, as reported by Bruce Catton in *The War Lords of Washington,* he wrote to Nelson: "We all realize that an all-out effort is needed and we all talk in terms of such an effort, but frankly I see no evidence of action consistent with such philosophy. Under war there must be a changed set of principles, and a strict adherence to fundamental principles irrespective of personalities. Frankly, either SPAB must take hold of the situation firmly, immediately, or there must be another agency to do the job." Nathan's suggestions were realistic and events proved them to be accurate.

No description of the job performed by the War Production Board and some of its top officials would be complete in this book without reference to the influence of Bernard Baruch during this period. And no better source is available than the head of WPB himself, Donald Nelson, who wrote: "Mr. Baruch headed the War Industries Board in World War I, and was, quite correctly, credited with the successful organization of industrial production in that war." Mr. Nelson, in describing an early meeting to which Baruch had been invited, goes on to say: "Perhaps the high point of Mr. Baruch's counsel concerned priorities, which he considered the 'synchronizing force' of any war production program. This lesson, too, we were to learn, although not as soon, perhaps, as we should have done. He talked at great length about price control, and declared that the big production program toward which we were heading could easily run away from us unless we arranged for price-control mechanisms. It is my opinion that hundreds of millions, perhaps billions, of dollars could have been saved and many headaches avoided if this recommendation had been adopted from the start.

"The former head of the War Industries Board knew what he was talking about when he expounded the ticklish subject of requirements and declared that they should be centralized in one agency so that each morning the agency could know just what had been ordered out of the nation's economy. Later on, when I was made head of WPB, I tried persistently to do this, but it was then too late. The program had grown so big that it was completely beyond control. I mention these considerations here in order to point out that we are too slow in taking advantage of other men's experience. Here was a man who had been all the way through the industrial production end of a great war, and I feel that on this occasion he gave us a precise picture of the essentials needed for coping with our future problems, although, of course, we had to do a comparable job in a war which was many times bigger than the one in which he served."

An important part of Donald Nelson's responsibility as WPB Chairman was delegated to Ferdinand Eberstadt when he was named Program Vice Chairman of the WPB, in charge of materials controls. A Wall Street investment banker, Eberstadt had been a young lawyer on Baruch's economic staff at Versailles. In World War II he became an active Baruch disciple.

"I was completely ignorant when I went to Washington in June of 1941 as Chairman of the Army-Navy Munitions Board," Eberstadt stated later. He soon found, he added, that "Baruch's works were the granite structures that covered the whole War Production field." Some of his associates, he continued, "paid lip-service to Baruch, but they hadn't studied his principles." His own study, on the other hand, had prepared him to work out the Controlled Materials Plan which, as Nelson stated, "proved so useful during the rest of the war period." A Brookings Institution bulletin summarizing Eliot Janeway's book, *Struggle for Survival,* said that Eberstadt's plan "brought much order out of chaos by controlling three key materials— steel, aluminum, and copper—and by regulating total production through the simple device of keying priorities to orders of finished goods."

Early in 1943, according to Nelson's own book, production scheduling had become the key problem. "The Army's increasing insistence that we restrict our controls to materials only led it to support the job Eberstadt was doing and to oppose Wilson's work ... and developed into a conflict between Wilson and Eberstadt themselves." Nelson then transferred Eberstadt's authority to Wilson, the Production Vice Chairman.

Commenting on this feud in his book *Roosevelt and Hopkins,* Robert E. Sherwood wrote, "Eberstadt had the backing of the War and Navy Departments who had come to the conclusion that Nelson must go."

241

This was the same kind of conflict, discussed in an earlier chapter, which resulted in the ousting of Frank A. Scott as the first Chairman of the War Industries Board in World War I and his replacement by Baruch. At that time Edward R. Stettinius, Sr., as Surveyor-General of Supplies for the War Department, was being backed by Secretary of War Baker to make "an empty shell" of the WIB, as Grosvenor B. Clarkson reported in his history of that Board. President Wilson intervened.

This time, President Roosevelt decided, just after his return from Casablanca in mid-February, 1943, that he too must intervene. He wrote to Baruch asking him to take over the WPB chairmanship. Baruch, then ill at his home in New York, was unable to get to Washington for a few days. When he did, he learned that the President had changed his mind.

Grace Tully, the President's Secretary, later suggested that this was Hopkins' doings. Sherwood reached the same conclusion. "It seems evident," he wrote, "that Hopkins backed Nelson and persuaded the President to give him another chance."

Nelson, it developed later, had received a warning call at midnight from one of his most trusted assistants. At breakfast the next morning, this informant told him that a letter offering the job to Baruch was ready for the President's signature. The Army, the assistant added, was determined to have Nelson fired that very day. Eberstadt would then be named Baruch's deputy. Byrnes, Secretary Stimson, Secretary Knox, and Under Secretary Forrestal were to ask the President to sign the letter at a White House conference that afternoon.

Nelson had his General Counsel, John Lord O'Brian, check the story with Secretary Stimson, and Stimson said he was sorry but it was the only course the Army could take. Nelson immediately called in Eberstadt, asked for and got his resignation, and announced it to the press. Roosevelt accepted the accomplished fact and the scheduled conference was not held.

Baruch's friends felt, for the third time, that he would be

appointed head of the WPB when Wilson and Nelson began to disagree early in 1944. Roosevelt later asked Nelson to go to China on an important mission, intending to appoint Wilson Acting Chairman of WPB in his absence. However, Wilson resigned. Julius Krug was made Acting Chairman and Nelson left for China.

Whatever might be Baruch's own interpretation of the fact that he was by-passed, he has never made any public statement on the matter. Indeed, each of his official recommendations that one man be empowered to mobilize economic resources and industrial production was immediately followed by a dignified disavowal of self-interest.

Nor is there any available account of the specific objections which Hopkins may have raised to Baruch's appointment. Three of Baruch's biographers, Carter Field, W. L. White, and Harry Irving Shumway, have surmised that Roosevelt's closest advisers never forgave Baruch for his forthright attacks on certain New Deal economic policies, and that they also held against him—however unfairly—the fact that two of his WIB associates and life-long disciples, George Peek and Hugh Johnson, campaigned for two Republican presidential candidates—Peek for Landon, and Johnson for Willkie.

There is no evidence that Hopkins blamed Baruch for hostile newspaper attacks on him by Hugh Johnson; Hopkins' own temperament provides a more likely explanation of his opposition. He shed past experiences quickly and must have grown restless under Baruch's constant references to World War I, as Abraham Lincoln's younger officers grew restless when Lincoln's first General-in-Chief, "Old Fuss and Feathers" Winfield Scott, kept referring to the Mexican War, of which he had been the hero. Hopkins, moreover, constantly sought concrete suggestions, not the kind of broad generalizations—"guiding principles"—which Baruch most favored.

Nor could it have escaped either of that vigilant pair that

Baruch's testimony on that occasion took almost no cognizance of the alarming European situation stressed in Roosevelt's special message to Congress in January of that year, which asked for a bigger Naval building program and increased Army materiel. Furthermore, several of Baruch's specific suggestions at that time were wholly out of line with his own record of foresight regarding preparedness. He attacked Government-built hydroelectric power developments; yet without TVA, Bonneville and Grand Coulee, could the war have been won? He called for reduced taxes, though increased revenue was surely needed for a larger Army and Navy. To reduce "technological unemployment" he favored the Technocrat proposal to tax industrial machines. (His ideas changed after Munich, it should be noted, to conform to the critical world situation.)

Sadly contemplating these matters, an admirer of Bernard Mannes Baruch can only turn to the Roman poet, Horace, for solace. Horace wrote, "In long works, sleep will sometimes surprise. Homer himself hath been observed to nod."

Yet, because no man worked more devotedly to straighten out costly blunders on the home front, Eliot Janeway could truthfully report in *Life* magazine in January, 1943 that Baruch was one of the few World War I leaders "whose prestige has been enhanced by this war." Janeway called him "a disinterested ambassador from the public to the War Administration," and the public knew how to appreciate his success in the crucial job of trouble-shooting that President Roosevelt assigned him early in 1942.

At that time, with supplies of natural rubber from the Far East cut off by Japan, nothing effective was being done about conserving our tragically inadequate rubber reserves, and the synthetic rubber program seemed to be moving at a glacial pace. "Honest Harold" Ickes, Secretary of the Interior, aghast at the procrastination and inefficiency, insisted that brains, integrity and energy be called in to find out what was wrong and to recommend the remedy. "Get Baruch," he said. Roosevelt named Baruch Chairman of the committee to investigate and make recommendations for the conservation of the nation's rubber supply.

A nation on wheels and an Army on wheels balked, at first, at some of Baruch's drastic proposals. "The Army insisted," Nelson stated later, "that we did not need the full amount of synthetic rubber called for by the Baruch Committee, and it insisted that if we tried to make that much we should interfere with the building up of 100-octane gasoline plants." But Nelson decided that Baruch was right in declaring, "We'll take that report or we'll take defeat," and proceeded with plans for bringing synthetic rubber production up to the levels Baruch called for. William M. Jeffers, President of the Union Pacific Railroad, was named the rubber czar. At cross-purposes with the War Department from the outset, Jeffers nevertheless fought for and got the material necessary to build the synthetic rubber plants Baruch proposed.

Charles E. Wilson at the WPB is credited with working out one part of the solution. He devised a plan for production of "critical components" so that rubber production could go ahead without cutting too much into Army and Navy aviation gasoline, or the landing-barge programs. Jesse Jones, head of the Reconstruction Finance Corporation, defended the work of the Rubber Reserve in a memorandum to the President on Baruch's Rubber Report. He said that RFC, authorized on June 28, 1940, to build up rubber reserves, had accumulated "more than 634,000 tons of rubber" by mid-summer 1942, and that this was "by far the largest rubber stockpile ever possessed by any nation in the world."

In his biography, *Fifty Billion Dollars, My Thirteen Years with the RFC,* Jones pointed out that John M. Hancock, a partner in Lehman Brothers, Edward Eagle Brown, President of the First National Bank of Chicago, and Clarence Dillon, head of Dillon, Read and Company, were also members of Baruch's Rubber Report Committee. He added, "In making his report, my friend Baruch was willing to give me a little dig—for reasons of his own, maybe. Probably Mr. Baruch and his committee colleagues . . . like some other Wall Streeters, were none too pleased that RFC, the biggest banking and industrial corporation in history, could be run without calling on some of them!"

An armistice may come eventually in this war of words as to who deserves the lion's share of glory for breaking the rubber bottleneck. The American people know there is enough to go around, and that much of it belongs to Baruch and his Rubber Report.

Every civilian was able to understand the highlights of Baruch's advice on rubber conservation. The technical aspects were aimed at the experts, but the general public could understand the wisdom in his broad recommendations. Baruch emphasized that the conflict between RFC's Rubber Reserve and the Office of the Petroleum Coordinator had to be ended at once, and an adequate staff employed for the new synthetic rubber industry, which involved an investment exceeding $600,000,000. He added that a complete reorganization and consolidation of the governmental agencies concerned with the rubber program must be made, and recommended a directive to that effect from the President. "Full authority must be centered in a single official," Baruch declared. "We therefore recommend that the Chairman of WPB appoint a Rubber Administrator and delegate to him full and complete authority in regard to the manufacture of synthetic rubber, including research, development, construction and operation of plants.

"This single official, who must be a man of unusual capacity and power, must also have full charge of all matters connected with rubber within the WPB. . . ."

Baruch's next important assignment was to help solve the manpower problem caused by the enormous expansion of war plants, especially on the West Coast. By the time Byrnes, as Director of the Office of War Mobilization, called him in on this one, it had become a pretty ticklish matter. Numerous unofficial advisers were letting their own authoritarian impulses get out of hand in their concern to destroy Nazi and Japanese authoritarianism. They kept clamoring for a Labor Draft, though they used the more persuasive phrase "National Service Act." The whole matter, they insisted, could really be handled democratically, and need be no harsher than the universal call-up English system. Frances Perkins, Secretary of Labor, and Judge Rosenman, among other influential figures in Washington, bluntly called this proposal a dangerous attempt to control human beings. Moreover, they said, such labor conscription was unnecessary. The War Manpower Commission, set up in April, 1942, with Paul McNutt as Director, listened to the official recommendations of Judge Rosenman.

But even in a democracy during a total war, totalitarian ideas keep springing up among the intemperate like wild garlic. They had to be uprooted again before fall, 1942, when Baruch's report was submitted. John M. Hancock, one of Baruch's associates, assisted in its preparation. Baruch recommended a labor budget system, charging the WPB with the responsibility of assigning no more contracts to communities where the supply of labor was already strained, a limit as to the number of persons manufacturers could employ, and the limitation of workers in their choice of jobs. "Without arguing the merits of a National Service Act which is for Congress to decide," he added, "it can be said that everything called for in the labor-budget plan would be necessary in the administration of such an Act."

Baruch called for enforcement of the labor-budget system by

247

local authorities. "There must be adequate delegation of power from all Washington agencies to their West Coast representatives," he declared, "and the communities themselves must get on the team." He also attacked cost plus contracts as an incentive to the hoarding of labor. "Until now," he continued, "the energies of the Government have been directed principally at reducing the five, ten, or fifteen cents of a production dollar that goes into profits. While not relaxing our efforts to prevent profiteering, it is time we turned our attention to the 85, 90, or 95 cents of the production dollar represented by costs."

Sober advocates of fiscal reform include some who have bluntly charged that Baruch's post-war adjustment recommendations made in 1944 helped erode "the ideal of public responsibility in the federal government," and paved the way for the most tremendous waste, colossal fraud, and shameless corruption in the nation's history. One spokesman of this view was Blair Bolles, author of the book, *How to Get Rich in Washington.* He devoted a chapter to a withering analysis of Baruch's post-war recommendations and to their effects. Bolles, a former top-flight reporter on *The Washington Star,* did not dispute the claim that the nation lost billions of dollars by its delay in following Baruch's advice on all-out mobilization in World War II. He was more concerned with what the nation lost by taking Baruch's advice instead of the advice of Lindsay Warren, the Comptroller General, on the termination and payment of war contracts and the sale of war surplus.

It is, therefore, well to have another look at the facts and at Baruch's own words. As to the inception of reconversion in 1943 while battles raged overseas, the varied popular and more ponderous accounts are in general agreement. Donald M. Nelson called the undertaking a "war within the war," an estimate which was somewhat softened by James M. Byrnes, who was

Director of the Office of War Mobilization and Reconversion. Byrnes said "a fog of controversy" hung over the post-war readjustment problems, and he reported, in a speech before the Academy of Political Science in New York on April 12, 1944, that the "constructive report of B. M. Baruch and John Hancock" on those problems "had gone far to dispel" that fog.

From the outset of the war, Byrnes was impressed by the need to wind up the bookkeeping on it within a reasonable period. He was an Associate Justice of the Supreme Court when it finally decided a Bethlehem Steel Corporation suit over a Government contract made in World War I. The 23-year-old case was being argued before the Court on the Tuesday after Pearl Harbor. How much did it cost the Government in litigation to lose that case in the end? Surely better procedures, Byrnes reflected that day, could be devised for the termination and just payment of war contracts.

Byrnes called in Baruch and John M. Hancock, to work out a policy on contract termination and various demobilization difficulties. Hancock was named Acting Chairman of the Joint Contract Termination Board. Many of the recommendations they made in their printed report, *War and Postwar Adjustment Policies,* became law in the Contract Settlement Act.

A pessimistic climate of opinion surrounded Baruch and Hancock as they worked on the report. Here is how Baruch summarized it later when he testified, in March, 1946, to the House Banking and Currency Committee: "Many could not make up their minds whether we were going to have inflation or deflation. The wonder to me is that things are not even worse than they are.

"Before the report on War and Postwar Adjustment Policies was made in February of 1944, practically every one predicted between 9,000,000 and 15,000,000 unemployed. That prophecy proved unfounded. This kind of thinking shows how momentary emotion can affect a whole people."

"Our country's position today is such that if the war terminated suddenly most of the factories in this country would be shut and there would be unemployment of the worst kind. Of course, the war will not end tomorrow, but peace jitters already are cutting into war production. Removing all uncertainties as to the Government's policy on settling terminated contracts is needed for the immediate conduct of the war."

Baruch was confident, however, that if his recommendations were put into effect, disaster could be avoided. His 1944 report said, "A postwar depression is not inevitable. One-half of the world will need rebuilding. Enormous demands, put aside during the war, and added to prewar demands, await satisfaction. Much depends on the settlement of the peace. . . .

"Much will also depend on the measures taken now to prepare for peace—and, as important as the measures, on the men who will carry them out. The mistakes and delays made in the mobilization must not be repeated in the demobilization. . . . America's productive capacity can perform still another miracle in a fine and lasting peace. . . .

"Speed in shifting this productive capacity from war to peace is our most effective attack against the two enemies which threaten in the transition and postwar period—unemployment and inflation. What are the things that need to be done to insure this speed, to set our feet on the right path towards work—not alone for those here at home but for the men and women who will be returning from foreign shores?

"The very first problem to be solved is how to get Government work out of the plant so civilian work could come back in."

One piece of advice Baruch considered so important that it was printed in his report in capital letters, is as follows:

"SO THAT THE LOANS MADE AVAILABLE CAN BE REPAID AND TO ENCOURAGE NEW ENTERPRISES, A POSTWAR TAX LAW BE DRAFTED NOW, DURING

THE WAR, AND PUT ON A SHELF FOR USE AT THE
END OF THE WAR.

"This tax law to make known in advance the reductions in
tax rates from the present wartime levels to normal peacetime
levels. That this tax law provide for reduction of the national
debt—the importance of reducing the debt being to return to
a strong position of national defense."

Congress acted upon this advice later, reducing taxes by
nearly $6,000,000,000, as he deplored in 1946. Baruch also
advised:

"Early engineering on public works to be ready if needed to
fill in the valley of unemployment. Provide credit means for
those requiring it during the adjustment period, particularly for
the smaller business groups and returning Service men."

A large part of the 1944 report was concerned with recommendations for "quick, fair and final settlement of terminated
war contracts through negotiations by the contractors and the
procurement agencies.

"Any course such as that proposed recently by the Comptroller General would quibble the nation into a panic," Baruch
declared. He added, "The Comptroller's suggestion, as we
understand it, was that he review every settlement before payment and that no payment be final until approved by him.
Pending this audit, the Comptroller proposed that advances and
loans be made; but the amounts would be entirely inadequate
to keep business and jobs going."

Instead of Warren's method, Baruch advised:

"Immediate payment—the full 100 percent—for all completed
articles. On the uncompleted portion of the contract, immediate
payment—the full 100 percent—of the Government's estimate
of factual items, where proof ordinarily is simple. . . . Immediate
payment—the full 100 percent—of settlements with subcontrac-
tors as soon as possible. Payment by the Government of interest
on termination claims, until settled. As insurance against delays

251

in validating claims, a new, simplified system of T (Termination) loans by local banks, with Government guarantees, to be available to all war contractors, primes and subs. For those unable to obtain such loans from their local banks in 30 days, the Government to make the loans directly."

The Baruch-Hancock report also recommended that Congress absolve officials from legal accountability for any error they might make in the settlements. Baruch, however, approved the authorizing of an audit after the money had been paid out for each settlement.

Baruch himself complained in 1946 that only one part of his post-war recommendations had been adopted—contract termination. He declared that if his plan for the disposal of surplus property had "been worked intelligently and courageously many of the things the public wants and which are available would have been distributed and become useful. Some of the factories which we built could have been put in operation long ago. The surplus problem has been so tied up that it is not yet functioning properly."

The pros and cons of how we disposed of war-built industrial plants are still quite hotly debated. But it is worth noting here that a step in the right direction was taken when Public Law 364 further strengthened the Industrial Reserve by authorizing the Department of Defense to make long-term leases of real or personal property. For example, this has permitted the Navy to include in the Departmental reserve plant classification some 140 installations with an acquisition cost of almost one billion dollars, in addition to the half billion in facilities sponsored by the Navy in the National Industrial Plant Reserve.

Baruch's advice to create a new post of "Work Director" to see that the "human side of demobilization is not forgotten" was also rejected. This new official, in Baruch's words, was to "work with Congress in the development of a combined program of legislation and operations to carry out the objectives that all of us share." Baruch added that "among the fields to be covered by this 'Work Director' would be personnel demobilization of the Armed Forces, developing adequate machinery for job placement of veterans and demobilized war workers; adequate care for returning veterans; physical and occupational therapy for wounded and disabled; resumption of education interrupted by war; vocational training; the special employment problems of the great war industries, and others." This "Work Director" proposal received no endorsement from Secretary of Labor Frances Perkins or officials of the Veterans' Administration.

The Brookings Institution, however, issued a pamphlet written by Lewis H. Kimmel which advocated post-war tax policies similar to those Baruch recommended in 1944. Interestingly enough, Baruch's concern over additional post-war problems was not shared by two other Brookings Institution experts, Harold G. Moulton and Karl T. Schlotterbeck. In a pamphlet entitled *Collapse or Boom?*, published in 1942, these men had concluded, "The first two years or so after a war, as past experience reveals, are the easiest, not the hardest. . . . Economic difficulties are more likely to occur after the replacement period is over and the demand cycle produced by the war has ended."

Whatever the merits of their case, it is the people who suffer most in war. Believing, like Abraham Lincoln, that it is the people, in the last analysis, who must "mobilize the momentum of victory," Baruch did his utmost to make his experience available to his countrymen until that victory was achieved.

"We are here to make a choice between the quick and the dead. That is our business. Behind the black portent of the new atomic age lies a hope which, seized upon with faith, can work our salvation. If we fail, then we have damned every man to be the slave of Fear. Let us not deceive ourselves: We must elect World Peace or World Destruction.

— From Bernard M. Baruch's speech at the opening session of the United Nations Atomic Energy Commission, June 14, 1946.

CHAPTER 7

"A Choice Between the Quick and the Dead"

ERNARD BARUCH was approaching his seventy-fifth birthday when he began to prepare himself for the undertaking he considered the most vital of his life. It was the two-fold assignment to shape a workable plan for effective international control of atomic energy, and, as United States Representative to the United Nations Atomic Energy Commission, to promote adoption of that plan by the U.N. Commission.

The assignment was first definitely proposed in January, 1946, in a discussion with his close friend, James F. Byrnes, then Secretary of State. Baruch, along with most public-minded men, had been grappling privately with the problem for several months. It had become of dominating concern, of course, to the peoples of the world when they learned—as he later stated it—that "science has torn from nature a secret so vast in its potentialities that our minds cower from the terror it creates." That terror-breeding knowledge, coming with the details of the almost complete obliteration of Hiroshima by a single atomic bomb on August 6, 1945, and of the devastation of Nagasaki by a second bomb dropped on August 9, was immediately expanded by the very scientists who had developed the bomb in the Manhattan Project, but who were burdened with horror at the almost illimitable destructive power they had unleashed.

257

These men realized, as Baruch stated, that "the terror created by weapons has never stopped man from employing them. For each new weapon a defense has been produced in time. But now we face a condition in which adequate defense does not exist." It was their conviction, moreover, that no real defense against atomic weapons could ever be devised; that men would learn to make even more destructive atomic weapons and make them more cheaply; that other nations would inevitably acquire the secret processes used in the Manhattan Project; and finally, that if another war broke out, atomic bombs would surely destroy civilization. On the other hand, the scientists were equally sure of the almost limitless beneficial peacetime possibilities of atomic energy, if it were harnessed to work for the good of mankind.

This conviction was shared—and is still shared—by Albert Einstein, the genius whose mathematical formula, announced in 1905, was the matrix in many lands for the indefatigable research leading to successful nuclear fission. The scientists voiced their conviction in ominous statements which, in the years since, they have continued to reiterate. When first issued, the warnings magnified both mankind's instinctive terror of this ultimate force and the spontaneous demand for renunciation of atomic weapons.

It was Japan's scornful reply to the Potsdam warning which forced the decision to use the bomb—a decision recommended by an Interim Committee on Atomic Energy appointed by President Truman shortly after he became President. The Committee was headed by Secretary of War Stimson who had personally supervised the Manhattan Project from its inception. Byrnes, then without portfolio, was the President's representative on the Committee. His responsibility in atomic energy matters was extended after he became Secretary of State, on July 3, 1945, and continued until his resignation from the Cabinet.

The Committee was assisted by scientists from the bomb project and by engineers and industrialists who had constructed the huge atomic plants at Oak Ridge, Tennessee, and at Hanford, Washington, and who had devised the necessary technical processes and equipment. From the combined information set forth by both groups of consultants, the Committee concluded that another government would need at least seven years and perhaps ten to produce an atomic bomb.

Meanwhile, our own military experts estimated that to invade and conquer Japan would cost at least a million American casualties, in addition to those of other allied forces and of the enemy. Informed of this, the Interim Committee recommended the crucial bomb tests at Alamogordo, New Mexico, and use of the bomb against Japan only where war plants or military installations were located. Secretary Stimson, with President Truman's approval, selected the actual targets.

At that time, it was reported that only two atomic bombs were ready, though more powerful ones were being developed. Four days after the first atomic bomb destroyed Hiroshima, Japan offered to surrender, and on August 14, 1945 accepted the terms of the Potsdam Declaration.

The profound relief in the United States that the war was over was mixed both with awe of the weapon which shortened the war and the utmost revulsion. The devout cried out that once too often the sons of Eve had eaten of "the forbidden fruit of the tree of knowledge." Extremists in every land insisted that all known atomic weapons, stockpiles and natural sources of fissionable materials, along with the records of the successful atomic experiments, be destroyed at once. Others, aware that the clock could not be turned back so simply, urged international agreement to guarantee the use of atomic energy solely for peaceful purposes, but all of these advocates "were not so particular" —as Secretary Byrnes later stated——"about safeguards necessary to protect" the world "against a violator of the international

259

agreement." Many of these, indeed, including Americans, actually proposed that the United States renounce atomic weapons and offer to share atomic secrets even before undertaking negotiations for international atomic agreement.

Yet, however varied were the proposals in details, the peoples of the world were united in the one demand that atomic bombs be outlawed. It was a demand, as Baruch said, that "sprang from the awakened conscience of humanity."

It was during a discussion by Byrnes and Baruch of world opinion and the firmer United States policy as it was then emerging in negotiations with Russia, that the new appointment for Baruch was considered. Byrnes waited two months to press for it. He was appreciative of the fact that his own most trusted adviser "had earned a rest from public service," as he later explained, but he felt that no other available American was equally qualified for the heavy responsibility. Agreeing, President Truman sent Baruch's nomination to the Senate on March 18, 1946. The appointment was quickly confirmed and widely acclaimed.

Meanwhile, carefully examining the many aspects of the problem, Baruch had evolved what he called "the bone and sinew" of an effective control plan. The details come later.

Sitting on a bench in New York City's Central Park near his home, he set the bones in place, one by one, for consideration by his younger associate, Ferdinand Eberstadt, former Vice Chairman of the War Production Board. As he finished, Eberstadt exclaimed in almost boyish enthusiasm: "Boss, you've done great things, but you're now on the verge of the greatest! Because you're offering the world one of the most elevated programs ever given mankind. And if it's followed, it can solve not only the atom, but the entire problem of war!"

Baruch required more solemn phrases to express his own feelings about the assignment—feelings akin to awe, as he voiced it in his two major speeches to the United Nations Atomic

Energy Commission. In the first address, presenting the plan, he emphasized that international agreement for effective control of atomic energy had become imperative in mankind's quest for peace and security, and added: "I was moved, in the afternoon of my life, to add my effort to gain the world's quest."

While both phases of Baruch's atomic energy assignment were difficult, the first demanded his characteristic working habits—habits which his close associate, Herbert Bayard Swope, had once zestfully summarized in these words: "Bernie is like an elephant at a bridge. He tests every board with the utmost care, and after he is fully satisfied that it will bear his weight, sits down on the bank and waits for somebody else to cross first."

In this case, Baruch had no choice. The bridge had already been crossed by a near-herd of atomic control advisers. He had to take account of their attempts and their accomplishments. It was—as he later called it—one part of the required "historical approach." His country's concern for enduring peace also obliged him to take account of the steadily accumulating evidence since the Yalta and Potsdam Conferences that Russia was bent on expansion—a consideration of utmost importance in devising effective safeguards against violation of any international agreement for atomic control. In addition, he was also obliged to conform with the law governing our nation's membership in the United Nations.

That law requires all our representatives in the organization and its commissions to follow the policy determined by the President and transmitted through the Secretary of State. Accordingly, Baruch asked for a directive on America's official atomic energy policy, and got the answer he anticipated. Byrnes said in effect: "First, the policy must be drafted. Help do that, please."

Conferences began between Byrnes, Dean Acheson, then Under Secretary of State, Baruch, and his long-time associate, John M. Hancock. Those conferences resulted in an eleven-page statement of policy which was submitted to President Truman. The President discussed it further with Secretary Byrnes and Baruch and, after some changes, gave it back to Baruch as his directive.

The policy, as described in that directive, had been gradually shaped. The first stage in its evolution had been made public on November 15, 1945, and was known as the "Washington Agreement." It was the accord of the three governments which had cooperated in developing the new bomb, and it was formulated—during a Potomac River cruise of the presidential yacht, the *Williamsburg*—by Clement B. Attlee, then British Prime Minister, Mackenzie King of Canada, Secretary Byrnes, Lord Halifax, and their advisers.

Baruch later called this group the legal "fathers of the concept" of international atomic control. He was especially impressed by their statement:

"We are aware that the only complete protection for the civilized world from the destructive use of scientific knowledge lies in the prevention of war. No system of safeguards that can be devised will of itself provide an effective guarantee against production of atomic weapons by a nation bent on aggression. Nor can we ignore the possibility of the development of other weapons, or of new methods of warfare, which may constitute as great a threat to civilization as the military use of atomic energy."

The Washington Agreement proposed international control under the auspices of the United Nations to insure the use of atomic energy only for peaceful purposes, to outlaw major weapons, including atomic ones, which were capable of mass destruction, and to provide effective safeguards through inspection.

The phrase "through inspection" is another one which won Baruch's full approval—for reasons to be discussed later.

Secretary Byrnes, in a speech made the day after the Washington Agreement was released, emphasized the aims set forth in the document. He called the agreement "a very modest first step in what is certain to be a long and difficult journey" and warned, "Without the united efforts and unremitting cooperation of all the nations of the world, there will be no enduring and effective protection against the atomic bomb."

His prescience as to the difficulties was officially confirmed in Moscow two months later when he and Foreign Minister Ernest Bevin conferred with Molotov. They took with them a definite proposal based on the Washington Agreement and calling for establishment by the United Nations of a commission on atomic energy and all weapons capable of mass destruction. Secretary Byrnes asked that this resolution be placed at the top of the agenda. Molotov insisted that it be placed at the end. Dr. James B. Conant, who was with Byrnes as his technical adviser, sat through ten days of discussion on other issues before the atomic energy resolution was finally reached. Then Molotov proposed a few amendments which after revision were accepted.

One of these amendments—though in conformity with the United Nations Charter—later became highly controversial and evoked Baruch's grave concern. This was a provision charging the Security Council with the responsibility for issuing directions to the Atomic Energy Commission in matters affecting security. Again the veto issue was to be joined.

Molotov raised serious objections to one paragraph of the resolution providing that the work of the control agency should proceed by separate stages, and that each stage should be successfully completed before the next could be undertaken. He finally yielded on this point—one which Baruch later insisted was crucial to his whole plan.

A few days later, the atomic energy resolution drafted at

Moscow was presented to the United Nations Security Council and was adopted without amendment by a unanimous vote, January 24, 1946.

Secretary Byrnes, meanwhile, had appointed a committee to begin the preliminary work on an international atomic control plan, and had named Dean Acheson to head it. The recommendations of this committee and its board of consultants—whose chairman was David E. Lilienthal of TVA fame—came to be known as the Acheson-Lilienthal report. The evidence appears to indicate that Byrnes accepted it unenthusiastically. Certainly, the foreword he wrote to the report tended to damn it with faint praise, for he called it merely "a suitable starting point for the informed public discussion which is one of the essential factors in developing sound policy." The document, he emphasized, "is being made public not as a statement of policy but solely as a basis for such discussion."

It is significant that this report struck out the proposal for inspection which was included in the Washington Agreement, the Moscow Resolution, and the resolution adopted in January that year by the General Assembly of the United Nations. Instead, as Committee Chairman Dean Acheson pointed out in a radio discussion summarizing the report: "All dangerous activities would be carried on—not merely inspected—by a live functioning international authority. . . . This monopoly of dangerous activities would still leave a large and tremendously productive field of safe activities open to individual nations, their industries and universities."

The timing of Baruch's appointment also would seem to be significant in view of the statement by Byrnes in his book, *Speaking Frankly,* that he recommended Baruch "for the task of translating the various proposals stimulated by the Acheson-Lilienthal report into a workable plan." Note the word "workable," remembering that Byrnes was kept informed of the Committee's progress in drafting the report and that

Baruch was nominated on his recommendation ten days before the Committee's report was made public, on March 28, 1946.

Baruch's plan, freighted with meaning for the security of the United States and the peace of the world, was the work of many weeks and many minds, with Baruch making the final decisions. At the outset, he told Secretary Byrnes, "I want my gang"—the men of unusual ability he had long relied upon. This inner circle included John M. Hancock, Herbert Bayard Swope, Ferdinand Eberstadt, and Fred Searls, Jr., the mining engineer who had served with Byrnes as special assistant both in the Office of War Mobilization and in the Department of State. Baruch also had the counsel of two other men who assisted in representing the United States at sessions of the United Nations Atomic Energy Commission. These were Dr. Richard Tolman, California physicist, and Major General Thomas Farrell, who had been Major General Leslie R. Groves' alternate on the atom bomb project. Because General Groves, the project's military director from 1942 to 1945, shared all its top secrets with Major General Farrell and with him alone, Army security officers had never let them risk flying in the same plane.

Baruch and his team, in their conscientious effort to consider all pertinent information, also conferred with Dr. Robert Oppenheimer, a member of the Acheson-Lilienthal committee, and Dr. Harold Urey. Dr. Oppenheimer was director of the Los Alamos atomic laboratory and co-ordinator of the bomb-making experiments after 1942. Dr. Urey, a Nobel Prize winner, was a member of the Institute for Nuclear Studies at the University of Chicago.

The scientists continued to warn that another nation would inevitably produce atomic weapons—perhaps within seven years—but Baruch, like Byrnes, President Truman, and many other leaders and articulate citizens, felt that the United States should not hasten that inevitable day by voluntarily sharing

265

atomic information until adequate international safeguards had been established. At that time, of course, it was not suspected that Russia was already in possession of much detailed information as to the actual methods which the United States, in cooperation with the United Kingdom and Canada, had successfully used in developing the bomb—information laboriously gathered over the years by traitors and spies, including the brilliant atomic scientist, Klaus Fuchs, a German-born Communist who had become a British citizen.

The devising of an adequate system of safeguards was the particular concern of Baruch and Byrnes as they reviewed the evidence—steadily mounting after Yalta—of Russia's greed for conquest. Neither had anticipated *that* sinister development quite so soon after the war, though both had forseen that the differences in fundamental concepts of liberty and economics among the allied peoples would again come to the fore. Both men felt as did the late President Roosevelt, who had often remarked, in justifying a domestic political compromise: "You cross a bridge with the devil—until you reach the other side."

The repugnance that Baruch has felt for Communist philosophy since the rise of Soviet Russia is exceeded only by Winston Churchill's. Indeed, the mildest criticism Baruch ever made of it was voiced in an interview with Bruce Barton early in 1929, and published in the June issue that year of *The American Magazine*. The Russian people, he said then, had in their revolution "experienced a rush of liberty to the head and attempted to beat economic laws that are as fixed and unbeatable as the law of gravitation."

But dislike of Communist philosophy was the smallest part of his concern in 1946. The real issue was the maintenance of world peace, and effective control of atomic energy was a prime essential. In establishing this control, the United Nations would be strengthened, he believed.

Bernard Baruch and a Blueprint for Security

Haunted for many years by the quarrels among the Allies at Versailles in 1919, by the failure of the resulting treaty, and by America's refusal to join the League of Nations, Baruch had agreed with President Roosevelt and other leaders that a world organization should be established at the height of allied unity in the war. In addition, Baruch had proposed two collaborative peace-making bodies, a Reconstruction Council in Europe, and an Advisory Council at home—a proposal which has been discussed in an earlier chapter. He outlined the idea to President Roosevelt soon after Roosevelt's return from Yalta. Two such councils, Roosevelt conceded, could be helpful. Soon afterwards, he sent Baruch to London to discuss a number of peace questions with Prime Minister Churchill, including relations with the Soviet Union. Baruch also tried, as Secretary Stettinius had requested, to win Churchill's favor for an economic and social council in the world organization.

A few days later, Baruch was in the East Room of the White House for the funeral services of the President. Writing of those services later, Mrs. Roosevelt said it seemed to her that everyone in the world was in that East Room except three of her sons, all of them in the Armed Forces. Elliott was the only son who had been able to get back. He had flown from London in the plane with Baruch and several officials.

The report Baruch had expected to make to Roosevelt he made to President Truman on April 20, 1945. In part, it repeated a brief communication he had sent from London: "Russia unquestionably is the gravest fear of British officialdom. The Prime Minister was reassured by Mr. Roosevelt's last message to Stalin—that we intended to insist that the Russians observe their agreements."

In his full report Baruch added, "I believe we can get along with the Russians, as I expressed it to many of the British, by doing three things:

" 'a. Keep our obligations, written or implied promptly, absolutely, and meticulously, making certain the Russians are kept thoroughly posted as to what we are doing and why.

" 'b. Insist firmly they do the same thing.

" 'c. Do our homework before going to conference so that agreements are free of ambiguity and so that we have concise grasp of the policies we wish pursued.' "

Re-stating this view, essentially, in later testimony before the Senate Military Affairs Committee, he declared: "I believe we can arrive at a full understanding with the Soviets. . . . *If it is not possible, the sooner we know it, the better.*"

That belief of Baruch's, however, was steadily weakened in the months preceding his work on the atomic energy control plan. Indeed, even before President Roosevelt's death, ominous gaps—not then fully reported—were developing between Russian and American thinking and aims.

Russia quickly began to hedge on the Yalta agreements and notably, first, on the understanding that the pro-Russian Lublin government in Poland was to be re-organized. Instead, Russia hastened to enlarge that government, an initial step in making Poland a satellite nation. Other Russian moves begun at that time eventually made Rumania, too, and Bulgaria captive states. To the last, however, Roosevelt made firm efforts to halt these developments.

Deeply offended in addition by the charges Stalin made regarding a conference which the Combined Chiefs of Staff had scheduled at Bern, Switzerland, Roosevelt replied bluntly, calling these charges "vile misrepresentations." When Stalin sent a more conciliatory message on this matter, Roosevelt replied with obvious relief.

The next day, just an hour before his death, he sent a message to Churchill in response to a request for advice on a speech the Prime Minister was to make soon to the House of Commons. Believing that it was unwise at that time—when the

Allied armies were closing in on Berlin—to highlight an apparent trend toward disunity among the Allies, Roosevelt suggested that Churchill's speech minimize the general Soviet problem as much as possible "because these problems, in one form or another, seem to arise every day and most of them straighten out as in the case of the Bern meeting. We must be firm, however, and our course thus far is correct."

Since then, the need to be firm with Russia has never lessened —a need the American people began to understand as certain differences came out into the open at the first meeting of the United Nations in San Francisco. In July that summer, however, hope for an enduring united front in peace was strengthened temporarily at the Potsdam Conference of the Big Three. The agreements reached there made the Conference seem a success, but Russia's eventual violation of those agreements prompted Byrnes at last to call that conference "the success that failed."

A discussion of other phases in the deteriorating relations with Russia following Japan's surrender is outside the scope of this book, but Baruch followed them as they developed. The public, too, early in 1946, began to learn more about the difficulties Secretary Byrnes was encountering in his efforts to negotiate with Russia. It was his view that "any lasting peace must be a people's peace," and only full information could prepare the people to help consolidate it.

News of disturbing international developments, progressively emphasizing the need for a firm policy toward Soviet Russia, gradually prepared the American people to understand and to support Baruch's atomic energy plan. Summarizing it the day after it was made public, John Hancock said, "In brief, the United States has proposed an international authority with unequivocal power to exercise full and effective control over atomic energy from birth to death, and a system of swift and certain punishment for violations which shall be stigmatized as international crimes."

The Baruch plan restored the provision for inspection safe-guards, as recommended in the Washington Agreement, the Moscow Resolution, and the United Nations General Assembly resolution establishing the Atomic Energy Commission. Baruch added other safeguards—notably, the denial of the veto to the Security Council in atomic energy matters. His plan also proposed specific penalties for specified violations.

Unfortunately, however, in the months before his plan was announced, numerous other proposals, including the Acheson-Lilienthal recommendations, were being advocated—and so zealously, that the public was inevitably confused. Yet most of the efforts in this country to educate the people as to the full implications of atomic energy were made by men and women of unquestionable good-will, who were concerned about enduring world peace.

In the forefront of these were the atomic scientists who had emerged from their laboratories in the hope of saving mankind from destruction. They were speaking, writing, publishing and raising funds to make their warnings widely available. Some were working through committees made up wholly of scientists. Others, undertaking unaccustomed political activity, had joined forces with civic, religious and educational leaders.

One such widely representative group—though termed the "Scientists' Lobby"—directed its efforts to passage of *national* legislation aimed at transferring control of atomic energy from military to civilian authorities so that it might be used to bless mankind. The bill they favored was fathered by Senator Brien McMahon, who had made this cause his own soon after the destruction of Hiroshima, and whose related efforts continued till his death on July 28, 1952.

Many of the influential men and women who were members of the "Scientists' Lobby" were also active on the international front to insure the beneficial uses of atomic energy. Some of these were committed to the Acheson-Lilienthal plan long before Baruch's plan was made public, and continued their agitation for it long afterwards. Another group on the international front included some military men who had bitterly fought the McMahon Atomic Energy Act to establish a national Atomic Energy Commission with exclusive civilian control—and who continued to fight it after the Senate, passing it unanimously, referred it to the House, on June 1. Two weeks later, part of this group launched most of their same worn arguments against Baruch's plan to establish international control.

Seldom in the nation's history had there been so many strangely assorted groups vying to create opinion, but the same momentous question had bred equal confusion in all other countries that permitted freedom of speech.

To rout this confusion and "find a meeting of the minds and hearts" of the peoples of the world, as Baruch stated it, the United Nations Atomic Energy Commission had been organized. In formulating and presenting his plan, Baruch made the greatest effort of his life to be both convincing and persuasive. He wanted to win world-wide enthusiasm for the plan—the kind of enthusiasm that Eberstadt had expressed that early day in spring when they first discussed the idea on a New York park bench.

Realism, however, told Baruch that once again his favorite George Washington quotation was appropriate: "It is too probable that no plan we propose will be adopted. Perhaps another dreadful conflict is to be sustained. If, to please the people, we offer what we ourselves disapprove, how can we afterward defend our work? Let us raise a standard to which the wise and honest can repair. The event is in the hands of God."

Baruch's speech embodying the plan did not include that

271

quotation—as so many of his previous speeches had done—but it was animated by that spirit. That speech to the United Nations Atomic Energy Commission at its opening session, on June 14, 1946, was presented with all the solemnity at his command.

"We are here," he began, "to make a choice between the quick and the dead.

"That is our business.

"Behind the black portent of the new atomic age lies a hope which, seized upon with faith, can work our salvation. If we fail, then we have damned every man to be the slave of Fear. . . . We must elect World Peace or World Destruction. . . .

"Science, which gave us this dread power, shows that it can be made a giant help to humanity, but science does not show us how to prevent its baleful use. Only in the will of mankind lies the answer. It is to express this will and make it effective that we have been assembled."

At this point, Baruch began to serve notice that the United States had shaped a firm policy. "We must," he continued, "provide the mechanism to assure that atomic energy is used for peaceful purposes and preclude its use in war. To that end, we must provide immediate, swift, and sure punishment of those who violate the agreements that are reached by the nations. Penalization is essential if peace is to be more than a feverish interlude between wars. And, too, the United Nations can prescribe individual responsibility and punishment on the principles applied at Nurnberg by the Union of Soviet Socialist Republics, the United Kingdom, France, and the United States —a formula certain to benefit the world's future.

"In this crisis, we represent not only our governments but, in a larger way, we represent the peoples of the world. . . . We must answer their demands; we must answer the world's longing for peace and security.

"In that desire the United States shares ardently and hopefully. The search of science for the absolute weapon has reached fruition in this country. But she stands ready to prescribe and destroy this instrument—to lift its use from death to life—if the world will join in a pact to that end. . . . The beginning of victory for the great ideals . . . lies in building a workable plan. . . ."

Without then developing the implications of these last tactful statements, Baruch continued his appeal for united action. No human being, he emphasized, "can escape war's devastation. Victor, vanquished, and neutrals alike are affected physically, economically, and morally. . . .

"The peoples of these democracies gathered here are not afraid of an internationalism that protects; they are unwilling to be fobbed off by mouthings about narrow sovereignty, which is today's phrase for yesterday's isolation.

"The basis of a sound foreign policy, in this new age, for all the nations here gathered, is that anything that happens, no matter where or how, which menaces the peace of the world, or the economic stability, concerns each and all of us.

"That, roughly, may be said to be the central theme of the United Nations. It is with that thought we begin consideration of the most important subject that can engage mankind—life itself.

"Let there be no quibbling about the duty and the responsibility of this group and of the governments we represent."

The United States proposal for the creation of an International Atomic Development Authority, as Baruch outlined it, first briefly set forth the functions of the Authority. To it "should be entrusted all phases of the development and use of atomic energy, starting with the raw material and including—

" '1. Managerial control or ownership of all atomic-energy activities potentially dangerous to world security.

" '2. Power to control, inspect, and license all other atomic activities.

" '3. The duty of fostering the beneficial uses of atomic energy.

" '4. Research and development responsibilities . . . intended to put the Authority in the forefront of atomic knowledge and thus to enable it to comprehend, and therefore to detect, misuse of atomic energy. . . . ' "

Baruch hastened to oppose the idea that "a treaty, merely outlawing possession or use of the atomic bomb, constitutes effective fulfillment of the instructions of this Commission. Previous failures have been recorded in trying the method of simple renunciation, unsupported by effective guaranties of security and armament limitation. No one would have faith in that approach alone. . . .

"Public opinion supports a world movement toward security. The peoples want a program not composed merely of pious thoughts but of enforceable sanctions—an international law with teeth in it."

He was almost ready now to make it clear that only after such a control system with teeth in it was at work would the United States give up atomic weapons, but he prefaced the announcement diplomatically. He said, "We of this Nation, desirous of helping to bring peace to the world and realizing the heavy obligations upon us arising from our possession of the means of producing the bomb and from the fact that it is part of our armament, are prepared to make our full contribution toward effective control of atomic energy.

"When an adequate system for control of atomic energy, including the renunciation of the bomb as a weapon, has been agreed upon and put into effective operation and condign punishments set up for violations of the rules of control which are to be stigmatized as international crimes, we propose that—

" '1. Manufacture of atomic bombs shall stop;

" '2. Existing bombs shall be disposed of pursuant to the terms of the treaty; and—

" '3. The Authority shall be in possession of full information as to the know-how for the production of atomic energy.' "

Any agreements by the United States, Baruch emphasized, would be "subject, of course, to our constitutional processes and to an adequate system of control becoming fully effective. . . .

"Now as to violations: In the agreement, penalties of as serious a nature as the nations may wish and as immediate and certain in their execution as possible should be fixed for—

" '1. Illegal possession or use of an atomic bomb;

" '2. Illegal possession, or separation, of atomic material suitable for use in an atomic bomb;

" '3. Seizure of any plant or other property belonging to or licensed by the Authority;

" '4. Willful interference with the activities of the Authority;

" '5. Creation or operation of dangerous project in a manner contrary to, or in the absence of, a license granted by the International control body.'

"It would be a deception, to which I am unwilling to lend myself, were I not to say to you and to our peoples that the matter of punishment lies at the very heart of our present security system. It might as well be admitted, here and now, that the subject goes straight to the vote power contained in the Charter of the United Nations. . . . The Charter permits penalization only by concurrence of each of the five great powers—the Union of Soviet Socialist Republics, the United Kingdom, China, France and the United States. . . .

"There must be no veto to protect those who violate their solemn agreements not to develop or use atomic energy for destructive purposes.

"The bomb does not wait upon debate. To delay may be to die. The time between violation and preventive action or punishment would be all too short for extended discussion as to the course to be followed. . . ."

A similar control system with a similar "guarantee of safety,"

Baruch said, could be established for "other weapons-bacter-iological, biological, gas—perhaps—why not?—against war itself.

"In the elimination of war lies our solution, for only then will nations cease to compete with one another in the production and use of dread 'secret' weapons. . . . If we succeed in finding a suitable way to control atomic weapons, it is reasonable to hope that we may also preclude the use of other weapons adaptable to mass destruction. When a man learns to say 'A' he can, if he chooses, learn the rest of the alphabet, too. . . ."

Peace, he continued, can be made secure only by "agreement fortified by sanctions. . . . We are now facing a problem more of ethics than of physics. The solution will require apparent sacrifice in pride and in position, but better pain as the price of peace than death as the price of war."

Baruch re-emphasized this theme in his closing appeal, "All of us want to stand erect, with our faces to the sun, instead of being forced to burrow into the earth, like rats. The pattern of salvation must be worked out by all for all. The light at the end of the tunnel is dim, but our path seems to grow brighter as we actually begin our journey. We cannot yet light the way to the end. However, we hope the suggestions of my Government will be illuminating."

He concluded with a paraphase of Abraham Lincoln, "We know how to save peace. The world knows that we do. We, even we here, hold the power and the responsibility.

"We shall nobly save, or meanly lose, the last, best hope of earth. The way is plain, peaceful, generous, just—a way which followed, the world will forever applaud."

Editors of the nation's leading newspapers and radio commentators called Baruch's speech and plan a masterly compound of imaginative idealism and tough practicality. That plan,

President Truman emphasized in a press conference, had the endorsement of both the White House and the State Department and was the official United States recommendation to the world. Referring to it sometime later when he laid the United Nations cornerstone, Truman declared, "I am for the American proposals until we get something better."

There was united approval of all the exalted sentiments Baruch had expressed, but many American citizens who could not in fairness be called either Communist or pro-Communist felt that at too many points in the speech the tone was aggressive. These spokesmen insisted that there is a distinct difference between appeasement and the conciliatory manner usually deemed especially wise at the initial stage of negotiations on a specific international issue. However, many of the sincerely patriotic citizens who expressed this view were either not then fully informed or sufficiently concerned as to the evidence of Russia's aim to expand.

In any case, Baruch had become accustomed since Versailles to state his recommendations to Congressional Committees forthrightly, if not on an actual "either or" basis. He usually included a warning on those occasions that failure to adopt his proposals would imperil the nation's well-being. He enjoyed follow-up conferences with old friends among Congressional leaders, but he was not too happy that summer and fall of 1946 under the international spotlight required—as his idol, Woodrow Wilson had stated it—for "open convenants openly arrived at," with open-eyed questioning of the view that absolutes can be wholly contained in any one human concept.

The definite proposals he set forth at intervals in his first major address to the Commission were seized upon for further controversy—in America and other lands—by various factions with various motives. Some were merely naive. Some were sinister. But Russian propaganda exploited the controversy.

A paramount issue with Russia, of course, was the announced

determination by the United States to keep atomic armament until after the control system was established. Another major issue was the insistence upon treaty safeguards—denial of the veto in atomic energy matters and prompt punishment for violations. In addition, a number of the fourteen specific measures Baruch outlined as essential to the control system—and, indeed, the very order in which all the measures were to be established —were also hotly debated.

Two of these measures included provisions for control and inspection by the IADA (International Atomic Development Authority) of "intrinsically dangerous activities"—even those concerned with the mining of fissionable materials—and complete "freedom of access, ingress and egress" for inspection in any area. In short, no iron curtain would be possible if these provisions became law.

Other measures provided for world-wide inventory by IADA of fissionable raw materials—uranium and thorium. In emphasizing that the comprehensive survey of these natural deposits should be "one of the earliest purposes" of the Authority, Baruch stated that "the precise pattern of control" of these deposits would depend upon the yet-to-be ascertained widely varied "geological, mining, refining and economic factors."

The Baruch plan expressed "neither an endorsement nor a disapproval of the creation of national atomic authorities," but recommended that any such national organizations should be subordinate to IADA. Both national and private enterprise, functioning under necessary IADA inspection, and using raw materials provided by IADA, would be free to operate "safe" power piles and to produce and use radioactive isotopes for research, clinical and other applications. Radioactive isotopes produced by IADA itself could also be distributed for peacetime use.

In an overall reference to national activities, Baruch specifically stated, "there should be as little interference as may be with the economic plans and the present private, corporate and state relationships in the countries involved." That loose statement went much too far to suit extreme nationalists in most countries, including America, and much too far to suit the Soviet government.

Another contested aspect of the plan was the provision that the work of IADA should proceed by separate stages, and that the Authority must be convinced by inspection that one stage of the work was proceeding satisfactorily before it began the next stage. This provision, preventing even the full exchange of atomic information until after the system of controls was in operation, was embodied in the General Assembly Resolution establishing the Atomic Energy Commission. It was the one provision to which Molotov objected when Secretary Byrnes first presented it at Moscow, but which he finally accepted. That agreement, however,—as Byrnes stated later—proved to be one "the Soviet wants the world to forget and which it urgently desires to see superseded."

The Soviet counter-proposal to the United Nations Atomic Energy Commission was definitely concerned with "stages." A crucial difference was that certain steps proposed in the Russian plan were to be taken in reverse order from the comparable stages outlined by Baruch. Specifically, Russia insisted that all existing bombs and atomic stockpiles be destroyed before other control devices were in operation, and within three months after the outlawing of atomic weapons by an international convention. Exchange of full information on atomic energy was another step that Russia proposed for early action.

In addition, the Soviet plan provided that within six months after the signing of the convention, legislation should be enacted to provide severe penalties for the violators—a provision immediately violated in Baruch's view by Soviet insistence on retaining the veto right in the Security Council on all security questions including atomic energy.

The Soviet plan was presented by Andrei A. Gromyko on June 19, 1946, five days after Baruch's proposal. Shortly afterwards came the Army-Navy atomic tests at Bikini, and the urgent need to reach an agreement was re-emphasized. Human imagination again proved unable to cope with the vast destructive potentialities evoked despite extensive radio, news and picture coverage of the tests. For these images were, after all, impersonal. A far greater assault on human emotions came in August with a detailed account by John Hersey of what had happened to the people of Hiroshima. *The New Yorker* devoted the entire text of one issue to this story of death, shock and anguish as Hersey pieced it together in talk with a handful of survivors. Quickly re-published in book form, it stimulated further public demands for the outlawing of atomic weapons.

Meanwhile, Baruch himself was deeply concerned. Apparently, he came to the conclusion that salvation from this superhuman force depended a great deal upon his renewed efforts. The debates in the Atomic Energy Commission reminded him too painfully of the wrangling at Versailles. Russia's insistence on retention of the veto brought back the bitterness of the fight in this country against Article X of the League of Nations Covenant—the article that put teeth in the agreement. It shocked him now to remember that he himself had urged Wilson to compromise on this point. At that time, his plea was "half a loaf is better than none," but Wilson saw reservations to the article as nullification and declared, "If I should accept that, I would be false to every young man who lies dead in Flanders."

"We know now he was right," Baruch declared. Actually he had taken an adamant position on the atomic veto question soon after accepting the assignment. When he first learned that the Acheson-Lilienthal plan made no provision for violation of the agreement, he decided, as reported in W. L. White's book,

Bernard Baruch, that it was—in Herbert Swope's words—"a set of pious platitudes like the Kellogg-Briand treaties." White stated that, in conference with Dean Acheson at Blair House in Washington, Swope asked, "What are you going to do if they don't behave?" Acheson, turning to Baruch, said, "Is this your question?" Baruch's nod brought the comment, "I suggest it be left to juridical interpretation."

Unable to accept that suggestion in the spring of 1946, Baruch was incensed in September by the suggestions of Henry Wallace, then Secretary of Commerce, regarding both the veto and the time-schedule for the proposed controls. These suggestions were made in a letter Wallace wrote to the President on July 23 about foreign policy. The letter, emphasizing his concern for world peace, was not published in the press until September 18 —at the height of the controversy over the speech Wallace had recently made at Madison Square Garden. The speech, like the letter, recommended a more conciliatory approach to Soviet Russia.

Wallace had long been widely criticized for views sympathetic to the Chinese Communists. He had aired those opinions in 1944 during and after his trip to the Far East, when he repeatedly stated that the Chinese Civil War had led to a great forward march by the "common man." At that time, he also began to assume a more vocal role as "apologist" for Russia— as critics interpreted his various attempts to influence foreign policy in the five-year period through 1948 when he ran for president on the Progressive Party ticket. It was not until the winter of 1950-51 that Wallace recanted in part through statements in *Coronet Magazine* and *Reader's Digest,* and not until September 5, 1952 that he made the full confession so proverbially good for the soul. Then, in an article published by *This Week Magazine,* he frankly declared, "I was wrong about" the Soviet Communists. Yet he emphasized that he was still proud of having risked his public career in an effort "to promote peace" at a time when it was "very unpopular to talk about such things." After 1949, he concluded, "I became more and more disgusted with Soviet methods and finally became convinced that the Politburo wanted the cold war continued indefinitely, even at the peril of accidentally provoking a hot war."

Wallace couldn't see the faintest sign of that Politburo aim when he wrote President Truman the notorious letter criticizing Baruch's atomic energy proposals.

Baruch's team, conferring with Wallace, asked him for a public retraction of certain statements in the letter, but failed to get satisfaction. Consequently, in a special memorandum to the President, Baruch denounced Wallace's letter, listing "misstatements under five headings," and pointing out "some mistaken conclusions which were the inevitable result of the errors of fact."

The most emphatic part of the memorandum was aimed at Wallace's statement, "The Russian counter-proposal itself is an indication that they may be willing to negotiate seriously if we are. In some respects their counter-proposal goes even further than our plan and is in agreement with the basic principles of our plan."

On the contrary, Baruch declared: "The U. S. delegation has hoped upon exploration of the Soviet plan it would be found to contemplate creation of machinery for holding violators . . . accountable before an international tribunal and for punishing them. . . ." However, he continued, the delegation had been unable to get assurance on this point from Soviet representatives whose idea of "serious international crime is not accompanied by any machinery for enforcement other than an appeal to the Security Council with the veto intact to serve as a possible shield to the violator." The Soviet proposal for national legislation, Baruch conceded, might "prevent misuse of atomic energy by private individuals within a country, but it would of course have no effect on the national governments themselves.

Moreover, the Soviet proposals contain no suggestions for international preventive control measures as contrasted with punishment after an offense. Obviously, prevention is the essence of control."

The memorandum closed with this warning: "any modification which achieved agreement but failed to provide effective control and safeguards . . . and to give timely warnings of violations would merely create a false sense of security. Such an agreement would be directly contrary to the specific and unanimous instructions of the United Nations. It would be a fraud on the peoples of the world."

Baruch also released a statement to the press blasting the Wallace letter as "misinformation or complete distortion" and upbraiding him for refusal to correct the errors. "You have no monopoly on the desire for peace," he pointed out. "I have given thirty years of my life" to search for it.

Byrnes wired Baruch, "I've seen blockbusters, but nothing so complete."

A month later President Truman was moved to repudiate Wallace and, though his exit from the Cabinet did not still the clamor over Wallace's views, it did ease Baruch's task in winning the support of the Commission for the United States plan. It certainly settled the question it had raised in the minds of some Commission representatives whose votes were not yet committed: Would the President repudiate Baruch?

Efforts to round up those votes continued from June until late September. Baruch refused to deal with one French delegate, the scientist and Communist, Joliot-Curie, who did not confine his pro-Russian talking to sessions of the Commission. He made one such speech at the July World Control Institute held in Washington by the National Committee on Atomic Information and seventy sponsoring national organizations.

After he and other French Communist delegates returned to Paris, favorable negotiations with Count de la Rose, the man they left behind, were speeded.

Baruch and Gromyko presumably got along well personally, but neither made any appreciable dent in the other's views. In fact, Eberstadt told Baruch in August, "Boss, we've got a short sale here." He was convinced by then that the Russians didn't want any real agreement, but Baruch insisted that a "decent respect for the opinions of mankind" required them to keep on trying for agreement till the facts were clear to the world.

Baruch's team seized numerous opportunities outside the Commission to explain the United States proposal and to influence world opinion. Baruch himself won more converts in his speech, on October 8, 1948, accepting the Freedom House award.

Mrs. Eleanor Roosevelt presented the award, and in turn he voiced this tribute. "She represents a spirit that was given flesh by her great husband, Franklin Delano Roosevelt, who was never more needed than at this moment of peril and confusion, for he was unafraid."

The words on the Freedom House plaque provided the text for Baruch's talk, "There must be no veto for those who violate their solemn agreements." He re-emphasized the fact that the American proposals—so "generous and just"—had the full authorization of the President, the Secretary of State, and Senatorial advisers. "America," he repeated, "stands ready to insure the world's security from atomic warfare. But it must be a realistic working pact—not merely a pious expression of intent.

"The Soviets," he added, "protest that inspection violates national sovereignty. Better that than international disaster. America is willing to accept inspection as a control measure and for some time America would be the one most inspected."

Another telling point followed, "It is important to understand that the methods of creating atomic energy for peace purposes and for war use are the same up to a very advanced point. In obtaining atomic energy for peaceful uses, you have gone about 75 per cent of the way toward a deadly weapon."

Soon afterwards, Herbert Bayard Swope explained the plan at a New York meeting of the Foreign Policy Association. The State Department quickly protested that one of his answers during the question period was regrettably undiplomatic. When asked what would happen if the Russians didn't agree to the American atomic proposals, Swope flatly said, "There will be no agreement."

It was by no means easy to get even British acceptance of all the American proposals. One British delegate gave this explanation, "We know you have the bomb, but the Russians have guided missiles." Naturally, the representatives from countries nearer the Soviet borders also hesitated to declare their support of the plan. But gradually the necessary votes came in sight.

Meanwhile, delaying tactics of the Russians were being displayed at sessions of the Council of Foreign Ministers, and at the General Assembly of the United Nations. Molotov, in the Assembly, had presented a proposal for general disarmament which Secretary Byrnes believed was obviously designed to combine the Atomic Energy Commission with a General Disarmament Commission—and so to prolong the debate endlessly.

In November, when the Council of Foreign Ministers met in New York, Baruch and his associates conferred with Byrnes. They pointed out that the terms of two members of the Commission would expire December 31, and if no action was taken by that date Gromyko would probably move, in January, to postpone further action on the grounds that the two new members would require time to study the problems.

"I knew they were right," Byrnes said, "and agreed that they should act at once."

Accordingly, Baruch on December 5, 1946 presented his plea for immediate action. His speech to the Commission set forth a series of general findings and recommendations that encompassed the original American plan and had resulted from over seventy meetings by the Commission and its committees during the six months' period.

"The debates on disarmament in the General Assembly," he pointed out, had "followed closely the proposals laid down by the United States on June 14 before this body. It remains, however, the responsibility of this Commission to submit definite plans to the Security Council . . . . I entreat all to join in the enterprise so that we may show speed, as well as vision, in our assignment. . . .

"I beg you to remember that to delay may be to die. I beg you to believe that the United States seeks no special advantage. I beg you to hold fast to the principle of seeking the good of all, and not the advantage of one."

He emphasized that "through the acid test of deliberation and debate, before this Commission and before the public opinion of the world," the original proposals of the United States had been proven generous and just and that the discussion had always come back to them. "We have heard words that sometimes seemed to be steering us away from our goal, only later to hear others that led us back toward it. . . .

"The price we have set upon the surrender of the absolute weapon," Baruch continued, "is a declaration of peaceful intent and of interdependence among the nations of the world, expressed in terms of faith and given strength by sanctions—punishments to be meted out by concerted action against wilful offenders. That is one of the great principles of the United Nations—justice for all, supported by force. But there can be no unilateral disarmament by which America gives up the bomb, to no result except our own weakening. That shall never be.

"It is for us to accept, or to reject—if we dare, this doctrine of salvation. It springs from stark necessity, and that is inexorable."

He emphasized, however, that the United States, first to lay down a plan of cooperative control, hoped for the adherence of all. "We seek especially the participation of the Soviet Union," he said. "We welcome the recent authoritative statements of its highest representatives. From these, we are justified in concluding that it no longer regards the original American proposals unacceptable, as a whole or in their separate parts, as its member of this body stated at an earlier meeting.

"I repeat—we welcome cooperation but we stand upon our basic principles, even if we stand alone. . . .

"The time for action is here. Each of us perceives clearly what must be done. We may differ as to details. We are in accord as to purpose."

Presenting resolutions including detailed recommendations for study and consideration, Baruch called for another special meeting of the Commission, as early as convenient, to act upon them "so that the position each nation takes on them may be recorded in this Commission's report which must be drafted by December 20, and presented to the Security Council by December 31."

The Commission, with the Soviet Union and Poland abstaining, voted to meet the deadlines and it did better. On December 30, again with the Soviet Union and Poland abstaining, the Commission voted to submit its first report to the Security Council. That report closely followed the second American draft, which differed from the original plan in phraseology but not in essence.

His mission accomplished, Baruch submitted his final report to Secretary Byrnes on the last day of 1946, promptly resigned and was lauded by the President and the people.

287

Now, six years later, the earnest prophecy Baruch included in his final appeal to the Commission has caught up with us. "Time," he said then, "is two-edged. It not only forces us nearer to our doom, if we do not save ourselves, but, even more horrendous, it habituates us to existing conditions which, by familiarity, seem less and less threatening.

"Once our minds have been conditioned to that sort of thinking, the keen edge of danger is blunted, and we are no longer able to see the dark chasm on the brink of which we stand."

The peoples of the world—unable through their governments to obtain the international atomic control agreement which alone could pull mankind back from the "dark chasm" have, indeed, become "conditioned" to living under this condition. Further evidence that the Soviet Union preferred the stalemate developed soon after Baruch's resignation.

The delaying tactics came in the Security Council of the United Nations. At about the same time that the Council received the recommendations of the Atomic Energy Commission in January, 1947, it also received a resolution from the General Assembly calling for action on the problem of general disarmament—the resolution which Soviet representatives had initiated and which they immediately insisted should be considered first. This proposal struck Byrnes as folly—the same kind of "folly it would have been, when gunpowder was discovered to start disarming by limiting the use of the bow and arrow." The majority in the Council, apparently feeling the same way, voted to begin debate on the relative merits of the two atomic plans—the one proposed by the Atomic Energy Commission and based on the American proposals, and the counter-proposal of the Soviet Union.

Unable during three months to reconcile the two plans, the Council on March 10 returned the subject to the Commission with instructions to report back by September. The Commission then appointed two committees, one of which attempted to work out the details of an atomic energy treaty based on the American plan. The other tried to reconcile Russian and American proposals. After negotiations in these committees eventually broke down, the problem of atomic control was assigned to the United Nations Disarmament Commission.

Meanwhile, Albert Einstein again warned, "The secret of the atomic bomb is the American Maginot line. It gives us security in imagination. To that extent, it is a great danger." Confirmation of this view came not long after with the White House announcement of the first explosion of an atomic bomb in Russia.

Then came the futile argument as to how much of that Soviet success was due to the information Russia received from Dr. Klaus Fuchs—whose Russian contact in London was instructed to carry a book appropriately entitled *Try and Stop Me*—and from other spies and traitors including Allan Nunn May, Bruno Pontecorvo, Ethel Rosenberg, Harry Gold, and David Greenglass. The one certain fact is that American, British, and Canadian security regulations failed to prevent the leakage of atomic data.

Now, however, it is the considered judgment of many of our scientists, including Dr. Ralph E. Lapp, that Soviet espionage probably shortened their A-project time-schedule by only a few months; that America tended to discount the ability of the Russian atomic scientists and of the Nazi scientists captured by the Soviets on the fall of Germany; and that, from the outset, we "sadly underestimated the Soviet technological and industrial capacity."

Are we still underestimating that capacity? Baruch's testimony of May, 1952, to the Senate Preparedness Subcommittee warned against that kind of over-confidence. It was another forceful reminder that we have no new Maginot Line in the hydrogen bomb—even though it may have about ten times the effectiveness of the bomb dropped on Nagasaki; nor in the other varied atomic armaments supplementing H-bombs, including the misnamed "baby" A-bombs. Some of the baby bombs are light enough to be carried by fighter planes launched from carrier decks, some are adapted to fit into howitzer projectiles.

Basing his warning on an authoritative statement by General Omar Bradley, Baruch declared that by 1954 "the Soviet atomic stockpile may be large enough so that our superiority in atomic weapons may no longer serve as sufficient deterrent against possible aggression."

But earnest efforts are still being continued in the United Nations Disarmament Commission for international agreement —with the essential features Baruch proposed—to stop this race in atomic and other mass destruction weapons. Benjamin V. Cohen, United States deputy representative to the Commission, said recently: "When one works in the field of disarmament one must acquire great patience . . . . I entertain great hope that we can make progress in the long run.

"Until that agreement is achieved, we must maintain a precarious balance by strength."

While this balance is maintained, it is still not too late to make the choice "between the quick and the dead"—between "world peace or world destruction."

As this account is written—on November 17, 1952—there has just appeared in the press an official announcement that "experiments contributing" to hydrogen-bomb research were completed recently during tests on Eniwetok atoll in the mid-Pacific. This announcement from the United States Atomic Energy Commission was necessitated because letters had been received in this country from personnel with the Bikini forces reporting that another and greater atomic explosion had taken place on the atoll on November 1.

There seems to be little doubt that either a hydrogen bomb has been exploded, or final tests have been completed which will make possible the explosion of this super-bomb. This, it appears, confirms the prediction made by Dr. Ralph Lapp, writing in *The Saturday Evening Post* of October 25, 1952, that "the greatest explosion the eye of man has ever seen" would one day soon take place.

Not only has Dr. Lapp provided the first reliable information on the structure, cost and development of the hydrogen bomb, but he publicized this startling fact: "So great an authority as Dr. Hans A. Bethe, the pioneer in the thermo-nuclear, or hydrogen field, has even said that the Soviet Union may explode the hydrogen bomb before this country. The intelligence experts are slightly more optimistic. They believe that we are still a little ahead of the Russians in this race, but their best guess is that the Soviet hydrogen bomb will be exploded next year, and at the latest in 1954."

Dr. Bethe obviously is wrong about who will have the H-bomb first, but it remains to be seen how long it will take the Soviets to produce such a bomb.

It is Dr. Lapp's opinion that we shall know of any Soviet hydrogen explosion as soon as it happens. He doesn't explain how—presumably for security reasons—but there is no reason to question it. In any case, we can be sure that this news will not come from Moscow. The Soviets have not to date confirmed our knowledge of their first atomic explosion in September, 1949, except in a radio broadcast, picked up in London on November 2, 1952, that declared: "Soviet scientific achievements in atomic energy are greatly outstripping other countries."

Since this announcement came less than a month after Soviet claims to having first invented gunpowder, the lawnmower, "beizbol," and other American achievements, one could be forgiven for questioning Soviet claims about atomic energy. However, it is clear that Americans might be well advised to reserve their opinions on this vital subject and not feel too complacent about our security.

"In all my life, now past the Biblical allotment of three score and ten years, never before have I seen so rich an opportunity for deathless service as is presented to us here. I want my country associated with victory in this great crusade. For myself, as I look upon a long past and too short a future, I believe the finest epitaph would be—'He helped to bring lasting peace to the world.'"

—Statement by U. S. Representative Bernard M. Baruch to the United Nations Atomic Energy Commission, December 5, 1946.

CHAPTER 8

"A Long Past and Too Short a Future"

I N EARLIER CHAPTERS the reader has had an opportunity to read selections from Baruch's own public testimony and writings. In this way, the basic outlines of his lifelong crusade for peace through strength have been provided. At this point, it should be possible to look into the future and correlate Baruch's long-held views with the immediate problems that face us today and will face us in the days to come.

Recently, much has occurred to justify a reappraisal of Baruch's opinions. A new President is taking over the reins of office. A Party long out of power has assumed again the responsibility of administering the domestic and foreign affairs of the United States. A world barely accustomed to the deadly potentiality of the A-bomb has been asked to face, in the experimental explosion of an H-bomb, a destructive force more deadly still.

In what respects will such new developments alter the recommendations of Bernard Baruch? Doubtless, there will be very little change in the fundamental concepts that Baruch has been preaching these many years. There may be changes in his suggestions as to how those fundamentals should be applied, but they are apt to be changes in application rather than design. So basic has been Baruch's original thinking, so direct and forthright has been his approach to the eternal problems of leadership among nations, that a forecast of a possible program he might recommend to President Eisenhower will serve equally well as a summary of the highlights of this book.

We have seen that Baruch fears inflation more than almost any other danger that confronts our domestic affairs. We know from his repeated statements that he believes wholeheartedly in military strength in being; in existing weapons, and in men trained to use them, rather than in paper plans and drawing-board designs.

We are aware that Baruch constantly has urged an ever-ready defense mobilization organization, prepared at any moment to throw our industrial might into high gear for the supply of necessary armaments. He has stated repeatedly that he believes such a defense mobilization organization should be headed by one man with authority to take prompt and vigorous action in the event of attack.

We know, too, that Baruch has long emphasized the need for waging peace with the same energy that we as a nation have always been willing to devote to war. Paul Hoffman, in his dynamic book, *Peace Can Be Won*, cited a typical Baruch admonition. "You'll never make people understand the true character of this fight," Mr. Hoffman writes, "until you stop talking about the 'cold war' and start talking about waging the peace." Baruch has told Congress many times that it is vital for our country to state its peace aims in terms so clear and so positive that no potential enemy can misunderstand them. He has always believed that those aims should be pursued as diligently at the conference table as on the battle field.

The reader knows how deeply Baruch believes that we must have the help of other nations in striving toward our peace objectives, and how convinced he has been of the necessity for helping our allies without reducing them to the level of dependents. Self-aid, Baruch has counseled, should be a condition of our aid.

Baruch's recommendations, as the U. S. Representative to the United Nations Atomic Energy Commission, demonstrated his absolute belief in the urgency of an agreed-upon international control plan which would turn nightmare weapons into useful sources of power for the whole civilized world. Advised of the successful H-bomb test, Baruch told reporters on November 15, 1952 that it was reassuring to know the United States was going forward with the improvement of nuclear bombs.

"But," he added characteristically, "I think we should speed up atomic energy for peaceful purposes. With a little more drive and courage we will soon accomplish what the United States has striven for—its useful peaceful activity that will lift the burdens from mankind's back."

Finally, the most casual perusal of Baruch's counsel to his fellow countrymen makes it plain that he believes we can and should pay as we go, no matter what the cost. Baruch has pointed out repeatedly that we must be prepared to make sacrifices, to syphon off excess spending power, and to eliminate profiteering as the price of peace.

With these facts in mind, the author has advanced later in this chapter a sketch of Baruch's probable recommendations to the new Administration. There is little doubt that his views will be sought. Indeed, much of his long-held philosophy has become a part of the credo of both major political parties almost without our being aware of its penetrating influence. In an article in the *New York Times Magazine* of November 2, 1952, Governor Adlai Stevenson, then campaigning for the Presidency, wrote a passage that was almost pure Baruch in its concept and phrasing. The Governor's statement read:

"Most people are now agreed on the basic direction of our foreign policy: to join in collective action, with other free nations and through the United Nations, in building strength—military, economic, moral—to prevent Communist aggression; to defeat Communist subversion; and to create free, viable, and progressive societies on our side of the Iron Curtain. This is a massive, costly and heroic policy, but it offers the only present hope of achieving peace and restoring liberty to the millions now dominated by the Soviet empire."

General Eisenhower, in his Los Angeles address to the Veterans of Foreign Wars, on August 5, 1952, outlined his hopes for the American people in a declaration which drew heavily upon the policies Baruch has been urging for years. As if to underline his source, the Republican candidate added: "I believe if Bernie Baruch were here tonight, he would subscribe to every one of them. He would be one with you in saying, 'We can do it.' We will do it because we are Americans. And let me assert my faith, this faith in America. There is no human task, nothing within the realm of possibility, that the combined strength of 156,000,000 people cannot do.

"If we will dedicate our minds to worthy purposes, lift up our hearts in determination that it shall be done, there is no foreign power that can challenge us. There is no task in the foreign field that can defeat our leadership, our efforts to make it strong to serve our interests and the interests of others in the free world."

Baruch himself could not have said it better!

In the work the author performed as Executive Director of the Institute on Economics of Defense Mobilization, he was exposed to many views of the problems Mr. Baruch has emphasized so consistently—the problems we continue to face as a nation. Top Government officials appeared to present their first-hand descriptions of the roles their agencies play in the defense mobilization program, and to answer questions from the audience. Leaders in other fields presented their judgments as to the impact of government actions on their respective segments of the economy. The Chairman of the Munitions Board, John D. Small, summed up the situation with clarity and candor when he appeared before the Institute and reported:

"Your Government is engaged in a task of building up its armed strength so that we, along with other free people, may be in a better position to preserve our liberties and our freedoms against the forces of aggression which threaten, and in fact have already broken, the peace of the world.

"We need to strengthen our armed forces quickly and because of this need for haste, the job is difficult. The heart of our armed forces is the American fighting man, but the muscle consists of the ships, tanks, guns, and bombers, the fighting aircraft and the other instruments of war with which he carries out his fighting mission. To provide these modern weapons is our job—your job and mine—through the joint effort of a team made up of Government, industry and labor. . . .

"We are in a stage now of very real and very great danger. We have been in that danger for a year or more. We do not know from day to day what will happen. It could well be by intention or by accident that we might be thrown into a state of all-out war at any moment. Or it may well be that we will have to undergo a long test of endurance, a long period of tension, during which we must maintain strength—strength in being, positive strength which will deter, and we hope prevent, the aggressor from striking.

"We are building that strength, we are using time to advantage, we are making very real progress, and we will achieve victory should the need arise."

To the author these words indicate, in addition to Mr. Baruch's statements, that the time is—and has been—ripe for the adoption of many of Bernard Baruch's most frequently repeated recommendations. Thus, some of Mr. Baruch's major proposals have been synthesized by the author into a nine-point program. Furthermore, as stated earlier, it is the author's personal conviction that these points may well be the type of counsel Mr. Baruch will have occasion to present to President Eisenhower and the new Administration.

In advancing this nine-point blueprint for security, the author wishes to indicate clearly that the list is advanced as his own estimate based on a review of previous statements made by Mr. Baruch. In essence, the items are a summary of his principal proposals, adapted to present conditions and supported by pertinent quotations from Mr. Baruch's own statements.

The estimate of Bernard Baruch's recommendations for action in the period ahead is as follows:

A BLUEPRINT FOR SECURITY

1. Mobilize sufficiently to guarantee the maintenance of our minimum security. The present defense mobilization organization, although an improvement, has not been adequately geared to perform this function.

> "Any budget cuts that are made must not reduce our fighting strength—in men or in weapons. Far from slowing down, our security requires that we step up our defenses both in speed and scale if the peace is to be won. There comes a time when you have got to have weapons in being and not on the drawing-board. Some clearly designated person must decide when to stop improving and start producing. . . . Under the program which was adopted, we have gotten neither adequate security, nor a healthy economy."

2. *The President must be provided with authority by the Congress to continue anti-inflation controls for as long as this country is in peril.*

"Needless inflation already has cost us 12 billion dollars in high costs of defense and is likely to exact another 10 billion dollars in needless tribute over the next fiscal [1953]. . . . We can still step up our defense program and avoid further inflation by reducing all unnecessary and postponable expenditures by imposing the necessary controls. . . . The inflationary havoc we have suffered has been mainly the result of the failure to mobilize properly."

3. *We can and should maintain such taxes as may be required to eliminate profiteering, pay all defense costs, and absorb excess spending power.*

"Our economy can do all that our security requires—and more—provided there is the will to do so and the courage of the administration to channel our resources from less essential to more essential activities and to share the costs of the struggle equitably. . . . Congress should adopt a defense budget which fits the risks we face. Cut the budget where you can, with safety—not where it will imperil our security."

4. *We must not only help the free nations of Europe in rebuilding their defenses during the cold war, but we also must bolster those who are opposing the Communists in the hot war raging in Southeast Asia.*

"We must organize ourselves so that first things come first through our entire economy, through everything we do. That is our responsibility to our men in Korea, in Europe, and other fronts."

301

5. *A general staff for peace should formulate a global stra-*
tegy for peace-waging with a single agency abroad to
coordinate our efforts.

"Even during the current state of undeclared war, the
extension of a stockpile of weapons would be an enormous
boon to the free peoples of the world. Such weapons would
enable us to render swift assistance to any nation threatened by aggression in the future. We could take instant
advantage of any opportunity that might arise for arming
some ally. We would be prepared if events forced an
abrupt increase in our Armed Forces, since men can be
recruited more rapidly than munitions."

6. *We still must have pools of trained men and quick pro-*
duction of all the weapons we need—plus ample reserve
stocks.

"No decisive victory in the cold war is possible as long as
the Soviets hold as terrifying an edge in military readiness
over the West as they do today. As long as this disparity
exists, there is no basis for peace in the world. This disparity is one of *actual* weapons on hand. It can be filled
by getting ready to produce or by merely expanding productive capacity. . . . Obviously, we must strive constantly
to improve our weapons. But no aggressor was ever stopped
by blueprints."

7. *A realistic control plan for atomic and hydrogen weap-*
ons, based on the U. S. proposals to the United Nations,
must be achieved soon.

"Our highest military authorities have stated, unequivocally, that from now [May, 1952] through 1954 will be
the point of maximum peril for this nation. . . . The Soviet

atomic stockpile may be large enough so our superiority in atomic weapons will no longer serve as a sufficient deterrent against possible aggression. . . . We must elect World Peace or World Destruction. . . ."

8. *We still must define our peace terms to the Kremlin, working through the United Nations. Only after we have done this can we determine whether Korea will be the only arena in which it will be necessary to defend our freedom.*

> "We must spell out our peace aims and at the same time be strong enough to support and enforce them. . . . In that way we achieve peace and avoid war, and only in that way. There are certain people who only understand strength. They sneer at weakness, no matter how noble the aim of the seeker after peace."

9. *To insure security in the free world, we must demonstrate, through resolute conviction and whatever sacrifices are necessary, our determination to preserve our freedom at any cost—to achieve that all-important condition of readiness: peace through strength.*

> "It is no solution of a problem to ignore it, and it is no argument against doing a thing to say that it is administratively difficult. . . . We have to stop backing into things, to stop postponing unpleasant decisions and trying to do things and not do things at the same time. Let us tackle the job that has to be done and get it over with. . . . Whatever organization or plan may be adopted for industrial mobilization, I know all Americans will join in endeavoring to make it a success. There must be no holding back or sulking because we do not approve of this or that particular plan or the personalities involved."

Most of the statements which have been quoted in support of the blueprint were in Mr. Baruch's testimony of May 28, 1952 before the Senate Preparedness Subcommittee. It is pertinent to note that, on the very next day, Manly Fleischmann, in his final press conference before relinquishing his position as head of the Defense Production Administration, remarked that the Government had moved as rapidly as possible in the early days after the Korean war began in obtaining an effective control over materials—the key to the mobilization problem.

Mr. Fleischmann, in commenting on Mr. Baruch's testimony of the preceding day, went on to say: "On many points of Mr. Baruch's testimony . . . I find myself in complete agreement." He agreed with Baruch that it would be fantastic to believe that an adequate armed program, maintained over a period of years, would bankrupt the United States, but not the Soviet Union. "We can afford," he added, "to do whatever has to be done in the munitions field. . . ."

He also mentioned his agreement with Mr. Baruch as to a remark the Elder Statesman had recently made in a speech at the War College that a solicitude for the civilian economy should not be allowed to prevent the maximum military production. Fleischmann significantly added that "there has been no occasion on which military requirements as presented to us and carefully screened have been disallowed because we wanted to make any material available for civilian production."

In answer to a reporter's query on Mr. Baruch's statement to the Subcommittee, Mr. Fleischmann commented: "While I am in general sympathy with his attitude, which is that we must do everything we can to get ready, I doubt whether it would have made a great deal of sense to produce the kind of planes that could have been produced in volume right after Korea, although that certainly is and was a debatable question. Every day that we go along and the nearer we get to the steam-up on production of the kinds of planes that we are now able to produce, it seems to me to indicate that that basic decision was defensible and a proper one . . . another aspect of his original statement [is] that at the time of Korea and right up to the present time we would have been better off to produce a great arsenal of weapons even though they might become obsolete, rather than put the time and attention that has been put in on building plants capable of producing the F-86, to use a good example. I did not participate in that decision and do not know all of the considerations that entered into it. It seems to me . . . that every day that goes along without a major war tends to support the decision that was in fact made, although I think if I had to make it right after Korea I would have gone along the way Mr. Baruch thought it should have been done."

Henry H. Fowler, who succeeded Mr. Fleischmann as Defense Production Administrator and who later was named Director of Defense Mobilization to succeed Charles E. Wilson, evidenced the same deep concern with the totalitarian threat to our freedom. Mr. Fowler has stressed time and again the urgency of achieving military and economic strength. In a talk before the Annual Convention of the American Federation of Labor on September 18, 1952, he presented a "forward look," stating:

"A survey of the increased availability of supplies of materials and industrial equipment which will become available in the year ahead due to the expansion programs, wisely undertaken in the years just passed, indicates the existence of opportunities to raise our security goals or achieve current security goals faster without any impairment of the civilian economy. Our choice now is not between building our mobilization base and turning out increasing quantities of key weapons and maintaining a healthy civilian economy. There is room now to achieve progress on all these obectives if the funds and the authority are made available in the period ahead.

305

"The decisions concerning the future of defense production will be made by the nation as a whole, acting through the President and Congress. Whatever the decisions, I should like to venture some comment on how we should arrive at them. . . .

"These decisions should not be predetermined or foreclosed by picking some attractive budget figure out of a hat on the assumption that the U. S. A. in this critical and dangerous period in world history can afford to devote only this share or that share of its resources to the national security. The question is not only what can we afford for national security. It is, also, can we afford not to make the provisions determined to be necessary for our security in this struggle for peace. The difference between the wise figure and an arbitrarily chosen figure may be the difference between security and disaster.

"One last thought. Our common pride in past progress in defense mobilization is overborne at times by our deep concern, lest the buildup in national strength, plus achievements in handling some of our worst material and equipment shortages, give rise to a false sense of optimism, security and complacency. These attitudes if they emerge in the executive and legislative branches of the Government or in the public mind can retard the completion of our scheduled military buildup, both of our own forces and those of our Allies in the Free World and prevent our maintaining the shield of strength. . . . It behooves us to fix definite objectives, challenging in time and scope for our future accomplishments for national security and to hold these objectives despite the alternating storms and lulls by an enemy who is a master of that art. Only by so doing can the attitudes that give rise to lethargy and confusion of purpose be dispelled. . . ."

As late as December 3, 1952, Henry Fowler reaffirmed that his views had not changed. He stated at a news conference that day that "it would be a grave mistake" to presume "that directions of this program are going to be radically changed, except as new facts and economic circumstances dictate." Fowler further emphasized that the Government's mobilization program since Korea had always been a non-partisan undertaking.

These purposeful convictions of Henry Fowler and Manly Fleischmann demonstrate the continued influence of Baruch. They stress action—not talk; clearly-defined objectives—not improvisations based on superficial observations. Bernard Baruch's leadership is still in evidence, inspiring and compelling.

Who else, at the age of seventy-six, could have talked with such youthful confidence, such boldness—and yet with such humility—as did Mr. Baruch in his speech to the United Nations Atomic Energy Commission on December 5, 1946?

"The elimination of war itself is within the range of possibility," he said. "I repeat: 'The man who learns to say *A* can learn, if he chooses, the rest of the alphabet, too.'

"But we must make a beginning. Let us delay no longer. The awakened conscience of humanity is our goal. In all my life, now past the Biblical allotment of three score and ten years, never before have I seen so rich an opportunity for deathless service as is presented to us here. I want my country associated with victory in this great crusade."

Humbly Baruch added, "For myself, as I look upon a long past and too short a future, I believe the finest epitaph would be—'He helped to bring lasting peace to the world.' "

Afterword

by

Charles E. Wilson

A S ONE WHO HAS HAD a little experience in the management of our mobilization program in World War II and again as Director of the Office of Defense Mobilization after Korea, it has long been a personal privilege to avail myself of the wisdom and accumulated experience of my old friend, the great mobilizer of World War I, Bernard M. Baruch. This privilege is one I have exercised informally and often during my work in government.

History has a way of repeating itself, and so has Bernard Baruch—who has himself become almost a part of our history. The Kaiser's forces of World War I, the totalitarian aggression of Germany and Japan in World War II, and the savage invaders from North Korea are essentially the same enemy; the differences are largely those of time and geography rather than of degree. And Mr. Baruch's hard-pressed truths are the same truths today that we faced in those earlier days, unpalatable as they may seem to some.

Therefore, when Bernard Baruch pounds away at the same dogma of preparedness that he has always preached, it is because he knows it is necessary. He recognizes that our military men, industrialists, financial experts and political leaders have not yet mastered the art of mobilization. This is an art in which Mr. Baruch's brilliant strokes of planning and improvisation were more than a match for the war-making ability of the tyrants of the First World War and since.

It is not surprising, I suppose, that a Democracy such as ours should be forced to learn over and over again the lessons Mr. Baruch has sought to teach; the obvious need for armaments in readiness and for armies in being; for manpower in training and for critical materials in stockpiles; for peace policies that the whole world can understand; and for wartime strength with which to back those policies if necessary. Experience is one thing which cannot be inherited, as shown by the Ten Commandments, which even at this late date seem to need constant repetition.

We have every right to be surprised and pleased, however, at our good fortune in having a "Dr. Facts" to guide us for so many years in the person of Mr. Baruch. The next best thing to being able to inherit our national experience in the immensely technical task of mobilization is to be able to keep with us, through seven Administrations, a man who has accumulated that experience at first hand and stored it in his own immensely efficient mind.

Imagine, if you can, how reassuring it has been to our mobilization officials—drawn as they often are from industry or commerce and newly arrived in Washington—to find guidance through the recommendations gained by a single American through long experience. Washington is a jungle to the average business leader, but not to Bernard Baruch. He knows the military, he knows the financial experts, he knows the leaders of both parties on the Hill, and he knows government procedure.

Moreover, they know him too—and they respect his judgments.

Is there an apparently insoluble conflict as to materials or methods? Mr. Baruch can tell you just how that same conflict was solved for Pershing and for Eisenhower, and is ready with an answer for today's problems, if you need it.

Is there a policy crisis in connection with our Allies overseas? Mr. Baruch has long since anticipated the possibility of such a clash, thought about it, arrived at a possible solution which might be agreeable to all concerned, and filed that solution away for future reference.

Is one of the heads of a foreign government an unknown factor in forthcoming negotiations? The chances are that Mr. Baruch has known the man for years, has possibly called on him in his own country, and may have entertained him during one of his visits to America.

In our day the old-fashioned reference to "encyclopedic knowledge" is likely to be dismissed as a cliché. Yet, range as you will over the files of finance, production, foreign affairs, taxes, manpower and government administration; you will find that Bernard Baruch has been there before you, and that he has contributed fresh, invigorating new concepts of the use to which that field should be put in the mobilization picture.

Mr. Baruch is not alone, of course, in rising above politics, above self-interest, in his activities on behalf of his government. It is one of the glories of our Democracy that so many able men are always ready and willing to drop their personal concerns for such periods of emergency service as our national safety may require. Few such men continue their active interest past the time when an emergency period appears to have passed, however, being understandably anxious to return to private life as soon as possible.

By contrast, Bernard Baruch's everlasting willingness to devote his time and energies to his country's problems is unique.

In season and out, with or without portfolio, he has worked to preserve the nation that means so much to him.

Sometimes his conclusions, arrived at by strenuous personal toil, have been unpalatable to those in power—but they always have made sense; they always have had the backing of hard facts; and they always have carried the aura of integrity that has become almost the hallmark of their author.

If, to some, Baruch has seemed a Jeremiah crying needless havoc, who is there today who would deny that his sharpest warnings have been justified by events? If there were those who scoffed at his demands that we tighten our belts in good times, surely our inflation-ridden economy has taught them soberer judgment since.

If anyone now alive fails to see the wisdom of Bernard Baruch's counsel that we keep our powder dry even during periods of international amity, let him read the news reports under today's dateline—or tomorrow's.

If there yet remains in this country any substantial body of our citizens that does not now regret the lack of readiness against which Mr. Baruch has so long inveighed, let that group look now at the world our boys are dying to save.

A great statesman has done his best to keep us free; to arm us against surprise; to alert our minds to the dangers that confront us in ever-increasing measure. A review of his counsel down through the years was never more timely than at this moment, and I am gratified to know that Morris V. Rosenbloom has prepared such a review in book form.

As Honorary Chairman of the Institute on Economics of Defense Mobilization, which Mr. Rosenbloom headed as Executive Director, I have had many reasons to know of his competence and of his distinct contribution to the mobilization field.

It is my sincere hope that, through this book, the lessons of the past will not be lost; and that we will thereby be aided in meeting our threatened emergencies with the cool skill and reasoned calm so often displayed in the past by that master mobilizer and prophet of peace through strength, Bernard M. Baruch.

Bibliography

RECOMMENDED BOOKS AND ARTICLES
ABOUT BERNARD BARUCH AND HIS TIMES

Baldwin, Hanson W., "Dissection of the 'Fortress America' Idea", *The New York Times Magazine*, August 17, 1952.

Barton, Bruce, "Bernard M. Baruch Discusses the Future of American Business," *The American Magazine*, June, 1929.

Beard, Charles A. and Mary A., *The Rise of American Civilization*, New York, The Macmillan Company, 1928.

Beard, Charles A. and Mary A., *America in Mid-Passage*, New York, The Macmillan Company, 1939.

Bolles, Blair, *How to Get Rich in Washington* (Rich Man's Division of the Welfare State), New York, W. W. Norton & Company, 1952.

Blum, John M., *Joe Tumulty and the Wilson Era*, Boston, Houghton Mifflin Company, 1951.

Brookings Institution, The, *Significant Books Summarized*, Washington, D. C., March, 1952.

Business Week, "Baruch, Enthusiastic Democrat, Helps Hoover in Emergency," December 23, 1931.

Byrnes, James F., *Speaking Frankly*, New York, Harper & Brothers, 1947.

Catton, Bruce, *The War Lords of Washington*, New York, Harcourt, Brace & Company, 1948.

Clarkson, Grosvenor B., *Industrial America in the World War* (The Strategy behind the Line 1917-1918), Boston, Houghton Mifflin Company, 1923.

Eisenhower, Dwight D., *Crusade in Europe*, Garden City, Doubleday & Company, 1948.

Field, Carter, *Bernard Baruch: Park Bench Statesman*, New York, Whittlesey House, 1944.

Gunther, John, *Roosevelt in Retrospect*, New York, Harper & Brothers, 1950.

Hauser, Ernest O., "Ridgway's Toughest Job," *The Saturday Evening Post*, October 25, 1952.

315

Hersey, John, "The Old Man", *The New Yorker,* January 3, 10, 17, 1948.

Hillman, William, *Mr. President,* New York, Farrar, Straus & Young, 1952.

Hinshaw, David, *Herbert Hoover, American Quaker,* New York, Farrar, Straus & Company, 1950.

Hoffman, Paul G., *Peace Can Be Won,* Garden City, Doubleday & Company, 1951.

Janeway, Eliot, *The Struggle for Survival,* New Haven, Yale Press, 1951.

Jones, Jesse H., *Fifty Billion Dollars* (My Thirteen Years with the R.F.C.), New York, The Macmillan Company, 1951.

Johnson, Gerald W., *Roosevelt—Dictator or Democrat?,* New York, Harper & Brothers, 1941.

Johnson, Gerald W., *Incredible Tale,* New York, Harper & Brothers, 1950.

Johnson, Hugh S., *The Blue Eagle From Egg to Earth,* New York, Doubleday, Duran & Company, 1935.

Kimmel, Lewis H., *Postwar Tax Policy and Business Expansion,* Washington, D. C., The Brookings Institution, 1943.

Lapp, Ralph E., "Too Many Secrets Spoil the Atom," *Collier's,* July 5, 1952.

Lapp, Ralph E., and Alsop, Stewart, "The Inside Story of Our First Hydrogen Bomb", *The Saturday Evening Post,* October 25, 1952.

Leigh, Virginia, "The Private Life of Bernard Baruch," *Collier's,* November 27, 1948.

Leighton, Isabel, Editor, *The Aspirin Age,* New York, Simon & Schuster, 1949.

Life Magazine, "Baruch's Christmas Present", January 4, 1943.

McCann, Kevin, *Man from Abilene,* Garden City, Doubleday & Company, 1952.

Moley, Raymond, *After Seven Years,* New York, Harper & Brothers, 1939.

Moorehead, Alan, "Traitor Klaus Fuchs, He Gave Stalin the A-Bomb," *The Saturday Evening Post,* May 31, 1952.

Morgan, John Davis, Jr., *The Domestic Mining Industry of the United States in World War II,* U. S. Government Printing Office, 1949.

Moulton, Harold G. and Schlotterbeck, Karl T., *Collapse or Boom at the End of the War?,* Washington, D. C., The Brookings Institution, 1942.

Moulton, Harold G. and Schlotterbeck, Karl T., *Should Price Control Be Retained?,* Washington, D. C., The Brookings Institution, 1945.

Nelson, Donald M., *Arsenal of Democracy,* New York, Harcourt, Brace & Company, 1946.

Perkins, Frances, *The Roosevelt I Knew,* New York, Viking Press, 1946.

President's Materials Policy Commission, *Resources for Freedom,* June, 1952.

Roosevelt, Eleanor, *This Is My Story,* New York, Harper & Brothers, 1937.

Roosevelt, Eleanor, *This I Remember,* New York, Harper & Brothers, 1949.

Roosevelt, Elliott, Editor, *F. D. R. His Personal Papers (1905-1928),* New York, Duell, Sloan & Pearce, 1948.

Ruark, Robert, "Bernard Baruch, Esq., Prophet Without Portfolio," *Esquire,* October and November, 1952.

Sherwood, Robert E., *Roosevelt and Hopkins,* 2 vols., New York, Harper & Brothers, 1948.

Shumway, Harry Irving, *Bernard M. Baruch: Financial Genius, Statesman, and Adviser to Presidents,* Boston, L. C. Page & Company, 1946.

Stettinius, Edward R., Jr., *Roosevelt and the Russians* (The Yalta Conference), Garden City, Doubleday & Company, 1949.

Sullivan, Mark, "Bernard M. Baruch," *Collier's,* January 31, 1920.

Tully, Grace, *F. D. R. My Boss,* New York, Charles Scribner's Sons, 1949.

U. S. Congress. Report of Joint Committee on Pearl Harbor, Appendix D, Washington, D. C., U. S. Government Printing Office, 1942.

U. S. Government, Civilian Production Administration; *Industrial Mobilization for War,* vol. I, Washington, D. C., Government Printing Office, 1947.

U. S. Government, General Services Administration; *Federal Records of World War II,* vol. I, Washington, D. C., Government Printing Office, 1950.

White, W. L., *Bernard Baruch: Portrait of a Citizen,* New York, Harcourt, Brace & Company, 1950.

Wilson, Edith Galt, *My Memoir,* Indianapolis, The Bobbs-Merrill Company, 1939.

SELECT LIST OF WRITINGS BY BERNARD BARUCH

The Making of the Reparation and Economic Sections of the Treaty, New York, Harper & Brothers, 1920.

Address at the reunion of the members of the War Industries Board at Washington, D. C., on December 10, 1920. [privately printed].

Putting Farmers on a Modern Business Basis. Pamphlet. New York, 1920.

Bibliography

Agricultural Finance, an address delivered before the American Farm Bureau Federation, Chicago, December, 1922.

"Taking the Profit out of War," *The Atlantic Monthly,* January, 1926.

"We Won't Have to Fight—If," *The American Legion Monthly,* January, 1936.

Taking the Profit out of War (A Program for Industrial Mobilization), New York, 1936 [privately printed].

Statutory Amendments to Natural Laws, Commencement Address at Union College, Schenectady, N. Y., June 14, 1937 [unpublished].

"Priorities—the Synchronizing Force", *Harvard Business Review,* spring, 1941.

American Industry in the War, edited by Richard H. Hippelheuser, New York, Prentice-Hall, 1941.

"All-Out Price Control", *Rotarian* Magazine, December, 1941.

Preventing Inflation (Statements and Writings on Controlling Living Costs and Preventing Inflation September 1941-December 1941), New York, Prentice-Hall, 1942.

"Report of the Rubber Survey Committee." House Doc. 836, 77th Congress, 2nd Session. Washington, D. C., 1942.

War and Postwar Adjustment Policies, (Text of Official Report and Related Documents). Washington, D. C., American Council on Public Affairs, 1944.

"Memorandum for the President, September 24, 1946" (concerning) Statements on Atomic Energy in Secretary Wallace's Letter of July 23, 1946, New York, 1946.

The International Control of Atomic Energy (Speech at Freedom House, October 8, 1946), New York, Freedom House, 1946.

"Toward Effective International Atomic Energy Control", statement to the United Nations Atomic Energy Commission, December 5, 1946.

"United States Atomic Energy Proposals," address to the United Nations Atomic Energy Commission, June 14, 1946, New York, American Association for the United Nations, 1946.

"What of Our Future?", *The Saturday Evening Post,* April 23, 1949.

Speech on National Security Resources Board at Armed Forces Industrial College, June 29, 1949.

"Our Last, Best Hope for Peace," *Look* Magazine, September 26, 1950.

"Spiritual Armageddon Is Here—Now", *Reader's Digest,* March, 1951.

"Baruch Answers 13 Questions," *Look* Magazine, July 17, 1951.

Bibliography

SIGNIFICANT TESTIMONY BY BERNARD BARUCH BEFORE COMMITTEES OF CONGRESS

Statement before the War Policies Commission, March 6, 1931; a Memo submitted to Joint Congressional and Cabinet Commission.

U. S. Congress. House. Foreign Affairs Committee. December 21, 1934.

U. S. Congress. Senate. Munitions Committee. March 27, 1935.

U. S. Congress. Senate. Committee on Unemployment and Relief. February 28 and March 1, 1938.

U. S. Congress. Senate. Foreign Relations Committee. April, 1939.

U. S. Congress. House. Banking and Currency Committee. September 19, 1941.

U. S. Congress. Senate. Committee on Military Affairs. November 1, 1945.

U. S. Congress. House. Banking and Currency Committee. March 26, 1946.

U. S. Congress. Senate. Banking and Currency Committee. July 7, 1950.

U. S. Congress. Senate. Preparedness Subcommittee of the Committee on Armed Services. May 28, 1952.

ADDITIONAL REFERENCES ON ATOMIC ENERGY

Man vs. Atom—Year 1. Pamphlet. New York, McGraw-Hill, 1945.
The Atom—A Tide in the Affairs of Men. Pamphlet. New York, McGraw-Hill, 1945.

Smyth, Henry D., *A General Account of the Development of the Methods of Using Atomic Energy under the Auspices of the United States Government,* Princeton, N. J., Princeton University Press, 1945.

Atomic Information, World Control Issue. Pamphlet. Washington, D. C., National Committee on Atomic Information, July 1, 1946.

Talk It Over: Atomic Peace or Atomic War. Pamphlet. Washington, D. C., National Institute of Social Relations, 1946.

Newsweek Magazine, "Atom: Einstein, the Man Who Started It All," March 10, 1947.

Bulletin of the Atomic Scientists, June, 1947.

12 Atomic Facts. Pamphlet. Washington, D. C., National Committee on Atomic Information, 1947.

Index

REVISED

(Writings by Bernard Baruch are italicized)

321

Index

324